Waltham Forest Libraries

Please return this item by the last date stamped. The loan may be renewed unless required by another customer.

Mar 2016		

Need to renew your books?
http://www.walthamforest.gov.uk/libraries or
Dial 0115 929 3388 for Callpoint – our 24/7 automated telephone renewal line. You will need your library card number and your PIN. If you do not know your PIN, contact your local library.

MARTIN FAULKS

The Path of the Ninja

A quest for the elements

CORONET

First published in Great Britain in 2015 by Coronet
An imprint of Hodder & Stoughton
An Hachette UK company

First published in paperback in 2016

1

A CIP catalogue record for this title is available from the British Library

Paperback ISBN: 978 1 444 76441 3
Ebook ISBN: 978 1 444 76442 0

Typeset in Minion Pro by Palimpsest Book Production Limited,
Falkirk, Stirlingshire

Printed and bound by Clays Ltd, St Ives plc

Hodder & Stoughton policy is to use papers that are natural, renewable
and recyclable products and made from wood grown in sustainable
forests. The logging and manufacturing processes are expected to
conform to the environmental regulations of the country of origin.

Contents

Introduction

N inja: the very word conjures up amazing images in the mind's eye. Cult movies, cartoon turtles or the vision of the dark-clad, masked master of deception and stealth: we all have our image of the ninja. Modern culture is awash with them; comic books, manga and anime films feature ninja heavily. They appear as powerful figures in Batman and James Bond and in popular video games such as *Mortal Kombat* and *Shinobi*. But who were the real ninja? Is there more to them than murder and masks?

In Japanese tradition, the ninja (also known as *shinobi*: I shall use the two terms interchangeably within the book) were covert agents and mercenaries, proficient in a wealth of skills, such as espionage, infiltration, assassination and martial arts. The first records in Japanese history show that they were highly trained warriors, with a reputation for enduring danger and hardship in the name of their mission. It was said that their sophisticated fighting techniques, combined with a high level of spiritual training, made them an invincible force. Perhaps the closest comparison to anything in the West would be the legend of Robin Hood – in effect, a band of warriors who used stealth to see justice done, then disappeared.

A traditional Japanese story that demonstrates perfectly this method of working is that of the female ninja, or *konuchi*, who had such skill in the art of human manipulation that she converted the second in command of the enemy to her cause in just two days. The story goes that she knew the enemy's commanding officer viewed himself as an honourable man. He was lonely, thoughtful, and, watching him from a distance for weeks, she saw that he had a weakness for women. With this in mind, she drew up her plans against him. She appeared in his house late at night, apparently injured, crying that one of the generals had abused her and pleading for help. He must take her home. The commander was overwhelmed. His emotions and sense of honour were so strong that he didn't question the situation, responding with his heart. But where was her home?

Home, of course, turned out to be far into enemy lines. A dangerous mission but he was a man of honour and had to get her back. He would deal with the evil perpetrator of the crime when he returned. He had to leave quickly without being seen, or the general would spot the girl and try to cover up his crime. He disappeared with her into the night on the back of his horse.

He felt such a hero with the grateful maiden clinging to his body. Soon they were setting up camp behind enemy lines. She held him close all night to feel safe, but in the morning they received bad news. It seemed that one of her friends had found out that the commander's absconding was viewed as desertion. His own side were searching for him to arrest him for treason. He couldn't go back. But he could, she pleaded, stay with her and work for her father, the commander of the local militia. He should stay, shouldn't he? After all, she loved him, and his own commander had turned out not only to be a brute but so disloyal that he didn't even trust him! After all his years of loyal service, didn't her rescuer deserve loyalty?

Little did he realise, in his state of despair, that he had been the victim of clever manipulation.

Compared with their contemporaries, the samurai – knights who lived by a strict code of honour and conduct with regard to combat – the ninja favoured more subtle methods that often allowed them to achieve more in a short time than those engaged in lengthy combat. A serious lack of morals freed them from restraint.

Another enduring tale demonstrates how the ninja used their cunning and adaptability to overcome superior odds. In this one, a ninja was sent on a mission to destroy a whole regiment of enemy samurai. He had been poisoning the water supply with an undetectable substance. For months, the samurai had been trying to find a way to prevent this. No matter what they did, whether dividing the water supply, controlling access to it or even hiring other ninja to set traps, nothing stopped him and he attacked repeatedly, devastating their forces.

Finally, they put together a special unit designed purely to catch him. It consisted of expert trackers and the most experienced samurai warriors.

The next time he attacked, he was detected. They were now on his trail and this time he couldn't throw off their expert trackers. After three days, he decided that if he could not be free of them, he would have to kill them, even though they massively outnumbered him. To do this, he would use the ultimate weapon: nature. He would utilise their number to his advantage but also their skills, equipment and personality. He alone would survive.

First he had to disarm them and arm himself. He started to move through the swamps, which meant that they would have to leave their horses and heavy equipment behind. Then he would circle back around them and gather anything of use they had discarded, checking the number of horses and the nature of the equipment, so that he knew what he was up against. He cut blades from the long *nagatta* or halberds they had left and carried on with his journey. As he moved swiftly through the night, he noticed that one samurai was out on patrol. This warrior had made a grave mistake: he had not adapted to the environment and had kept on his full armour. As he moved through the swamp, with the rain beating down on him, his bamboo armour filled with water and he sank at every step. It took little effort for the ninja to jump on his back and ease his face forwards into the water to drown.

Now he knew how thoughtless and unadaptable his enemy samurai were, which meant they would be slow. He led them through a ravine that forced them into single file. He climbed above them, doubled back and harassed them with falling stones and missiles. His stealth and ease of movement meant he was always one step ahead of them . . . or one step behind.

In the darkness, he slit the throat of a warrior at the back of the pack, a strong warrior wearing heavy armour, unused to night fighting.

I remember my growing awe as the story continued, the ninja using everything at his disposal to aid him. He wore them out, causing them to turn on each other and, one by one, slaughtered them all.

The story shows the ninja's resourcefulness, that he had skills comparable with those of modern SAS or Navy SEALs troops. But this was ancient warfare, without precision weapons and technology. He had relied on sheer skill and fortitude.

Where had this elite fighting force learnt their arts and what were their origins?

Etymology reveals much about their actual way of being: the word *ninja*, in original Japanese script, is constructed in two parts: *nin*, 'to do quietly' or 'to do so as not to be perceived by others', so with 'stealth' and 'invisibility'; *ja*, meaning 'person'. So ninja means 'a person who is stealthy and invisible'. Further still, if we look at the art of ninja, *ninjutsu*, 'the skill of going unperceived' or the 'art of stealth', we may translate 'ninja' as 'one skilled in the art of stealth'.

As with many words, though, there can be more than one meaning: *nin* can also mean 'to endure', so we could say that ninja is the 'art of enduring'. As we shall see, anyone who has done such training can relate to this.

The first mention of the word 'ninja' occurs in a text from 1367 called *Taiheiki* (太平記), an account of the Nanbokucho wars (the 'wars between the courts'): 'One night, under the cover of rain and wind Hachiman-yam was approached by the highly skilled ninja who set fire to the temple.' It goes on to tell tales of warriors who used the kind of skills we associate with the ninja today.

Some scholars assert that the ninja may have been around as early as the twelfth century but, according to records, they were most active from 1460 to the mid-1600s, known as the Sengoku or 'Warring States' Period. Iga, a province now located in what is today part of western Mie Prefecture, became known as a centre for ninjutsu. With another town called Kōka (or Koga, now Shiga Prefecture), Iga was said to be the birthplace of the ninja clans. They wielded great power in the province, until they were effectively destroyed in 1581 when warlord Oda Nobunaga launched an attack on Iga with around sixty thousand men. Shortly afterwards the ninja clans scattered across Japan.

Primary source material on who or what the ninja were is hard to find: accounts of ninja activity are third-hand, and the exact evolution of the tradition is hard to ascertain. It tells us that they were reputed to use secret hand signs and words, which allowed them to channel magical powers, becoming invisible, reading minds, mastering and controlling the forces of nature. In their heyday, some Japanese people wondered if they were spirits or demons evolved from beaked goblins called *tengu*.

Interestingly, we have writings by the ninja, albeit from far later. These eighteenth-century historical records show us that ninja believed in the development of mystical powers and honed techniques of magic, divination and achieving enlightenment alongside their skills in assassination, illusion and stealth. It seems that the ninja didn't see themselves as immoral, demonic assassins but as men of morals and virtue. In their eyes, they were secret heroes and protectors, who were restoring harmony to the world.

There is a great paradox. They would kill – with fire, poison and blade – trap, trick and frame others. How can this coexist with a code of ethics? Ninja texts talk of keeping good heart (*seishin*). How could this be compatible with a life of deception and violence? We have records of ninja sending young girls to seduce enemies purely so that they could gain access to the man's bedchamber and leave the window open, thus allowing a team of fully armed ninja to enter the room and chop their target to pieces. Their path often involved hurting innocents to get to their goals.

When I started this adventure, I wanted to understand that paradox. Little did I know that, in a way, I was investigating the same paradox in myself.

Japanese martial-arts authorities declare that today there are no genuine ninja schools. The West, however, begs to differ. Thanks to Bruce Lee, we have hundreds of authorities claiming to be ninja grandmasters, dressed in outlandish costumes and affecting Japanese titles. This has been big business in America ever since the ninja boom in the seventies. Most modern Japanese would respond to someone coming to Japan to train as a ninja in the same way as a Westerner would if someone came to the UK to train as a knight.

As I will show, the schools and methods of training still exist. Of course, by the very nature of ninja, they are hidden and hard to find. It is hard to believe that an art such as *ninjutsu*, practised to such a high standard, would simply vanish.

However, thanks to the proliferation of organisations *claiming* to be ninja, the true ninja and his arts are hard to find. For any would-be seeker it is a matter of extracting the wheat from the chaff. The best way to find a true ninja must be to test him: what is he truly capable of?

If I tracked down the remaining living ninja masters, would all the myths turn out to be true? Could the teachers in Japan teach me to be very silent, to enter anywhere I liked, to be invisible? Would they know secret skills that would allow me to do supernatural things? Or would everything turn out to be a disappointment?

This book is the story of my quest to answer these questions. It is an attempt to know the truth by *being* the truth: the path to becoming a true living ninja.

To do this, I have dedicated myself to practising the ancient arts of ninja. In my quest, I have spent extended periods away from my home and my wife, invested money in my search and travelled across the world to seek instruction from many different teachers. I would test and question everything. In writing about my quest, I have sometimes had to change names and locations. Sometimes I have combined multiple trips to the same teacher into one for the sake of the narrative; and I have changed events to avoid revealing secret identities.

I found the challenges I faced along the way tested me to my absolute limit. Some parts of my journey were far more difficult than I had ever imagined. The art of *ninjutsu* is not just a martial art or system of physical combat: it is a form of spiritual training. It requires the student to rethink not only the way he views the world around him but also the way he sees himself. I do not view myself as a great authority on the art of *ninjutsu*, but as a beginner. My understanding of the art is always evolving. I attribute my successes to the kind attention of my teachers. Misunderstanding or areas of confusion are entirely my own.

Prologue

I'd stood and watched as they rained blows upon him, totally rooted to the spot and unable to lift a finger to help. Outnumbered, my best friend cowered, now curled into a ball as they continued to kick, punch and drag him further into the wood.

They'd come from nowhere while we were walking home through a small copse near my house. Two, three, then more, the leader striding in front, lip like a bulldog, screaming at us. Something about us having pulled a knife on their mate? We had no chance to answer. They grabbed Josh by the neck of his sweatshirt and hauled him backwards, fists and feet already starting to flail. I ran – not towards him but away. What kind of friend was I? I could hear dull thuds as fists and boots met their target. My breath came in ragged gasps and I stopped and turned.

One of the guys had leather gloves on, a kind of pseudo biker-style with studs. He had Josh pinned to a tree and was screaming, 'I'm gonna hit you! I'm gonna hit you!' The boys' faces were contorted. Spittle flew from the leader's mouth as he continued to scream and kick. They threw Josh into a bramble bush, then dragged him out, thorns ripping into his arms and face. He managed to escape their clutches and ran towards a break in the trees. Like a pack of dogs, they headed after him, one threw a stump of wood, which hit him squarely on the back of the head. He crumpled like a rag doll.

I was so transfixed I didn't hear the dull thud of horses' hoofs on the moss-lined path behind. Only when a branch snapped did I look round – just in time to be knocked flying by a swinging whip. I picked myself up, as the rider circled for another swipe, and ducked into the undergrowth, my face smarting. I recognised her as the sister of the boy kicking my friend.

They left as fast as they had appeared. The last I saw was the receding back end of the horse vanishing down the bridle path.

Josh was still on the ground, covered with leaf mould and resembling a pile of old clothes. I ran over to him. He turned his head at my voice, eyes glazed but burning with resentment and silent accusation. In that moment I realised I could never stand to see someone beaten or hurt again.

For months after the attack on my friend, I felt waves of guilt. How could I have left someone I cared about to be beaten almost senseless? This experience, when I was just twelve, changed the way I lived my life for ever.

1

In the Beginning

———◆———

> *Know the enemy and know yourself; in a hundred battles you will*
> *never be in peril. When you are ignorant of the enemy, but know*
> *yourself, your chances of winning or losing are equal. If ignorant both*
> *of your enemy and yourself, you are certain in every battle to be in*
> *peril.*
>
> Sun Tzu, *The Art of War*

'Martin?'

Thump-thump . . . thump-thump . . . thump . . . thump. I lay rigid in bed wondering why every morning my heart would beat like an out-of-step soldier. I was afraid it would go too fast or just stop. The room was getting light, the sun creeping round and under the gaps where the curtains never quite pulled together. I didn't want it to be light: I wanted to bundle back down, for time to reverse and night to fall again.

Ever since Josh and I had been beaten in the woods, getting up in the morning terrified me. Before it had happened I'd often lain in bed dreaming of being Batman or Spidey, transformed from geeky kid to high-swinging hero. In my dreams I'd always won, always been able to beat the bad guys: that was how it was meant to happen. Days later my face still hurt from where I'd been hit and I rubbed it. I hated the idea that I wasn't actually a superhero – I hadn't even managed to hit any of the boys who'd chased us.

In my heart I was Batman or Superman. I wanted to right wrongs. Now, in the waking world, my mouth was dry, stomach churning in anticipation of another day of fear.

'Martin! Breakfast!' Dad's voice echoed up the stairway. He really had no idea. To him, my desperate attempts to avoid school were futile: he just wanted to get to work. I trudged downstairs.

Mum was more sympathetic – we'd talked about the fight. 'What about self-defence classes?' she asked suddenly, glancing up from a textbook propped on the table.

I looked at her blankly. The toast I'd been chewing tasted of nothing.

'Or there's a martial-arts class starting at the college.' She looked expectant.

I swallowed and nodded. OK.

We went to watch a class and I ended up joining in. Soon Mum had decided to take part too. From that moment I was hooked, and over the weeks my confidence grew, though Mum never again moved from the seats surrounding the training hall.

The class wasn't huge – there were five or six of us in a room for fifty. It was normally used for college gym classes and basketball, so the walls were high enough for climbing ropes and hoops. Kicks, punches and martial-art 'shouts' (called *ki-ups*) filled the room. The instructor's voice boomed into corners, ricocheting off the ceiling: '*Hana, dul, set, net, dasot, yasot, ilgup, yodol, ahop, yeol!*'

I looked at Mum, confused. 'It's counting,' she mouthed. 'One, two, three, four . . .'

I spent a long time watching and memorising the moves: powerful squats with vicious punches from the hips, sweeping kicks. Then one day I saw people doing something that made my jaw drop. They were practising a move that enables you to fall without hurting yourself, known in martial arts as a 'break fall'. This was a form of somersault, combined with a break fall, involving a run-up, a jump, then flipping in the air and landing flat on your back. I had watched a few of the black belts perform it repeatedly, with no sign of pain or winding.

I had to try it. The class was coming to an end so I took the opportunity – run, leap, kick feet backwards to make a spin and, wham, onto the mat. That was it in theory but when I tried it I missed the mat. Pain, anger and humiliation flooded me, and I lost it. The instructor came to help me up but I reacted with pure rage.

He was having none of it and grabbed me by the back of my tracksuit pants. I swung at him, arms flailing, months of frustration and fear pouring out. 'Whoa, whoa, whoa!' He had me almost in a headlock, then shoved my face into his armpit. Jeez, I was trapped! All I could do was breathe slowly and keep still, which had the desired effect of making the anger slip away and calming me down.

When I emerged from the armpit, the rest of the class had disappeared. Mum stood stony-faced in the doorway, slipping her arms into her jacket, ready to leave. 'I don't believe you did that,' she hissed. 'I thought you'd grown out of the "tigers" – you're your own worst enemy!' She gripped my arm, practically pulling me through the double doors.

It dawned on me that, very publicly, I had had one of my tantrums (known in my family as 'tigers') but something had shifted inside. Instead of feeling frustration at the world and an underlying rumble of anger, I realised I now had an outlet.

Riding home on the back of Mum's moped, I thought about how my love of superheroes, ninja turtles and mythical characters could blend. If I couldn't be Batman or Hercules, I could at least be the best martial artist possible. I'd always been pretty disciplined – or maybe that should be obsessive – but that could work in my favour . . . or could it?

2

The Fantastic Four

◆

In the beginner's mind there are many possibilities, in the expert's mind there are few.

Shunryu Suzuki, Zen Master

There we were all sat, round the dining-room table, and my whole world had gone into slow motion. My sister, aged ten, who was three years older than I, was smiling. What on earth was wrong with her?

Dad looked me in the eye. 'Daddy loves Mummy and Mummy loves Daddy but Mummy also loves someone else . . .' The words hung in the air, like thick, choking smoke. I had no idea what to say or do, looking from one parent to the other, desperately wanting them to explain.

I knew it was bad but didn't really understand why or what was going to happen. Was this a way of saying they were splitting up? After the talk was over everyone seemed so . . . normal. Kate was still smiling and happy – I suppose it was her way of dealing with it. I had a sudden flashback to a few weeks earlier when we had been in the car with Mum and her 'friend'. Kate had prodded me and pointed to them holding hands; I now remembered thinking, This is not right. Now I had a horrible sinking feeling in my stomach. Things were *definitely* not right.

The next day Mum left, and the slow-motion world finally ground to a halt. I had no idea where she had gone and I was just a ball of pain.

I remember my evenings at the martial-arts hall. They had *kuk sool won* lessons every night of the week and one extra on Sunday. I went to them all. *Kuk sool won* (or National Martial Art Association) is a Korean martial art that was created in 1958 by Suh In-Hyuk, the *kuk sa nim* or grandmaster. When I was at home, I spent every minute in my room, surrounded by comics.

I used to watch endless martial-arts movies and try to do the movements I saw on the screen. I had no idea that most of them used wires, trampolines and clever camera work.

I loved to look at the syllabus for the *kuk sool* belts and dream of what I was going to learn. I could see there were knockout strikes at blue belt called *mek chigi* and *mek chagi*. A set of instant knockouts for kicks and punches – that would be amazing. I looked at advanced sets of flips and acrobatics.

I used to buy different martial-arts magazines and scour them for courses. Bodybuilding, knife-throwing and hypnotism – you name it. I loved the idea of progressing and gaining abilities. I remember reading a copy of *Black Belt* magazine; it had an article on *ninjutsu* by Stephen K. Hayes. It was about how four elements were used in the ninja arts: earth, water, fire and wind. It talked a lot about things I didn't understand like 'trans-personal psychology' and 'self-actualisation' but the essence was clear. If you trained in *ninjutsu* you gained amazing abilities. You could be as solid as a rock and super-strong, deceptive and flexible, like water, invisible and evasive, like air, or aggressive and unstoppable, like fire.

I looked at Stephen Hayes standing there forcefully, with his full beard and ninja uniform, and could almost believe he had such powers. It made me think of the Fantastic Four – each has a power of an element. The 'Thing' was a giant rock man; the Human Torch could flame and become fire; Mr Fantastic had a body like rubber, which could flex and bend, with the flexibility of water; the invisible woman was the epitome of wind or air, becoming invisible and creating force fields. With *ninjutsu* you could have all the power of the elements, and to me these were the ninja's super-powers.

My interest in ninja was ignited. I used to visit the local video shop and search the basement for the crazy martial-arts movies from Japan, like *Black Ninja* and the *Red Shadow*. I practised the magical hand gestures and tried out the moves.

Kuk sool won involved wearing black suits and learning amazing skills. I started collecting books on historical *ninjutsu* and the ninja. I became a martial-arts maniac, practising constantly, opening doors at school with head-high kicks.

My parents had split up, which I found very hard, but school was an added hell.

'So where's your mum gone, then?' John looked at me over his sandwich. 'My mum says she's run off with a nigger. Is it true?'

'No!'

I had no idea then what that racist term meant but my mother's new partner was a great ally to me and I was not about to hear him insulted. I had the playground gauntlet to run. I should say that my school was not the best in Norwich. It was actually one of the roughest in the city, serving a local overspill of social housing. I didn't live in that part so to some of the kids I was a middle-class upstart.

Over the next few years, I began to watch what was going on around me and saw other children being systematically tormented. The teachers didn't seem bothered and all I wanted to do was get even for my previous bullying experience. So part superhero, part reckless semi-trained martial artist, I decided to become the playground vigilante.

Josh was as inspired by the idea of martial arts and heroic adventures as I was, so we spent each lunch hour conjuring up crazy workouts and pseudo martial-arts routines. We were even given permission to train in the PE hall. The other kids thought we were strange. We sat and watched the bullies. Their targets changed but the format was the same: verbal sniping would lead to physical attacks, escalating as they gained confidence. No one would step in. But when one of our friends, Jules, became a target, we manned up. We came into the classroom to see him being hung out of a window three floors up. It was time to retaliate.

Josh and I saw red and, with just a nod between us, we launched a well-timed attack. Looking back, it was probably the most stupid thing we could have done, attempting to disarm four guys while they were holding another boy out of the window, but somehow it worked. I had actually picked up a piece of wood from near the blackboard and started whacking them. As soon as this happened they brought Jules back inside with haste. Seeing this, Josh had piled in and gone crazy. We had no thought of what we were doing and no fear of the consequences. The whole gang were totally taken off guard – you could see in their eyes complete disbelief that they were not only being challenged but that we were beating hell out of them. Suddenly the rules had changed and we were fully in control. Falling over themselves, they fled, Josh and I tearing after them.

We expected to be in deep trouble but there was no hint of retaliation or retribution. Next time we saw those boys they sidled past us. I suppose they didn't know what to do about two *kung fu* nerds.

3

The Tournament

By letting it go it all gets done. The world is won by those who let it go. But when you try and try, the world is beyond the winning.

Lao Tzu

'**W**hat do you mean you haven't brought your uniform?' Richard Roper, our *sa beom nim*, or instructor (this term translates literally as 'master instructor' but also referred to his rank of fourth *dan* in *kuk sool won*) was incredulous.

Josh and I were prepared for this and smugly trotted out our rehearsed speech. We'd decided that competing was not in the spirit of our idea of martial arts and we were making a stand: we weren't going to compete in the tournament. We were fourteen; we knew our minds.

At this point my dad, who had given us a lift to the massive sports centre where the annual *kuk sool won* championships were being held, interrupted: 'OK, let me get this straight. You've spent *six* days a week, *fifty-two* weeks a year for the past five years training to "make a stand"?' My confidence slid. I recognised that slow, deliberate and *very* calm voice – it was the one that came before nuclear meltdown.

'Get . . . back . . . into . . . the . . . car. We are going to pick up your uniforms.' The words shot out staccato. If they'd been bullets, we'd have been dead.

I glanced at Josh, who was looking decidedly less comfortable (and smug) than he had a few moments ago. Then, miraculously, his uniform appeared from his bag. 'You bastard,' I mouthed at him. I got back into the car.

Half an hour later I was back, clad in my well-worn black cotton *dobok*.

They had actually held up the event until I returned: girls, boys, men and women of all ages were clustered in the main hall, stretching and practising techniques while they waited for the tournament to start. I wasn't sure I was ready for it, even though I had spent years working towards it. Suddenly I felt like that kid in the woods again.

I didn't have a chance to think much more about anything because John Ives, a tall Ichabod Crane of a guy, hauled me by the collar and dragged me into a line. I had no idea what I was doing, when I was meant to be doing it or why he'd put me there. I looked around, hoping to catch sight of Josh or Gavin. Gav was always good for a laugh and had the unnerving habit of vomiting copiously before and after every challenge. Why we found this endearing was beyond me, but he always seemed to do everything with good humour, including throwing up. There was no sign of either of them but across the room I saw one guy we had a lot of respect for – Darren Hart. He was a mountain of a man, a flat-topped army fitness instructor and *kuk sool won* veteran, who always won the championship. While the rest of the students were bouncing around warming up, he was sitting in full splits in a kind of Buddha-like Zen state. I waved in his direction; he raised an eyebrow in return.

Back in the line, I was rapidly trying to work out what I was about to face – it could be anything: forms, weapons, sparring or self-defence demonstrations. I was second in the line and getting anxious. Then I saw Josh: he was talking to the grandmaster's son – it's definitely a family business. The grandmaster was also in attendance, wearing his official gold and red uniform resplendent with tumbling embroidered dragons; he resembled an exotic bird, with a beady eye on the proceedings. *Kuk sool* is not just a style but an entire system not limited to a single discipline – the grandmaster sums it up as a structure that 'integrate[s] and explore[s] the entire spectrum of established traditional Korean martial arts, body conditioning techniques, mental development, and weapons training'. We all learnt this like a mantra. Everyone knew that much *kuk sool* history.

As I waited for my name to be called, I reckoned I had a half-hour to kill so I explored a stall next to me selling T-shirts, weapons and souvenirs. There was a new book: *The Complete Kuk Sool Manual*. It was so big it was hard to handle and the dust-jacket kept coming off.

At first, I tried to swot up on the forms and techniques I would be asked to demonstrate in the tournament. My mind wouldn't settle and I found myself questioning my original plans and getting confused. But I decided to read on. That would prevent any uncomfortable conversations with others I was about to compete against and calm my mind.

As I read I found the history fascinating; according to the official *kuk sool won* manual, Korean martial arts date back to the prehistoric era. In Korea, Buddhist monks developed a martial art known as *boolkyo musool* to improve their health and defend themselves while travelling. It included internal training, such as meditation and breathing techniques, as well as effective self-defence strategies.

The book also told me that royal families and high-ranking government officials had bodyguards who practised *koong joong mu sool*, an esoteric martial art that used both easily portable weapons (including short swords and fans) and weaponless techniques, such as pressure-point striking and joint-locks. Apparently this system had found its way from Korea to Japan and given birth to the Japanese art of *jujitsu*, which in turn had led to all Japanese martial arts, including *jujutsu*, *aikido* and *ninjutsu*.

I liked the idea that there was a link between *kuk sool* and *ninjutsu*. I flicked through the huge tome, looking at the exotic weapons and forms techniques. It had everything.

Hand striking: palm, fist, wrist, finger, closed hand, open hand, arm, shoulder and pressure-point striking techniques.

Kicking: spinning, jumping, double-leg, and pressure-point kicks.

Throwing and grappling: body throws, projection throws, leg throws, pressure-point grappling, grappling for defence, wrestling and ground-fighting.

Falling: *kuk sool won* teaches its practitioners to fall into a variety of positions that minimise the chance of injury.

Animal-style techniques: tiger, mantis, crane, dragon, snake, bear, eagle, etc.

Traditional Korean weapons: sword (short, long, single and double, straight and inverted), staff (short, middle and long, single and double), *jeol bong* (double and triple sectioned; also known as *nunchaku* and *sansetsukon*), knife, spear, cane, rope, fan, bow and arrow (taught in the traditional style, using a thumb draw).

Martial-art healing methods: acupressure, acupuncture, internal energy and herbal medicine.

Meditation and breathing techniques: meditation and breathing postures along with concentration techniques.

Could the martial art I was spending every night of the week practising be the basis for the arts of the ninja? But, if so, where were the stealth techniques?

After the initial first few weeks of training, I'd been bitten completely by the *kuk sool* bug. Each day after school Josh and I would walk to the martial-arts centre and do three classes back to back. Sa Beom Nim's motto was 'We always need more practice!' So that was what we did: night after night, weekends and every school holiday. Each class would be made up of loads of different techniques, from joint-locking/breaking, kicking techniques, animal style, weapons.

Josh's and my favourite technique was one of the palm strikes; we had secretly learnt it while watching some of the higher-grade students and spent all our spare time practising on each other. We weren't meant to perform techniques above our grade but we were fireballs of energy and nothing was out of bounds for us, or so we believed.

Eventually my name was called to get in line for sparring. It was time to focus on the challenge ahead of me. *Kuk sool* sparring is semi-contact and based on points. You need to demonstrate ability to win but also good technique in the style. If you fought like a kickboxer or *jujutsu* fighter, you would be marked down. I put on my matching blue gloves and footpads. My plan was to take advantage of my flexibility and score many hits to the head, as these would get you double points. I would also use some traditional *kuk sool* moves to impress the judges.

My first match was about to start and Sa Beom Nim was watching. I was about to be attacked: I had to rise to the occasion and show perfect form by kicking the guy's backside. Before me stood a slightly overweight but still muscular boy who, like me, was in his early teens, an easy target. The match started and I instantly scored my first point with a roundhouse kick to the head. The game was on. Soon I was winning every round and every match using kicks, lots of them! I had to lie down between matches but my cardiovascular fitness and enthusiasm were too much for most people to handle well. That – and almost all of my opponents were people who practised *kuk sool* as a hobby. They weren't obsessives, like me and Josh.

I wasn't the only one doing really well. The girl in front of me impressed the judges by jumping into the air and striking people from above. Those not seeming to defend themselves were often finished off with a flying sidekick. There was no way I was going to be beaten by a girl with pigtails – and, sooner or later, we were to face each other.

The match started and we both went for it with our normal method. I kicked and she jumped so close that my kick failed to land – *whoomp*. Point went to her, the red side.

Damn! I decided to attack faster, harder, and jump too. Higher and . . . wham! Point to red.

OK, ready . . . Another failed kick.

Point to red.

I was going to lose. I was trying my best but I was going to lose to this irritating girl.

'He's just too fiery.'

I didn't know who'd said it, but I could hear someone talking about my performance.

'She's a kick-boxing champ. He just attacks all the time and that's not going to work on her.'

They were right. I had to change tactic or I would lose. I can't explain why but in that moment I felt that if I were to win I would have to become the opposite: become like water. Retreat, be calm and pick my shots. I knew what she was going to do. I would shorten my stance, cover up tight and raise my guard high, like a Thai kick-boxer or old-school boxer. So I moved continually. When she was in the air I knew she could not change direction, so I could step to the side and strike.

Next round, I gave the perfunctory bow – *gyeong rye* – and, adrenaline coursing through every cell, I listened for the command: '*Junbi!* Ready!' We were off. She was launching towards me with a leap. I barely registered her movement before I heard, '*Son deung pyeong soo* – backhand strike.' It was Josh, trying to remind me that in *kuk sool* the best way to win points was to fight in the traditional manner. Just remember your forms, *remember* the forms. I repeated it like a mantra to myself. I'd spent years practising these movements: I couldn't let myself down now or I was going to be tasting rubber flooring.

When she jumped, I would see this as a target for me to strike. Whatever direction she chose, no matter how aggressive she was, I would accommodate it. It all seemed good in my mind's eye but I needed to wait for the first jump to see if it worked.

Yes! I executed a *sa ma gwi mak-bi* – a praying-mantis block – no problem. I had no idea what my opponent was thinking: all I could do was react and it was seamless. Echoing commands flooded from brain to body – *sang dan dol-a cha gi*, high spin kick, *ha dan dol-a cha gi*, low spin kick, *ssang pyeong soo*, double palm strike, and so it went on. The air seemed thick, too hot, and it was beginning to smell of the combined sweat of two hundred hyperactive martial artists.

Confusion and a slight tinge of nausea threatened to disable me but determination won out and I finished with an awesome *dwi dol-a yeop cha ci*, backward turning side kick, and then . . . a roar of applause. All of a sudden we were bowing and that was that. I walked off, dazed, desperate for a drink and in search of Josh. I was halfway to the refreshment table when I saw him standing on a podium to the right: he was having a gold medal draped over his head by the grandmaster! I was just about to head over when, for the second time that day, I was hooked by the collar. 'Get over to the podium. They're calling your name!' I swivelled on my heel and turned back to where I'd just come from in time to hear, 'And winner of the gold medal for forms – Martin Faulks!'

I couldn't believe it. Josh and I had turned up determined not to compete and ended up winning. The rest of the day was a flurry of activity, and by the end I had not only a gold medal but a bronze for techniques too. This was to be the first tournament of many in which I would succeed against the odds.

Sa Beom Nim was pleased, but as I looked around expectantly for my dad's face in the crowd, Josh gently took my arm. 'Martin, he left soon after he dropped you off . . . I'm sorry.' I felt as if I'd swallowed a hot stone. 'Oh, no problem, I just wanted a lift home . . .' Josh and Sa Beom Nim exchanged a glance that I ignored. I must have upset Dad with the rigmarole of the missing uniform. Josh was used to lack of parental interest, but for me hope sprang eternal that I would impress my mum and dad. It still does.

I loved and will always love *kuk sool won*. People criticise it for being too commercial: the incessant testing and the need for equipment can be a real financial drain. Each testing and each belt cost me hundreds of pounds, including a bizarre silver and black uniform, which made me look like an extra from *Flash Gordon*. My dad used to semi-joke that the Koreans had turned up with a sackful of belts and left with a sackful of money.

Later, Josh and I sat on the wall outside his house with the *kuk sool* manuals, learning about the techniques with a naïvety that only two teenage boys can muster. When we read about moves needed for our blue belt, we saw some were listed as knock-out strikes and kicks. We really believed that when we got to that point we would gain the ability to knock anyone out at will, as if we would gain a magic off-switch over the human body. Then there were meditation techniques, which the grandmaster said could give you the power of seven men. Again, we thought we'd be lifting cars and bending iron bars! Imagine how disappointing it was when the only knock-out strikes we could get to work involved hitting someone very hard on the chin or the temple. We even went as far as hiring an acupuncturist to mark the spots on our bodies, then hit them as hard as we could. Nothing happened.

When we were seventeen, we re-read the manual with new eyes. It was no longer a list of exciting abilities to master but, rather, a list of disappointments. We *hoped* these things could be done but we were not being taught the methods. We were disillusioned because we did not know how to pursue our dreams. Also, the violent aspect of the fighting, plus performing and constant training, was beginning to wear me down. I began to accumulate a catalogue of minor injuries, which eventually culminated in a more serious back problem. My view began to change: I wanted something to help me grow as a person, not just try to do acrobatic things with my body.

Then something happened that changed my world, something that *really* complicated things. I fell in love.

4
Alchemy

*When the sun and the moon, the male and the female join together
to make a third magical state that is alchemy.*

Anon

Meeting Pip moved me into a different world. Here was someone who shared my love of all things mystical, who inspired, encouraged and made me feel I could do anything. But there was a problem. She was nine years older than me – I was eighteen at the time – and she had a child from a previous marriage. I was torn. Not knowing what to do, I made the mistake of asking other people's opinions.

'Listen, Martin, I know you feel you're in love with this woman – hmm, although she is pretty amazing . . .'

'Whoa, stop right there.'

Josh laughed at my obvious discomfort. 'No, seriously, have you thought this out? You've just been asked by Sa Beom Nim Richard to go to America to run the *dojo* in Texas. That's a huge step forward.'

He was right. I'd been offered the opportunity of a lifetime. Our instructor, Richard Roper, was leaving the UK to set up a new *kuk sool won* training centre in Houston, Texas, and he'd asked Josh and me to go with him as instructors. However, there were already problems with those plans. My focus was moving from *kuk sool* to more internal disciplines. My quest was going in a different direction and my body, as well as my spirit, was not happy.

'I know, but my back is *really* bad and I'm not sure I'm going to be up to it. I've been to the physios and they're saying that any more serious fighting is possibly going to cause permanent damage. I need six months off or to change to something less violent.' I hated situations I couldn't fix immediately and the dilemma of 'Should I stay or should I go?' was almost as crippling as my back pain.

Pip was upset when I mentioned going to the USA. We'd formed quite a close bond, even if we weren't officially 'a couple', and it was pretty obvious to everyone around us that we were developing strong feelings. Being so young I was in conflict: I wasn't sure I wanted a serious relationship; I should be focusing on my career. After all, I was one of the most promising students in Richard's class, and the idea of going to the USA was seductive. As Josh said, I could go there, become an instructor and find a hot American chick.

'Well, I guess we can stay friends and just write or phone . . .' Pip was making all the right noises, being stoic and totally unconvincing. It made me feel better, yet I still couldn't decide. I was smitten. I had a woman who was supportive of my obsessions with martial arts, fitness and spirituality but who also liked wrestling: what a catch! Friday nights had become a ritual of WWF, French beer and the hospitality of my mum, who had a huge TV and, more crucially, Sky channels.

After six months of anguished to-ing and fro-ing emotionally and physically, I had a moment of realisation. Pip and I were opposites, her *yin* to my *yang*: she was practical and down to earth and I was full of adventure and big plans. It was time to let my heart take care of matters that concerned it. You wouldn't use your heart to do maths, so don't let your head deal with love. I decided I was staying. I would carry on training with Josh and the other *kuk sool* class in England. But Fate had other ideas.

One day I was walking with Josh through Norwich. It was early evening and we were going to visit my mother, taking a shortcut through the local council estate. I felt what I thought were drops of rain, but when I looked up, two drunken men were spitting on us from the flats above.

'Argh, that's gross!' I gestured angrily.

Josh was shaking his hair, thin specks of spittle still clinging to it.

'Bet they aren't man enough to come down and do it.' I was furious and we stood, considering our mode of revenge.

We didn't have to consider long: they had come down to the street.

It was as if the universe had been listening: we had our chance. Much older and full of drunken bravery, they wanted to fight.

'Oi! You do all that kick-boxing stuff, don't you? What's that all about, hard man?'

A squat, shaven-headed, muscular yob in a bright yellow T-shirt and ripped jeans moved towards me, his head pecking, like a cockerel's.

I evaluated him and his mate. They were both monstrous but the second guy towered over all of us and he was definitely the one to be afraid of. He stood stock still, eyes narrowing, and motioned with his fingers at Josh. 'Come over here.'

Josh was going to do nothing of the sort but suddenly, with an ease of movement rare in one so large, 'the Hulk' practically shepherded Joss into an area behind a shop where the bins were kept.

This was not going to end well so I decided to use distraction. Letting out the most insane yell, I ran like a man possessed and grabbed his mate, swinging him round and head-butting him as hard as I could, my forehead striking at the base of the skull where the brain stem rests.

As bone met bone, the voice of Sa Beom Nim echoed in my head, 'Now, boys, promise me you won't ever use that move.'

I'd broken my word, but I couldn't let Josh get beaten senseless for the second time in our friendship.

The guy slumped to the ground but tried to stand up. I grabbed him by the hair and smashed his face directly into the concrete path.

By now Josh had realised the game was on. He jumped through the air and grabbed the Hulk in a headlock, using his weight to pull him down to his height, and punching him as fast and hard in the face as he could.

As I had been dealing with my opponent, I'd only seen a blur of movement. Turning to see how Josh was doing, I misinterpreted the situation, thinking he was being beaten, not the other way round.

I rushed to his aid and kneed the man in the floating lower rib as hard as I could repeatedly to make him let go. As my leg tired, I switched to elbowing him directly in the lower back.

All this time Josh was choking him and hitting him in the face. The guy finally fell to the ground, and I knew it was time to escape. 'Josh . . . run!'

We sprinted into the distance, expecting to hear pounding footsteps behind us. Nothing. After a few hundred yards we turned. No one was following us – neither man was capable of doing so.

Both lay on the ground, one retching, the other struggling to stand. Blood was smeared all over the smaller man's face.

What had we done? Who had we become? My body had outgrown my discipline and my skill overpowered my judgement. I had been hurting myself and now others. This wasn't what it was supposed to be like. It was time to give up *kuk sool* and develop more balance.

I hadn't been to *kuk sool* for some time and was beginning to get restless at not doing any form of martial arts. I needed something, but I knew it was time to follow a new path: one of healing, for myself and others. Something with calm, gentle goals. I had spent years trying to master violence. Now it was time to master myself.

I decided to try *tai chi*, a much gentler combat technique based on pushing the opponent. The full name of the style is *t'ai chi ch'uan* or *taijiquan*, or *tai chi* in English usage; it means 'infinite ultimate' and relates to the concept that two opposite principles, '*yin*' and '*yang*', can join together to form a third principle that is greater than the sum of its parts. *Yin* is a hot, fiery, outgoing male principle, as I mentioned earlier, while *yang* is a cold, watery, receptive feminine principle. Originating from China and known for its gentle slow movements, *tai chi* is often called an 'internal' martial art as it focuses on developing *chi* or spiritual force. This spiritual force is believed to flow through our entire being, keeping our body healthy and balanced.

Tai chi is practised for its value as self-defence training but is also known to have healing and health-promoting effects on the mind, body and internal organs. The art is steeped in the ancient philosophy of Daoism, which teaches us to go with the flow and value simplicity and flexibility over brute force and strength. I tried a few classes but the lessons I went to taught *tai chi* as a form of health exercise. No pushing, no martial side and no *chi* development. After a lot of thought, I decided I didn't want a Western teacher. But how I would find an authentic Chinese master in rural Norfolk was another matter. Was I setting the bar too high? Would I have to travel to China to find what I wanted?

Sensing my frustration, Pip encouraged me to try something less stressful on the body. She worked as an assistant manager in a whole-foods shop and, as a former massage therapist, she often knew what was going on at the local alternative health centres. 'Did you know there's a traditional Chinese master teaching in Norwich?' She handed me a city directory. 'It says they trained in Beijing and are teaching *tai chi* and *qi gong* at this health centre. Their name is Bo Ou Mander.' I read the directory and learned a bit more about Bo.

Bo was trained in a form of *tai chi* that was popularised as part of a system called *wushu*, which the Chinese government had invented because they didn't like the term *'kung fu'* due to its spiritual associa-tions and wanted to standardise the practice of traditional Chinese martial arts. *'Wushu'* translates as 'martial arts' (武 *'wu'* = military or martial, 术 *'shu'* = art). Recently it has become an international sport through the International Wushu Federation (IWUF); the first World Championships were held in 1991 in Beijing. That piqued my interest, and as I reached for the phone, I saw a sly smile of triumph slip across Pip's face. She knew I'd be back in my element soon, which meant I'd stop complaining.

So I made an appointment. It turned out that the teacher was a woman, not that I had a problem with that but I'd been expecting a wise, venerable master. However, while I was sitting in the waiting room four days later, I read about her and, to all intents and purposes, she sounded like the real deal.

Bo had grown up in China during the Cultural Revolution and attended a *wushu* boarding school from the age of eight. Following a four-year degree course, specialising in the teaching of *wushu*, she had moved to Beijing to deepen her study of *tai chi* and *qi gong*. Bo later trained in traditional Chinese medicine and had done her clinical practice in both China and the UK. Her pedigree was impressive: she had been trained personally by Li Tian Ji, Kan Gui Xiang and Niu Shen Xian, some of the finest martial artists in modern China – and I was excited at the prospect of being taught by someone of such calibre.

After reading about Bo, I was expecting a rather robust martial-arts warrior but was pleasantly surprised to meet a tiny, gentle, seemingly ageless woman, who emanated calm and tranquillity. She was so peaceful she seemed to make the air stand still. As I stood there in the living room in Norwich where she taught her students, I felt as if I was in a temple in China.

The air definitely began to move when I tried to get her to fight. My arrogance and pride went ahead of me and I challenged her. The more I rebelled and wanted to spar, the closer she got to teaching me a valuable lesson: never underestimate a petite, quiet woman! This gentle stream became a fast-flowing river, complete with the odd boulder. We began an exercise called 'pushing hands', a *tai chi* form of combat where no one gets hurt. If boxers box and wrestlers wrestle, then *tai chi* people 'push hands'.

Pushing hands is said to be the way for students to experience the subtle aspect of internal martial arts – the tradition based on the spiritual, mental and energy-related arts such as *qi gong*, which focus on the flow of energy within the mind, body and spirit. Pushing hands encourages the student to relax the natural instinct to resist force with force and teaches the body to yield to the force and redirect it.*

So there we were, doing something completely out of my comfort zone – I found that the more she redirected my blows, the more I

---

* It also teaches you to be aware of your own vital organs, the associated energy flow and especially the crucial acupressure points; it introduces students to the principles of *chin na* (the technique of locking joints so that the opponent cannot move) and aspects of *tui na*, a manipulative therapy also taught in the traditional *tai chi chuan* schools. Pushing hands also begins to take on aspects of *qi gong*, the practice of aligning breath, movement and awareness for exercise, healing and meditation. Originally, like all the techniques, pushing hands had a martial application and could be used empty-handed or when armed with a spear.

wanted to punch her. She was defeating me at every turn – I wanted a fight and she wanted me to calm down! My goal was to win at pushing hands. My ego wanted me to defeat this woman. I was a martial-arts champion, and a five-foot female was thwarting me. I actually got to the point where I thought, I need to hit you to prove a point – how arrogant was that? Eventually my agitation and pride began to recede and we slipped into a rhythmic war dance – push, block, pull, sweep, push. I was hooked. I also had carpet burns from continually being knocked to my knees by a woman eighteen inches shorter than me.

I went for lessons every week, and after six months or so, Bo opened a clinic at her house where she also gave acupuncture treatments. It became more informal but no less enthralling. Each lesson began with a cup of steaming jasmine green tea, a ritual that I still incorporate in my training. Bo's house was a bit of a refuge from outside life. There was nothing ostentatious or overstated. She was a consummate professional. I could have been in a simple acupuncture clinic in China: rows of books lined up on one wall, pale-wash watercolours of old Chinese paintings dotted around others, and the smell of *moxa* (Chinese mugwort, used in acupuncture) filled the air.*

For me, traditional Chinese medicine seems the epitome of precision and order, and the energy of the room reflected that thought.

Bo exuded a calm maternal aura, which was combined on occasion with girlishness when we discussed something metaphysical or discovered a new way of applying a technique, which sparked her innate love of learning and sharing wisdom. Often just a few sentences would send her running for a book, carefully chosen from her extensive collection and laid open to confirm a theory or resolve our curiosity. Unlike some Western teachers, Bo was always open to new things

---

* Moxibustion is a traditional Chinese medicine therapy, using *moxa* made from dried mugwort. The mugwort is aged, ground to a fluff, then formed into a cigar-shaped incense stick. The therapist lights the *moxa* and holds it about two inches from the body, usually over acupuncture points (with or without needles) or meridians. This allows the skin to be suffused with warmth.

and eager to enhance her already extensive learning. She had no discernible ego and was one of the most gentle, genuine and naturally gifted masters I have ever encountered. After years of training, the regular practice of internal martial arts (we practised various types of *qi gong*, including *tai chi*, *ba duan jin*,* the Small Circulation, and *yijin jing* or muscle/tendon change) helped to heal a lot of the chronic injuries I had sustained from the hard martial arts. It also gave me much-needed balance. I'd gained more flexibility. I could now be gentle and receptive, retreating, soft and adaptable, like water, or firing and attacking, like fire, aggressive and connecting, like a bolt of lightning.

Love and *tai chi* had taught me that two opposites could combine to make something different and better – but I needed something further to help me reach the next level. I wasn't sure what but, however much I loved the internal arts and the gentleness of *tai chi*, I still craved more. That childhood yearning to become more than a normal man still haunted me.

After much musing and months of research, I boiled it down to *ninjutsu*. It was time to follow my dream and train as a ninja.

---

* *Ba duan jin qi gong* is one of the most common forms of Chinese *qi gong* used as exercise. Variously translated as 'Eight Pieces of Brocade' or 'Eight Silken Movements', the name of the form generally refers to how the eight individual movements characterise and impart a silken quality (like that of a piece of brocade) to the body and its energy. The *ba duan jin* is primarily designated as a form of medical *qi gong*, meant to improve health. This is in contrast to religious or martial forms of *qi gong*. The categorisation does not preclude the form's use by martial artists as a supplementary exercise.

5

Immovable Heart

◆

Know that patience comes first.
Know that the path of man comes from justice.
Renounce avarice, indolence, and obstinacy.
Recognise that sadness and regret are natural and
therefore seek to develop an immovable spirit.
Do not stray from the path of loyalty and familial
Love, and pursue the warrior and literary arts
with balanced determination.

Toda, 'The Law of the *Dojo*', *Shinden Fudo Ryu*

So there I was four years later, once more in Bo's waiting room but this time worrying about her reaction to my desire to study not only a more aggressive martial art but, worse, a *Japanese* one. I was hoping she would give me her blessing to go on my quest, but in Oriental traditions, it is a big thing to ask permission from your instructor to seek tuition under another master, let alone one from a different culture.

I was so involved in mentally rehearsing my 'I want to train as a ninja' speech that I didn't notice the previous student leave. Suddenly Bo was calling me in. As I entered the room, she was tidying up after her last client. Any hopes I had of remaining cool vanished, and I blurted out my plan, explaining to her everything I knew about ninja and why I felt it was important that I embark on this quest. When I finished she looked stunned and took a few moments to absorb what I'd said.

Finally she spoke, 'So you want to train as a ninja?'

I nodded, ignorant of how this would go from there.

Bo paused again. We sat together for what was probably only a few moments but time seemed to stretch out in an interminable stream. I kept glancing at the Chinese art on the walls – watery glimpses of life in bucolic provinces I'd never visit. Why now did I suddenly feel drawn to Japan? I'd always thought I'd be off to Beijing to train in the artful footsteps of Bo and her masters, doing *tai chi* in the parks and searching the markets for pungent healing herbs.

'I suspect you may need to search many different places to find the true art of *ninjutsu*. You will have to travel to different countries and undertake many hardships.'

I said nothing.

Eventually Bo gave a small smile, dipped her chin in a sweet nod and said, 'Go ahead with my blessing, but be careful your heart does not become corrupted by these skills.'

I nodded respectfully but curiosity had the better of me: 'How do I protect my heart?'

'Ah, these skills are very powerful. To protect your heart you have to make sure you know what your true motives are. Ask yourself what makes you want to go on this quest.'

That took me by surprise. I had spent so much time trying to gather the courage to tell her I wanted to train as a ninja but hadn't really taken the time to work out exactly what my motives were. I'd read the books, seen the films, done the hard and soft martial arts, but what exactly did I have in mind?

To me, the whole spectrum of martial arts is based on the same dream. They focus on the principle of becoming stronger, faster and more skilled. I'd learnt that, in an ideal world, a martial-arts student would succeed and become more disciplined than a normal man. From my studies, I'd deduced that a true student of martial arts could stand up for the common good; he would take it upon himself to help and protect others and his actions would demonstrate justice and honour. In hindsight, I can see my childhood dreams of dealing out justice like Batman reflected these thoughts. But there was obviously more to it than that. There was the element of danger that appealed; then there was the subterfuge and myriad techniques to overpower and disable the enemy. Far more than just a martial art, this tradition taught mind control and distinctly esoteric techniques. Also, if I was really honest with myself, I just thought ninja were pretty cool.

The concept of protecting my heart appealed to me. I knew Bo was well read and understood more about other cultures than she let on. So, before she went to make some jasmine tea, she had a look through her bookshelves. Lo and behold, she pulled out a volume that was wedged between two tomes, one on medical herbalism and the other on Chinese folklore. It was a book on the sacred sites and shrines of Asia. She handed it to me. 'This will show you the spiritual root of *ninjutsu*.'

As I flicked through the book I soon discovered more about the way *ninjutsu* was connected with Buddhism. I learnt that one of the mainstream major schools of Japanese Buddhism was called Shingon Buddhism. It was a tradition full of magical powers, mystic hand signs and metaphysical abilities. It seemed that in Japan a philosophical and esoteric dimension drawn from Buddhism was used in certain martial-arts training called *fudōshin* (不動心). It is a state of equanimity or imperturbability, even when faced with danger or evil, which effectively translates as *fudō*, 'no move', and *shin*, 'heart/spirit/will'; therefore *fudōshin* is 'immovable mind/will or spirit' or 'immovable heart'.

I couldn't put my finger on it but something was falling into place. During my earlier research, I'd noticed that the *kanji** for '*nin*' is made up of the pictograms representing the heart ('*kokoro*') and the blade ('*ken*'). *Nin* can translate as both 'endurance' and 'stealth', so the ninja must keep his heart and mind in complete control. In this case we can associate the blade with the sharp mind, the perfect weapon, and the heart must be immovable or incorruptible. In the context of *ninjutsu*, it is a vitally important state of mind, a place of determined and almost permanent meditation, whereby the mind is calm but disciplined, focused and ruthless in its clarity. *Fudōshin* is a state of mindfulness whereby the ninja is aware of everything happening in his sphere of consciousness without becoming disturbed by anything and remaining purely focused on his goal; will-power and strength of character are paramount.

* One of the three scripts used in the Japanese language. They are Chinese characters, first introduced to Japan in the fifth century via Korea.

The blade, or sword, would become a much-used focus for me in the years that followed, not just as a weapon but also as a metaphor for the mind. The sword in action reflects the state of mind of the person wielding it; controlled, ever-vigilant, able to outmanoeuvre and defeat the enemy, whether that enemy is physical or mental. Negative, unproductive or destructive thought and action are sliced through with the sword of the mind so that balance and discipline prevail. The term *fudōshin* comes in part from the deity Fudō-myōō, depicted with a sword in his right hand, used to cut through delusions and ignorance. Now, sitting in Bo's presence, I understood completely. The ninja aimed to be enlightened warriors with clear vision and immovable determination. This was amazing.

FUDŌ-MYŌŌ

I'd obviously been deep in thought because Bo had to clear her throat to attract my attention. 'I see you found answer?'

I felt like a kid caught with his hand in the sweetie jar. 'Erm, yes. It's actually telling me about the process of protecting the heart, as you mentioned.'

She nodded. 'It's a very important concept and one you find in many different religions. It is about being true, straight and unmoved by the world's problems.'

'Is it like the Buddhist concept that all is suffering and we need to accept it?'

Bo never really frowned: she focused on a complex question or thought with a subtle movement of the body – a deep inhalation followed by a squaring of the shoulders, almost in preparation for a gentle battle. 'I don't like the word "suffer". It seems too harsh.' She shook her head, almost as if perplexed by the idea. 'No, it is more that we are moved too much by the impermanence of things – how can we expect never to break a vase or for a loved one to live for ever? We get too caught up in our own lives and those of others and expect never to be upset or hurt. The heart should be guarded against these things and to protect you against the world and its illusions.'

I needed to think more about this and my motives. Bo was watching me like a hawk.

'Consider your intentions. They must always be good. If you do not cultivate a proper or correct heart it will cause confusion and distress.'

I learnt later that a 'correct heart' implies adherence to virtue, righteousness, loyalty and sincerity. Without these qualities, it is impossible to have good intentions and to protect ourselves from the dangerous games people play.

'The way to ensure your heart is protected is to make sure that your intention is correct. This does not mean having absolute purity of intention, as this doesn't exist, but we need to make sure that our primary motive is the direct cause of our actions.'

I looked at her quizzically.

'Imagine a man wishes to be famous so he chooses to raise money for charity to achieve his goal. Part of him also wishes to do good and we must respect him for choosing a noble vehicle for his ambitions. However, in time, this will result in negative outcomes because his primary motive is not correct. Another man wishes to do good for the world but also enjoys attention and fame as a side effect. His work will have good outcomes because the heart cannot be corrupted.'

I had heard much about the heart in other traditions. Pip, now my wife, being obsessed with ancient Egypt, often spoke of how the heart needs to be pure and filled with *maat*, a principle the Egyptians held dear; it roughly translates as 'truth, justice and order'. It was imperative to the ancients that their heart was uncorrupted so that they could live a good life and go on to become immortal in the realm of the gods.

Well, it all sounded correct to me, but it still didn't seem to match. I could understand the ninja wanting to have clear vision and immovable resolve. But how could you steal and kill people if you were Buddhist? Weren't ninja supposed to be tricksters and assassins? How could purity *and* deception co-exist in their world?

6

In Search of a Class

Always follow that quest. The one set out by the burning question you have in your heart.

An-shu Stephen K. Hayes

The mission was on! I needed to learn the true art of *ninjutsu* and, after reading the book at Bo's and listening to her, I had more questions than answers. I was thirsty for more understanding. The martial arts I'd already mastered had certainly given me great enjoyment, and the spiritual arts Bo taught were very valuable, but I was still drawn towards *ninjutsu*. I carried with me an ideal of the ninja: an ordinary man, freeing himself from the normal limitations through his skill and secret knowledge; he can go anywhere, remain invisible and have mental, physical and spiritual powers beyond the realm of most people.

I believe that knowledge bestows power, so I continued reading and watching everything I could lay my hands on. My passion grew with each book and DVD but I was confused by the wealth of information on offer. Thanks to the ninja boom of the seventies and eighties, the Western world was flooded with self-proclaimed ninja authorities. Probably the only populist ones to whom we can give credence (who are still teaching various forms of *ninjutsu*) are Masaaki Hatsumi, Stephen K. Hayes and their students. The other schools I found looked like *karate* or *kung fu* and offered no evidence of Japanese heritage. My focus narrowed to a lineage known as the *bujinkan*.

I wanted to know more about those masters. What inspired them? Where did they come from? More importantly, what and where did they teach?

Masaaki Hatsumi claims a serious pedigree, but also demonstrates a very distinct martial style and skill-set to back it up. Any martial artist can look at what he does and know instantly that it is a different style, that the range of movements and weapons is more than could have been made up by one man.

The story goes that Hatsumi took over the teaching of *ninjutsu* from his teacher Takamatsu in 1972, having spent fifteen years studying with him on Honshu Island.* At this point, I discovered that Stephen Hayes, that enigmatic figure from my childhood, was Hatsumi's ex-student. Here was the man who had started the Western obsession with all things ninja. Upon returning from Japan armed with Hatsumi's teachings, he had started teaching the world. Later he became a figurehead for the ninja art and inspired Liam Neeson's character Ra's al Ghul, in *Batman Begins*, or so the internet forums would have you believe. Hayes also felt a burning desire to 'find' the real ninja, and his travels to Japan during the seventies and eighties led him to train extensively with Masaaki Hatsumi. He took his skills back to North America where he founded the Shadows of Iga Society and, through his numerous books, introduced the Western world to *ninjutsu* and the teachings of Hatsumi. In the late 1990s, Hayes phased out the

---

* Hatsumi was named as 34th Soke, a Japanese term for head of the school of *togakure-ryu*, and later founded *bujinkan ryoha* (*ryo* or *ryoha* is a suffix which roughly translates as 'school/school of thought'). Much of Hatsumi's lineage and historical claims to *ninjutsu* have been challenged over the years but, in true ninja style, no one really knows for sure where the truth lies.

His school, the *bujinkan*, is most commonly associated with *ninjutsu* but the term *budō* (meaning 'martial way') is used more commonly as the nine schools of teachings descend from both samurai martial techniques (six) and ninja tactics (three). Just like his history, Hatsumi's *bujinkan* is viewed with some suspicion and neither of the two organisations (Nihon Kobudo Kyokai and Nihon Kobudo Shinkokai) that recognise and verify the history and validity of Japanese martial arts recognises its nine schools as being *koryu* (old-school Japanese martial arts with verifiable lineages that predate the Meiji restoration in 868). The scrolls that would be handed down for such a school have never been seen but that didn't put me off wanting to know more: after all, what ninja school would live by samurai rules?

Shadows of Iga Society, and founded the Quest Centers, now a world-wide organisation offering *to-shin do*, a Western system of *ninjutsu*.*

The more I looked into it, the more I started to believe that Hatsumi was the real deal. When I read about him, something rang instinctively true. I did not really care about the off-shoot schools: I wanted to find the source. I knew that if I went to ninja classes, I would quickly find out if the skills were genuine by pressure-testing them. There was no real way of proving that a ninja school was historically correct without evidence of extant textual scrolls handed from teacher to student; so surely the only criterion for truth must be if the techniques worked. It was time to stop reading and start doing.

* Hatsumi and Hayes definitely became my focus of attention but to finish the roll-call of ninja teachers and 'schools' there are a few others worth noting: Genbukan – as mentioned above, this worldwide organisation was founded by Hatsumi and Takamatsu's student Shoto Tanemura, who left *bujinkan* after a disagreement with Hatsumi. Genbukan is a huge organisation spanning thirty countries and twenty states in the US and has thirty-six divisions called '*ninja sanjurokkei*', teaching a wide variety of techniques.

Kage No Michi Ninjutsu – which translates into 'The Way of the Shadow Ninjutsu', is a modern derivative of traditional *ninjutsu*. This style was founded by Tafan Hong in 2005; he holds rank in the traditional *bujinkan ninjutsu* system and was inducted into the USA Martial Arts Hall of Fame in 2008. It is based on the principles of traditional *ninjutsu* but executed in a modern style.

7

You Can't Kick in Samurai Armour

Not everyone can be ninja. That takes an understanding of the whole history and science of ninpo. You have seen the whole forest; the technique is only one tree. To be ninja you must see the whole thing.

Hatsumi Sensei

I had visited Google and found a school that looked perfect for my needs. The school advertised itself as Bujinkan Budo Taijutsu, which translates roughly as 'Divine Warrior Hall; martial way of unarmed combat'. However, the advertising used the Japanese pictogram for ninja and pictures of ninja. According to the blurb, the instructor had practised the art for more than thirty years and trained with Hatsumi Sensei in Japan, so I knew he was the right man for the job.

As I entered the village hall, the senior instructors were putting away basketball hoops left over from the last occupants. We, however, standing in our black uniforms, looked the part and many of us had patches with ninja symbols on them. Unlike other martial arts, there were only two types of belt, green and black. I was told this came from the times when people used to train outside until their white belt turned green with grass stains. Having trained outside in the UK, I suspected a dirty brown colour would be more appropriate.

The place reminded me of school, with a strong smell of bleach and floors worn from years of heavy activity.

Everyone was making small-talk, nothing about martial arts. As I listened, I could tell something was different from the *kuk sool* schools I had attended. Something felt uncomfortable.

The teacher walked in. He was a tall, thin man of about fifty, with long grey hair in a ponytail, which hung almost to the middle of his back. His martial-arts uniform was black but his black belt was worn white around the edges. He had a big red ninja patch on his chest, showing the Japanese *kanji* for 'ninja'. In his hand, he held an enormous sports bag, full of swords, sticks and an array of exotic weapons.

'OK, lads, line up!'

We did so. He clapped twice, mumbled something in Japanese and everyone repeated it. I couldn't work out what had been said but it sounded like '*Shiken haramitsu daikoumyo.*'

One more clap and another bow, then half the class bowed again. I'd no idea what was going on.

'Pair up. Today we're doing some techniques from *gyuku ryu.*'

I was dumbfounded. No warm-up, no stretching, no conditioning. In every other martial-arts class I had been to, we had spent a long period warming up. Long training sessions could place serious strain on the body unless the muscles were warm.

I was opposite a Greek-looking man; he had serious deep-set eyes and didn't seem particularly friendly.

'John.'

'Martin. Nice to meet you. Don't we do a warm-up?'

'Um, not really . . .'

'Why's that?'

He regarded me blankly. 'Let me ask Ray.' He interrupted a very overweight man, who was talking to another student. 'Ray, this is Markus, it's his first lesson. Why don't we warm up?'

Behind them, I could see the instructor reading something from a book while everyone continued talking, this time in pairs.

Ray puffed out his chest and squinted. 'Well, Markus, you don't get to warm up in a fight now, do ya?' He paced backwards and forwards as he talked.

I started to say, 'Actually, it's Martin,' but he blustered on.

'I mean you can't ask the mugger to stop while you stretch, can you? Ooh, excuse me, Mr Mugger, I just need to warm up for thirty minutes before you beat me up!' He smirked at John and they gave a patronising snigger.

I was not amused. This was the stupid, macho posturing I was trying to avoid.

He looked at the *kuk sool won* badge on my uniform. '*Some* people spend most of the lesson warming up.'

He was right on both counts, I guess, but if we were about to do some serious training I thought we should warm up.

The teacher wandered in front of the class and read the technique from the book. Then he performed it for us. Couldn't he remember it? What was going on? Having come from a martial art where gradings were given on the ability to perform techniques from memory, I was appalled. The technique itself was strange, the movements slow and jerky; no spinning, no jumps or rapid movements. One man stood in a low stance, one hand over the heart and the other arm held out, pointing at the eye of the opponent, his hand out in a *karate* chop position but with the fingers bent. He lowered his rear hand to belt level in a fist shape but with one thumb pointing out. He then stepped towards his opponent with a giant lunging punch. I had never seen anything like it before and it seemed unbelievably impractical. His opponent, in the same starting position, took an exaggerated step back and, in a jerky motion, back-fisted the held-out arm of his assailant. He then stepped in with his back foot and kicked the attacker on the leg and then, stepping in with the front foot which was still in the air from kicking, struck the arm that was still held out using a knife-fist. The whole thing looked like something from a badly programmed computer game. I had so many questions. Why were we squatting so low that we could hardly move? Why would anyone punch like that? Why would the attacker keep his arm in that position after punching? What purpose is there in back-fisting or blocking an arm from a punch we had already avoided? Why do we step in with the back foot then kick from the front rather than just kicking from the back foot? Kicks are better off the back foot anyway. Why are we kicking to the leg and attacking that wrist? What was going on? I didn't want to ask. That would be construed as rude and it was time to show discipline and practice.

'You need to lower your stance.' John nodded at my positioning. I tried my best to imitate his. Back foot very bent, front foot less bent, weight almost all on the back; hand over heart, front hand held out. So, back arm and leg bent, front arm and leg straight.

'OK, that's good, but you need to line your feet up so that your front knee is past your toes. Your feet at exactly a ninety-degree angle to each other. You can use the line of the mats to help you. Just practise this until you have it exactly right.'

I did as I was told but as I practised I had more questions and my attitude towards the class was sinking rapidly. Why would we choose to fight in such an unnatural stance? What's to be gained by fighting in such a stupid position? Would the perfect 90-degree stance make the opponents scared?

I knew I had to change my attitude if I was going to get anything out of it. The truth is that we all expect things to be as we were educated or brought up. How we live at home is how we expect other's lives to be. In this case my martial-arts education had been so different that I was looking at everything negatively. But, still, as I watched the others training in that room, I couldn't help but be disappointed. I had expected a room full of elite athletes fitter than most martial artists, more alert, dedicated and skilful. As I tried the techniques I felt hobbled, limited and handcuffed. I was expecting to learn the secrets of fluid movement, methods to allow me to move faster and more naturally. Instead I was playing a game of 'robot fighting' with John.

As the teacher came to ask how we were doing, we demonstrated and I naturally kicked off the back foot and was immediately corrected.

Rather than taking it, I blurted out, 'Sensei, why do we kick off the front foot here? It seems natural to kick from behind, rather than add in the extra step.' Bad move. The whole room sniggered at me for calling him 'Sensei'. Of course, they just used his name. As I stared at him, he appeared like a character from a film, the ponytail, the scraggy physique, his uniform hanging off him – like a poorly acted baddie from a seventies martial-arts B movie. He grasped at his goatee and said loudly, so everyone could hear, 'This . . . Grasshopper,' more sniggers, 'is the traditional technique, in which you kick from the front foot after a step. If you wish to play with the technique and think up variations, go ahead . . . after the class.'

He started to walk away but then, in a *Colombo* moment, he had an afterthought and stopped in his tracks. 'The kick has to come from the front foot because you are wearing armour and you can't get the back foot through the *fauld*, which is the skirt-like armour covering the legs. So, this step-through is common. That's also why we only really see a small number of kicks in *ninjutsu*.'

Well, that told me – but I hadn't finished yet: 'So why do we strike to the wrist so much, Teacher?'

'It's because that is the only part of the body not armoured – the inside of the wrist.' He indicated the point on the arm.

I thought for a second. So that was why we were kicking to the leg – we were both in armour and weighed down and just wanted to make the other person fall over. Might that also explain the strange stances? Would they work well in armour and in a battlefield situation when one slip meant death? 'But what's the point in striking the wrist?'

'There are vital points there that, if hit correctly, have a devastating effect. Remember also you would have gauntlets so it would really hurt.' With that he was off.

The thing was, I knew that most of the 'vital points' thing was a load of rubbish. As I've mentioned, Josh and I had spent a whole day with an acupuncturist who had marked those points on our body. There were some basic anatomical ones that worked – the temples, the neck, the solar plexus, the pit of the stomach – but on the rest there's no effect, even if hit with a hammer! Perhaps in this technique we were aiming to disarm the opponent with a couple of giant thumps on the wrist.

Nevertheless, it still seemed strange to me. Why would ninja be wearing armour? Should we not be practising how to jump down from a wall and strangle someone?

As the teaching continued I hated every single moment of it. The techniques were all like that one. The class was like some kind of performance art where we were focusing on minute factors of body alignment. We stepped in such strange stances that it was hard to get any momentum or flow – all very un-ninja. By the end of the class, I was through. I would never come back: it was madness.

After the lesson everyone settled at a table to talk, so I took the opportunity to ask the teacher more questions. 'Thank you for allowing me to come to your class. Tell me, do we do any of the other ninja arts?'

He smiled at me as if I were a child asking to ride in a fire engine. 'Sure, you can do all that in a weekend course.'

Ray interrupted, 'If you want to crawl over walls and hide in mud and stuff, why don't you just join the army?'

He was drinking Monster Energy, the first of two cans lined up before him.

In that moment, I hated him.

I turned back to the instructor. 'But don't you think that these things take daily practice? So many weapons to learn, all those different arts and philosophies?'

'We teach all the weapons here, Markus, but you do need to get the basics of *taijutsu* down first. I myself have been studying the school of Miyamoto Musashi, the famous sword master.' He got up excitedly from his seat and took two wooden swords from his bag, one long, one short. I was fascinated.

Ray was not. 'Listen, *mate*, why don't you join the army?'

Greek John joined in: 'Yeah, this is a martial-arts class.' He shook his head witheringly and grabbed Ray's second can, aggressively pulling the ring and swigging at it.

Ray had obviously got his macho *mojo* up with the caffeine and sugar and was on a roll. 'So, you want to dress up like a ninja, throw blinding powders and death stars and jump around?'

A thin-faced, aggressive woman, with straw-like blonde hair, moved her chair closer, eyes narrowed. Our teacher had given up talking about his sword methods and was reluctantly putting the weapons away.

'Yeah, I would like to learn the traditional arts of a ninja – stealth, weather prediction, spying, tracking, meditation—'

I never got to finish my list.

Ray roared with laughter. 'He wants to be a weatherman!'

The blonde woman cut in, 'A ninja weatherman! But would we see him or would he be hiding in the trees sniffing the wind?'

The whole group was laughing at me now.

John piped up again: 'So, why don't you join the army if you want to do all that?'

I looked at him incredulously and shook my head. Join the army to become a ninja weatherman?

The teacher had sat down again and, thankfully, took the situation under control. He clasped his hands together and leaned forward. 'Markus . . .'

'It's *Martin*,' I corrected him, through gritted teeth. These guys were really beginning to annoy me.

He gestured impatiently, 'Sorry, Martin. Look, no one's laughing at you here.'

Well, they blatantly were but I wasn't going to argue: he was trying to be kind.

'I understand what you're saying. I was once like you and wanted to learn all this old stuff but, Martin, it's not sensible or useful. Nowadays you can learn what the weather is doing from your smartphone. There is no use in the modern world for stealth, studying poisons and assassination methods. No one needs to learn to ride a horse while firing a bow at a moving target and it's impractical to do so. Ninja weapons, like throwing stars, are banned here in Britain. We ride motorbikes, not horses now!'

'Crazy people acting like loonies sneaking about at night . . .' Ray interjected, but was silenced by a look from his teacher.

'In the seventies, during the ninja boom, people started doing all sorts of crazy things and causing trouble. People were throwing *shuriken* at football matches. We teach *taijutsu*, self-defence and traditional weapons of the ninja, but we are not a historical re-enactment society or—'

'We once had some guy come here dressed in full ninja uniform,' the blonde girl interrupted, finding her voice at last, 'mask and all!'

As I exited the room, I heard John call out, like the proverbial broken record, 'Why don't you join the army if you want to do things like that?'

8

The American Dream

If he holds on to the tail of a horse even a bug can go far.

Hatsumi Sensei

'Ladies and gentlemen, we are about to begin our final descent into Dayton International Airport. Dayton is proud to be the home of the famous Wright Brothers. Without them, you probably wouldn't be flying with us today! Currently at DIA the weather is a balmy seventy-two degrees. We have certainly enjoyed having you on board today and hope to see you again real soon. Thanks again for flying American Airlines.'

I had been drifting in and out of sleep on the last leg of the journey but came to just in time to catch the captain's witty drawl. I rolled my shoulders, cramped from the economy-class micro-seating, and strained to see out of the window. Toy Town buildings came into view, dotted among a patchwork of fields. So this would be my home for the next month.

I'd read about students of the martial arts who go on great pilgrimages to find the true secrets but that was usually somewhere exotic – distant mountains or unexplored lands. I, however, had flown to America to spend time under the tuition of the great ninja master, Stephen K. Hayes. If rumours were to be believed, he had not only studied with the very last ninja grandmaster, Masaaki Hatsumi, but was also the first Westerner to be given a *myko kyden*, an award showing total knowledge of the ninja ways.

As I sat there, I wondered what I would say to him when we met. Since I was a child I'd heard amazing stories about him. Some I knew to be true but others were just the stuff of legends. I knew that he had taken part in a documentary about ninja on the Discovery Channel, in which he had been challenged to 'assassinate' a hostage being held by a Swat team. The bullets were fake but his skills were real and he won the day.

I reflected on how much for me rested on Stephen Hayes living up to his reputation. I was exhausted after nearly eighteen hours of travelling but was also pretty fired up by the thought of the training ahead. I couldn't wait to get started but I was filled with trepidation; I hadn't had a chance to relax, never mind get much sleep. Nevertheless, I was excited to meet the expert who, I was sure, could teach me the secrets of the ninja. After my experience with classes in the UK it was time to go to the man who had started it all, whom I had seen in *Black Belt* magazine so many years ago.

Hayes had been born in Wilmington, Delaware, but had spent most of his early years in Dayton where his main *dojo* (training centre) was now based. He'd started training in martial arts as a teenager in the mid-1960s when he attended Miami University in nearby Oxford, Ohio. He had begun with the Korean art *tang soo do*. Then in the 1970s he had ventured to Japan to seek out authentic ninja masters. It was in June 1975 that he had met and begun training under Masaaki Hatsumi, the renowned thirty-fourth grandmaster of *togakure-ryū ninjutsu* and founder of the *bujinkan* organisation. In the latter part of 1980 Hayes's residency visa had expired and he had returned to the USA with his wife, Rumiko; he then began teaching and has since authored numerous books and magazine articles, and produced a set of DVDs.

His martial-arts credentials were manifold and I was seriously impressed. From what I'd read about him, he appeared to be one of the few genuine authorities to have come out of the 1980s Ninja boom. After training for more than a decade in Japan, he had gone on to travel in Tibet, where he had met the Dalai Lama and become proficient in Tibetan Buddhism. Later he had met the Dalai Lama again at a conference in the USA. It was at this meeting that the Dalai Lama learnt he had won the Nobel Peace Prize and, due to the subsequent media frenzy, Hayes was quickly asked to assist with security.

Afterwards, throughout the 1990s, he was called upon regularly to escort and protect the Dalai Lama. I had also heard that Hayes had learnt secret Tibetan martial arts and esoteric lore. I didn't know if I should believe that or not but it was possible: he is also an ordained practitioner of esoteric *tendai mikkyo* Buddhism.* Hayes had clearly followed a personal quest that had led him to travel the globe for tuition from the greatest spiritual masters. Now I was hoping that I could learn as much from him.

Further research demonstrated that Stephen Hayes never did anything half-heartedly. He seemed to dedicate himself 100 per cent to whichever cause he chose to follow and I saw parallels in this with myself: why be a mediocre teacher when you could be the best? Why not strive to be the most skilled martial artist in the world? He threw himself into whatever he followed, had true focus and didn't seem to be swayed by social status or popularity. Clearly, he was a successful man who had amassed great wealth – enough to live a peaceful and comfortable life. It was also obvious, though, that that wasn't his prime motivation: his dedication to his art and the way that he was reputed to teach made plain that he was not just a businessman or power-hungry.

So here I was in Dayton, Ohio. Perhaps now I'd found the *dojo* where I could start my ninja training with a real master. After the embarrassment of the class in the UK, I hoped this would be different. I had a month, all the time I could get off work: would it be enough? Well, for starters it would have to do. I would listen to everything, observe everything and, hopefully, I would gain a grounding in the spiritual side of things. I was no stranger to the more esoteric teachings but, as no two paths are alike, I certainly had much to learn.

I had surprised myself with my almost immediate affection for America. Naturally it was far warmer than the UK but I also found the people friendlier – I was even told to 'Have a nice day!' with my breakfast.

I'd woken early. I couldn't work out if it was nerves or excitement,

---

* *Tendai* is a Japanese school of *mahayana* Buddhism. *Mikkyo* literally means 'secret teachings, esoteric Tantric Buddhism'.

perhaps a combination of the two, but I was buzzing with adrenaline. I was staying in a Holiday Inn near a large shopping mall, with endless tarmac stretched across the car park but no pavements. I decided to drop in on the mall for a drink to take to the *dojo*. I guessed it would take me about half an hour to walk to the Dayton Quest Center. I armed myself with several soda bottles and some protein bars, then headed off to meet Stephen Hayes.

My previous observation of no pavements was reinforced when I got to the main road but by then I had no option but to walk down the verge of the highway. It soon appeared that no one in the USA walked anywhere and this was confirmed when I heard a slow cater-waul of a police siren behind me. A patrol car crawled to a stop beside me and two cops with the obligatory aviator sunglasses peered at me suspiciously.

'Excuse me, sir, can you tell us where you're going today, please?'

I raised my hand in greeting, 'Hello, good morning!' I sounded like someone from the 1950s – my English had suddenly become perfectly enunciated, as if I'd just come from a top-notch private school. Inwardly wincing, I continued, 'Erm, I'm heading to the Dayton Quest Center on Far Hills Avenue. I'm going to train as a ninja!' They stared at me. I saw my hot, sweaty reflection in two pairs of mirrored shades. The reflex exaggerated martial-arts stance and nervous laugh had obviously done me no favours.

'Sir,' this was Cop Clone One, 'on this occasion we can give you a ride.' I gratefully hopped into the back seat – even at that early hour the heat was almost unbearable.

'So you're over from *Eng-a-land*?' Cop Clone Two's shaded eyes fixed on me in the rear-view mirror.

'Yes, sir. I'm here to train with Stephen Hayes.'

He nodded slow approval. 'Yeah, I know Stephen. Ma boy trains with him too. He's a good man.'

They cruised to a halt and I thanked them profusely for the ride. As I slammed the door shut, Cop Clone One leant out of the window: 'Sir, we were more than happy to give you a ride today but I respect-fully ask you not to walk on the highway again.'

Funnily enough, he said that to me several times over the course of the month.

I was early. Classes started at ten-thirty and I looked around uncomfortably, hoping that no one had seen my arrival in a police car. I had noticed on the drive that many of the buildings in Dayton were spaced in clusters but with a fair gap between them. I guess I hadn't expected the *dojo* to look as it did: a single-storey plain stuccoed building situated next to a couple of fast-food joints. I suppose we're used to Hollywood interpretations of great spiritual masters, teaching their students in mystical surroundings, deep in a forest or amid misty mountains. Shrugging off a sense of disappointment, I leant into one of the windows, shading my eyes against the reflection. Through the glass I was surprised to see a vast, fully equipped *dojo* with mirrored walls, life-size dummies, body pads, practice weapons, the lot. It was the real deal.

Behind me, a car pulled up. I squinted into the light and saw that it was not Hayes, who is a big man with a trademark white beard, but someone small and wiry, with hardly any body fat. I noted, with interest, that he bore no resemblance to the overweight ninjas I'd met back in the UK.

'Hey! You must be Martin. Pleased to meet you. I'm James Norris. An-shu Hayes will be heading in to meet you later.'

Eager to get started, I followed him into the *dojo*. It was really well organised, with a wooden counter to the front, stacked with Quest Center merchandise, books, DVDs and some really cute Japanese floral-print *tabi* socks, that I mentally earmarked as a gift for my stepdaughter. Further along there was a waiting area, and still further, the changing rooms, office and a side room. I peeked inside and saw a row of glass cases but my eye was immediately drawn to the wall where what looked like the front of a Japanese-style house was hanging.

James followed my line of sight and smiled. 'You like the *kamidana*?'

'It's beautiful. What exactly is it? A shrine?'

'Yep. It's also known as a "god shelf". It's a traditional piece that most people have in their homes in Japan, kind of a house for the *kami*.' When used in the *dojo*, he told me, it was also a spiritual focus for the *kami*, the spirits of nature, and the place it was situated was called the *kamiza* – the 'seat of the gods'.

'You'll find out more when we work on the elements.' He pointed at the various objects surrounding the shrine. 'This,' he said, gesturing at a small round mirror on a stand just in front of the doors to the shrine, 'is the *kamidana shintai* – it houses the deity. You might get to see a ceremony while you're here but, if not, it's quite simple but beautiful, with prayers and offerings of flowers, rice, water and fruit.' He began to wander away. 'Oh, don't touch anything unless your hands are clean!'

'Wow, James, what are these?' Three magnificent Japanese paintings took up the better part of the opposite wall. The first was of a monk in a bright orange robe sitting on a rock seemingly in meditation. The second portrayed an enigmatic figure riding a giant toad and wearing a multi-coloured kimono, his hands in what seemed a magical gesture. The third painting was of a man standing under a waterfall. The icy water was raining over him and depicted a struggle against the freezing torrents.

'They represent the three traditions – Buddhism, *ninjutsu* and *yamabushi* – all these are influences for us. The first is Bodhidharma – you know him, the founder of Zen Buddhism?'

I did – I had read that Master Hayes had trained in the Japanese Myoko Buddhist path and taught in a school called the Blue Lotus Assembly.

James Norris went on, 'Bodhidharma founded his branch of Buddhism in China in AD500 at the Shaolin Temple. His school of Buddhism has a focus on meditation and self-control. When his teachings came to Japan they were protected by the ninja families and incorporated into their own wisdom.'

He pointed at the second picture. 'That's *ninjutsu*, which, as you know, is the native Japanese ninja warrior tradition. The figure on the toad is Jiraiya, a character from Japanese folklore. He reflects mystical power and cunning.'

'What does the toad signify?'

'It has many layers of meaning. You've heard the saying "as cunning as a fox". The Japanese believe that the toad is cunning and resourceful.

It also signifies "return" and is a good-luck figure, probably showing that money can return to you. Here, the man is riding the toad. So it could mean that he has taken on the power of nature. For the ninja, uniting with nature holds a great deal of power. You might say that if you are united with nature, nothing can defeat you.'

He moved on to the final piece of art. 'The third picture shows a follower of the *yamabushi* way.'

I already knew that the *yamabushi* follow a path called *shugendō*, an ancient Japanese religion whose name means 'the path of training and testing or magical powers through hardship'. The focus or goal of *shugendō* is the development of spiritual experience and power. *Yamabushi* means 'he who lives in the mountains'.

James filled me in: 'The whole path centres on a mountain-dwelling lifestyle and incorporates teachings from Eastern philosophies. Mountain priests are part of an ancient tradition involving the practice of rigorous mystical disciplines to cultivate psychic and spiritual powers. This is a special path whereby the followers believe that spiritual attainment can be gained through the mastering of the five elements of earth, water, fire, wind and void. They test their will and develop self-mastery through trials involving the elements. Their most famous training method is an amazing feat: standing under a waterfall and learning to control the pain. With hundreds of tons of freezing water passing over your body and beating down on you, the pressure and cold are so unbearable that this is the ultimate test.'

I listened with interest as he explained how these ancient methods helped to control and discipline the mind.

'This is what we do here.' He gestured around the *dojo*, obviously proud of his role in all this. We'd walked the length of the public area and on the wall I read the *to-shin do* mission statement:

To-Shin Do® is a thorough system of personal preparation for winning conflicts and overcoming opposition that can surprise us in everyday living.

To-Shin Do training leads to the ability to live life fully, fearlessly, and freely. The martial arts were developed as a way to promote peace, security, and well-being in the world – command over adversity – never as a way to practice violence. The world needs more protectors, not more predators.

In an over-stressed society, balancing a clear mind, fit body, and centred spirit is the pathway to becoming a *tatsujin* – a fully actualised person operating masterfully in all areas of life.

From the few moments I'd spent in his presence, it was clear that James knew his stuff. I was delighted that I had come to a place where people had such thorough knowledge. The concept of *tatsujin* moved me, inspired me. This was what I was looking for.

Before I could get too carried away at having found what I considered to be an official ninja school and bombarded James with even more questions, I was brought back from my thoughts.

'An-shu is here.' James was making a bow, hands clasped in respect. Stephen Hayes was striding purposefully into the *dojo*. He seemed taller and more commanding in the flesh than in his DVDs but his face was the same: neatly trimmed white beard, eyes that reminded me of an owl's. He seemed earnest, no flicker of emotion, but there was a sense of calm even if it had the taut quality of a bow-string ready to loose an arrow. Respect and admiration flowed through me. Something in his demeanour reminded me of Bo, my master in England.

As we made our introductions Stephen leant forward. 'Martin, I want you to know that I'm impressed. Many people talk about coming, but very few do.' With that, he disappeared almost as quickly as he had materialised. According to James, he was attending to another matter out of town for a few days but I was told not to worry: An-shu Hayes wanted to reassure me that we would have plenty of time together. In his absence I would be under the guidance of Master Norris.

I suppose I was a bit star-struck. I had met *the* Stephen K. Hayes, and he had told me I'd impressed him. I hadn't even showed him any of my skills yet. What struck me immediately, though, was that Stephen had read me so easily – *very* ninja. From some basic email correspondence and a brief meeting, he had hit the nail exactly on the head. I had come here intending to impress. He had seen how driven I was and I respected that – a lot. I was filled with an even greater resolve to keep impressing him; I wanted him to notice me.

But I didn't have time to analyse things too much: other people were steadily arriving and my first lesson was about to start.

9

The Elements of *Ninjutsu*

Move swift as the Wind and closely formed as the Wood. Attack like the Fire and be still as the Mountain.

Sun Tzu, *The Art of War*

Master Norris got straight down to business. It was my first day at the *dojo* but he was not going to cut me any slack. He had an abrupt and commanding manner, which wasn't entirely comfortable. I noticed that he barely made eye contact with me and was unsure what his first impressions of me had actually been.

'Ninja training in *to-shin do* is based on the five elements. Each element represents an archetypal state of being and the names of the five elements are: (*chi*) 地 earth, (*sui*) 水 water, (*ka*) 火 fire, (*fu*) 風 wind, and (*ku*) 空 void.'

He barked out the elements and I turned to see what the other five students thought of his delivery. Everyone sat poker-straight, legs folded under them. No one looked back at me. I wondered how much they knew about me. Had An-shu Hayes mentioned my 'pilgrimage'? The whole place was completely still. Just a single spiral of incense smoke broke the inertia. Nothing wrong with that, but it did seem a bit contrived. I suppose I was used to typical UK classes where perhaps the discipline was slightly more lax and people tended to be less . . . engaged?

Master Norris was explaining that the Japanese Buddhist elemental philosophy was collectively known as *godai* (literally 'five great') and is perhaps best known in the West for its use in Miyamoto Musashi's famous text *Gorin-no-sho* (*The Book of Five Rings*), in which he assigns each element to different aspects of swordsmanship. The five elements are, in ascending order of power, earth, water, fire, wind/air, and void. They were different from the classical elements in the Western tradition of earth, air, fire, water and spirit, I mused. Void was another divergence from the classics: nothingness as opposed to spirit, which seems to embody *something*.

'Earth!'

My attention was jolted back. Earth is the densest of all the elements. 'Earth represents the hard, solid objects of the world. The most basic example of this is a rock. Rocks and stones have inertia and they are highly resistant to movement or change. Emotionally speaking, earth also represents this quality of stability. We instinctively use the elemental classification for some types of people. You have heard the sayings "salt of the earth" or "solid as a rock". In England, I am told, they call someone who is really reliable "a brick". At this point, he looked directly at me; I looked directly back. *Was* there some underlying tension between us?

He went on to say that most people with an earth-type personality are stable and solid, although this can sometimes mean being stubborn or persistent. Often, people who are of the earth element have physical strength and athletic capability. As for our minds, James likened the element to confidence and certainty in our own actions. However, he added, 'Emotionally, earth is a desire to have things remain as they are, a resistance to change. We all use the earth approach to varying degrees in life. Some of us find it easier than others.'

Barely pausing for breath, he then moved on to the second element. 'Water represents the liquid, flowing, changeable and formless things in the world.' Like earth, water can be attributed to human personality traits – 'soppy', 'drippy' or 'wet' are sometimes used to describe someone who is over-emotional. Characteristically, the water personality resonates with emotion, being defensive, supple and adaptable. 'Physically, this element manifests itself in muscle flexibility, grace and fluidity of movement.'

I found myself nodding in agreement. I totally understood the correspondence of the elements so far; no one else had so much as blinked.

Next, James described fire, with suitably animated gestures, his arm movements big and bold. 'Fire is a forceful element with aggressive tendencies. Physically, fire represents the heat of the body and the electricity in our nerves. You've all heard someone described as a fiery character, a firebrand or firecracker. Someone who has a hot temper or likes to have an intense argument. We're "warm" when we're friendly and "cold" when we're not! The fire personality is also characterised by ambition, drive and passion. They tend to be dominating, outgoing and aggressive.' He paused for breath. I could see that he really identified with fire – but was it his 'natural' element or one that he aspired to? I decided to try to categorise everyone by their real and apparent elements. I knew that we modulated between them all but it would be fun. A ninja game.

The wind element represents things that fill space and enjoy freedom of movement. He explained, 'Air, smoke, steam and all gases represent this element. It can in some ways be best represented by the human mind.' A 'wind' person is optimistic, knowledgeable and logical. However, someone with too much of this element may be said to be 'spaced out' or an 'airhead'. Similarly, those who talk too much or talk endlessly about a particular subject are said to be 'full of hot air'. James continued, 'In our bodies, air obviously represents breathing, and all internal processes associated with respiration. Wind represents an open-minded, carefree attitude. It can be associated with will, elusiveness, compassion and wisdom. Wind represents a free, creative mind. With wind, you can outwit an opponent – you can get so close that they can't see you. You can literally disappear.'

Void was the final element, the most intriguing from my Western point of view. 'Void represents things beyond our everyday awareness. In the physical body, this element represents mental force and creative energy, our ability to think and to communicate, as well as our willpower and spontaneity.'

In the Buddhist tradition, void is the highest of the elements and should reflect our spiritual values. He explained, 'Void demonstrates how spiritual values should come above all other material things such as power (fire), knowledge (wind), emotions (water) or possessions (earth). In martial arts a warrior who has mastered the void element can fight without thinking, respond to situations spontaneously and intuitively, and overcome all other opponents.'

To me it seemed similar to the Western premise that in mastering the four elements you can become at one with the divine or even, if you are magically inclined, become divine.

I considered this for a moment. It seemed to me that the elements were different strategies, ways of being and of coping with life. Part of the mission statement I had read was to become a *tatsujin*, someone who had reached their full potential. Could this result from being able to master all the elements, becoming fully in balance, as stable as earth, as adaptable as water, as connected as fire and as in tune as wind?

My thoughts were interrupted. James Norris hadn't finished: 'At this level of learning, we hope to give you an introduction to the first four of the elements as physical training. A depth of understanding can only really be achieved by using the associated moves and practising the responses. The first level of *to-shin do* training is to learn the earth-level response. This will be the focus of your first week of training.'

We stopped for a 'comfort break' and I took the opportunity to try to break the ice with some of the other students. I wanted to know how much they had already learnt and where I stood in the great scheme of things. One guy was leaning against the wall in the social area, which had chairs and tables for families and guests to watch the training. I wandered over and introduced myself. It turned out that he had flown from Germany to train so, in that respect, we were both 'outsiders'. He explained that he'd been there a week already and was staying, with a boy from Texas, with a family who were all members of the *dojo*. So I wasn't the only one who was there on a quest! I asked if he felt out of place but he shrugged. 'It's kind of cool here. Everyone's so nice and they just want to help you learn.'

I hoped I might feel less like a square peg soon. There was no real reason to feel 'different' – everyone had been cordial. Maybe I had jet-lag and just needed a good sleep. We bantered a bit, exchanging our martial-arts credentials, but as we were summoned back to class, I realised I hadn't retained his name. I was not on form.

The main training area was really well padded and smelt faintly of plastic and ammonia, which was good: it showed they cleaned the place. The amount of classes I'd been to in England where you ended up with your face wedged against sticky mats covered with a variety of unidentifiable substances! The first lesson was to be based upon the earth element and focus on the concept of strength. Master Norris was insistent upon starting at the very beginning and I'd noticed he had a very particular way of doing things. He began explaining *to-shin do* fighting techniques, which are taught as methods of self-defence against the most common forms of attack.

According to Master Norris, we would be focusing on skills that would lead to successful confrontations. We got into pairs and stood opposite each other. I was with Master Norris.

'Hold your ground solidly. You are so firm that, no matter what the onslaught, it will not affect you. You know that your strength will prevail. Your adversary feels as though he is fighting against a rock impervious to anything he does.

'OK. Now, stand straight. Here is your first *kamae* or attitude position.'

That didn't make any sense. James Norris was simply standing in front of me. From what I could tell, he hadn't adopted any martial-arts position. As requested, I copied him.

'Correct! A *kamae* is a position that represents the fighting attitude, the natural standing posture of the human body. The mind is alert, the body is relaxed, ready to move and adapt to any situation. Your body weight is equally distributed by both legs. The shoulders are down and the arms hang naturally at the sides.'

James looked me in the eye and continued, 'From this natural posture you can react to even the most sudden attacks and defensive actions. This stance is all about stability and strength. Your opponent is *not* a challenge – don't imagine them to be. Instead, your attitude should be "I am as strong as the mountain."'

I was completely thrown. The whole thing was so simple that it confounded me. I could understand the need to be able to fight and respond from a normal standing position, but I felt very vulnerable in that stance and not at all ready for any martial-arts action. It was unlike the usual fighting stances I was used to. However, as Master Norris started to take me through some basic movements, I began to understand more. It occurred to me that the *kamae* were more than martial-arts postures. Unlike other martial arts that have formal ways of positioning the feet, the *kamae* are a reflection of a mental outlook. Through a physical stance I was able to show my true thoughts and feelings. It took some getting used to.

Following my years of *kuk sool* training and thousands of hours of practice, the earth idea of standing your ground and refusing to take action was more than slightly foreign to me. We were encouraged to state our verbal intent during lessons. This was also alien to me – I had never seen it done before. I'd moved on to be paired with Bret, a muscular southern American, who lived on hamburgers and soda. When he roared, 'Stop! Stay back!' as he moved to block my punch and defend himself, I noticed how effective it was. I was completely distracted and unnerved. I found that shouting my intention added clarity to my mind and underlined what I wanted to accomplish, as well as cementing my earth position. I started to realise that verbal expression had a greater significance: as well as keeping my mind clear, my shouts would grab the attention of an opponent, preventing him or her from taking control of the situation.

As I practised, I started to feel more relaxed. My mind was affected by my bodily positioning and the opposite was true as well. When we use the terms 'mind' and 'body', we separate our sense of self. I was beginning to grasp that a shift in your posture prompts a change in your attitude. I realised that if I had truly understood the earth element, and what it stands for, I wouldn't feel such continual impatience. I found the positioning unnatural because I hadn't yet mastered how to use it.

As my month at Dayton got under way, things started to come into focus. I recognised the inner structure of everything, and all was not as it would seem to the casual observer. It took me a while but each class I attended was underpinned by a specific routine, although its outer expression varied. For example, a combat situation would be the subject of a class. The attack would be drawn from something that takes place regularly on the streets but the response would be simple and devastatingly effective. The teaching method varied. Sometimes it would involve pads, role-play or a form of competition.

What struck me most about *to-shin do* was its practicality. I was constantly thinking, Now that would work. In more than two decades of martial arts, I had never seen anything so effective.

There was something else too. Rather than practise drills and techniques, as all my previous martial-arts training had taught me to do, *to-shin do* demanded that each student throw themselves completely into the actions and reactions. So, if we were working on a self-defence technique with a partner, both parties would be throwing themselves into the task with all their might. In most classes, there would normally be one person performing the technique, the other playing the part of the attacker. In that class, it was different. When you attacked, you were learning to attack; when you defended, you were learning to defend. It was always *your* turn. Our classes were about dealing with situations that we might realistically find ourselves in. We were told to imagine nightclub scuffles, street muggings and drunken brawls, all of which I had encountered at home in the UK. Instead of using my martial-arts skills, we were taught to punch, kick and attack, just as a thug might. So simple but devastatingly effective. The martial-arts stances we used were the same as those taught in the class in the UK but more natural, relaxed and fluid. They freed you up rather than hampered you.

Rather than go through the motions, one opponent would be doing their best to assault the other while they did all they could to block and defend themselves. This soon became exhausting. At the start of my time at Dayton, I found it hard to embrace this way of working so ended up catching a few blows here and there. My sparring (or fighting) partners were not trying to hurt me but they weren't taking any prisoners either. Each strike was aimed for real, so I soon learnt to put my all into every practice session, whether I was attacking my opponent or defending myself.

This method of using effective movement is based on the 'five Ds', as Stephen Hayes refers to them. These, in turn, are: discern, defend, disrupt, deliver and, again, discern.

Your first challenge as an opponent is to *discern* and work out what the threat is. The process begins from the moment you encounter your would-be attacker by calculating whether or not they pose a threat or are someone you can simply avoid. Then, if the would-be attacker launches an attack, your first reaction should be to *defend*. In order to gain time and distract the attacker from his intention, you must *disrupt* his focus. This can be a defensive strike or a shout to take his attention elsewhere. The instant at which his or her attention has been disturbed is when you *deliver* your own attack, blow or kick, which must disable his or her intent to harm you. Clearly, sometimes, one or two jabs or kicks may not do the trick. If that is so, you must return to the beginning of the process, to *discern* and work out the threat from there. Are you likely to sustain an injury? Is your opponent tiring or simply waiting to strike again? Does he have an accomplice waiting in the wings?

I repeated the drills for the five Ds constantly. I wanted to perfect my defence skills to protect myself from any future attackers. I wasn't learning the exciting new tricks I had originally expected to find at Dayton. There were no flashy movements, just practice with a variety of opponents of all shapes and sizes, but by the end of my training I would be able to defend myself against any spontaneous attack in any situation without prior warning. Unlike many modern martial arts, where you train in a situation that makes everything clear, I was learning to work under pressure, trusting my instincts and improving my reactions. After all, on the streets, would-be attackers or robbers don't give you any notice before they attempt a crime. That is a very different situation from when you are both in a wrestling ring in your shorts and you *know* the rules, or when you are scoring points with kicks and punches.

Our days consisted of repeated practice, and then we would be tested by one of the centre's most senior instructors: Shane Stevens. Where James Norris was thin and wiry, Shane was tall, broad and bear-like; his muscular physique was that of a professional athlete. I was soon convinced that he was stronger and more skilled than any martial artist who had ever previously taught me. Even more impressive was that he suffered from a degenerative eye condition: he was effectively going blind. Nevertheless, he exuded energy and enthusiasm and was happy to encourage all of the students. His positive attitude certainly left an impression on me, and his manner made us all believe that we could achieve whatever we were striving for.

On a personal level, I clicked with Shane in a way that I hadn't managed to with James. Where James was rigid in his views and followed certain systems to the letter, Shane exuded a positivity that affected the whole room. He was enthusiastic and I warmed to him immediately. No one, however, could mistake his enthusiasm for an easygoing nature. Any practice drills or role-plays we did were lifelike and believable. If you ended up opposite him on the mat, any sense of playfulness would evaporate and I found myself putting every ounce of training and the *to-shin do* I had acquired into practice. Shane was a formidable aggressor, which, in turn, forced me to fight realistically.

From moments like these, I began to discover the chinks in my own martial-arts armour. Until now, I had only ever had one or two ways of responding to attackers: in the past I had either attacked or retreated before launching a counter-attack. I had never measured my responses before and I was struggling to employ the new techniques. However, something else was forming inside me, something I didn't understand. The phrase 'it's always your turn', meant something to me, something beyond the idea of keeping focused, no matter what your role was. I found myself pondering it and repeating it often to myself.

Every day we would meditate on the appropriate element and, despite focusing my attention fully on the earth element, trying to remain calm and apply the expert techniques Master Norris and the team at the *dojo* had begun to teach us, I would still let myself down. It was so frustrating: whenever I was put under pressure I would find myself either laughing and trying to lighten the situation or going to pieces and attacking aggressively – both of these being fire element tactics. Bret, whom I was paired with more often than not, was getting totally exasperated with me. 'For God's sake, Martin, stop pissing around!' I couldn't help it: I kept lapsing into the most aggressive form possible to make the most powerful attack. I was finding it supremely difficult to embrace earth, and I noticed this was true in other areas of my life too. All of my success had come from charging into things with great force. If that didn't work, I applied more force. If I was to get anywhere with this, I had to change.

It was at this point that I learnt something from the examples set by others: Stephen Hayes and his students really *lived* their art. They seemed always to be aware, full of cunning and direction. When they walked, they moved far more silently than others. Everything they did appeared to be an exercise in discipline and self-development; their calm in the meditation hall extended into everyday life. The elements they were teaching – earth, water, fire and wind – were put to use in everyday life. They were *being* ninja, not just studying *ninjutsu*. Rather than wade in and ask questions, I was beginning to see how valuable simply sitting back and watching from the sidelines could be. I'm not sure it's even possible to absorb knowledge like this, but what I saw had an impact on me. From keeping a close eye on those around me, I noticed that each person was slowly assimilating themselves into the ways of a ninja. Their movements, actions and intentions all became inter-linked, and all they learnt became a part of them. That struck a chord in me, and has remained with me ever since.

One afternoon I was sitting drinking iced tea between classes. I had become friends with the family Bret was staying with and the daughter Kathleen came and sat with me. She was a quietly serious girl of around eighteen and I could see that she took her training seriously. In fact, the whole family did and, interestingly enough, I found I could put a dominant element to each member. Dad was air – reserved and intellectual; Keenan was water – fluid, quick, and adaptable; Brigit was fire – full of early teen energy and aggression;

Kathleen was earth – grounded, serious and logical; Mum was void – spiritual, creative and dynamic.

Training with Master Norris and Shane, though, wasn't enough for me. I had journeyed to Dayton to learn from Stephen Hayes himself and, up to now, I had spent barely a minute in his presence. I was determined to wring as much out of the experience as I could so, after days spent in the *dojo*, going through drills, being flung backwards onto mats and fully directing my aggression towards others, I would return to my hotel room and watch a stack of Stephen Hayes DVDs. I made sure that, although Stephen Hayes was not in the training hall during the day, with the aid of the TV in my hotel room, I had hours of his tuition every evening.

I felt a bit downhearted, though. I was in a strange town, not doing quite what I'd expected to do, and I was missing my girls. Pip had packed my bag for me, as usual, and had slipped in a letter, photo or note for every day of my stay, which kept my spirits up, but I wasn't sure that my quest for knowledge was being fulfilled. As valuable and wise as Stephen Hayes's words were, I was growing impatient. My only access to him was through DVDs that I could watch from my sofa in the UK. I hadn't travelled thousands of miles to watch him on TV but to learn from him in person. Like the ninja, he had disappeared.

10

Earth

◆

Nothing in the world can take the place of persistence. Talent will not:
nothing is more common than unsuccessful men with talent. Genius
will not: unrewarded genius is almost a proverb. Education will not:
the world is full of educated derelicts. Persistence and determination
alone are omnipotent. The slogan Press On! has solved and always
will solve the problems of the human race.

Calvin Coolidge

I might have been teaching myself the ways of Hayes, but my classes
were still not going to plan. Here I was with years of martial-arts
experience but I couldn't deal with an attacker calmly or firmly. It's
hard to explain why I couldn't but it just seemed so alien. I couldn't
be earth. Something about the reality of the situation, when someone
was shouting at me, and being threatening, made it hard to respond
imperturbably rather than attack or retreat.

Master Norris saw that I was struggling and offered assistance. 'One
of the most powerful techniques is how to bring us into the correct
psychological state to give us an advantage over our opponent. For
this we use the *kuji-in.*'

Anyone who has studied ninja and *ninjutsu* even briefly would be
aware of *kuji-in*. A magician has a wand, while the ninja were said to
have secret hand positions and words that would give them magical
powers.

I had read about this briefly. Apparently the *kuji* (meaning 'nine
syllables') are the mantras often used in conjunction with a set of
nine hand seals/gestures/*mudras* associated with the nine syllables,

which are said to have miraculous effects. When the combination of mantra, *mudra* and meditation are used together in a ritual, known as *kuji-ho*, they are supposedly able to control nature and help the ninja read minds. This was the stuff of legend. What seemed certain was that they had been used for centuries. My reading had told me that they exist to help a ninja channel his or her energy and focus on the task in hand. You learn to focus your whole being, creating a sense of calm and control. Given my problems at remaining earth-like for periods, I knew I had to master *kuji*.

Master Norris, as ever, had plenty of exercises up his sleeve to make me see the point of this. According to him, creating a picture and visualising the outcome I wanted would motivate me to achieve my goal. He also advised that the stronger and more vivid the visualisation, the more effective my actions would be. He showed me the special hand position for 'earth': hold the hands in a prayer position, then bend the little finger and thumb on each hand to touch the tips together and form two interjoining rings. To achieve the greatest and strongest earth-like ability I could muster, I tried to imagine myself as a strong, immovable object. An image of an ancient oak tree sprang to mind, deeply rooted and able to withstand the strongest winds. Something really had changed inside me: I was grounded and calm. I felt as if parts of me had connected for the first time: the exercise seemed to have summoned something from inside me. James was pleased: finally, I had learnt how to work with my instincts.

'Remember, Martin, this is *totally* natural. All animals know how to fight instinctively. If you grab a dog by the paw, it will bite your hand. If you grab it round the muzzle, it will claw at your hand to free itself. It knows instinctively what to do. It has never learned martial arts. It doesn't know dog-*jutsu*, it just does.'

According to Master Norris, it was good practice to observe animals: they naturally and fluidly fight, defend and interact with whatever and whoever is around them. Unlike humans, they don't require specific training: they react to their innate instincts. So, in truth, a lot of what we were doing was a return to nature – finding it inside yourself and bringing it out, rather than learning to stick to any set form.

'You're going to have to find your own natural way of getting into this earth mind-set.' He was clearly relishing his wisdom over my inexperience. 'It may be through another visualisation, it may be something else that you've used in the past. Maybe you can imagine a time when you've been solid. Or maybe you can imagine a fictional or divine figure that could make you feel this way.'

His next analogy caught me off guard. According to him, all humans were either big dogs, like St Bernards, or small dogs, like Chihuahuas. I nodded, but wasn't wholeheartedly convinced of this. Perhaps he had a secret soft spot for all things canine.

'I want you to imagine a big dog.' He spread his arms wide. 'Have you ever seen a big dog in the park? Then a little dog, like a Chihuahua, comes up to it, yapping away. Do you know what the big dog does?'

My knowledge of dog behaviour didn't extend too far. 'Erm, no.'

'The big dog does nothing. Do you know why the big dog does nothing?'

I shook my head.

'Because . . . it's a big dog!'

What was this dog fixation? I must have looked confused.

'I'd like you to think about the analogy of the big dog, and the Chihuahua barking away, being really, really verbal, while the big dog does nothing.'

As he walked off, one of the foreign students mocked me, chuckling and flapping his hand in an opening-and-shutting-mouth movement. 'Ha, he just used the dog analogy on you, yeah? Bark, bark, bark! What do you reckon?'

I was loath to admit it but now I could see Master Norris's point. In the past, I had been in situations when a verbal attack or aggressive behaviour had provoked a reaction in me and I'd snapped. I had got used to a certain type of bloke squaring up to me, eager to start a fight. Sometimes I'd be wound up enough to lash out, thanks to their verbal insults. James must have seen this in my character, and it was true: in the past I had found it very hard to ignore the allegorical Chihuahua and not lash out. If I let situations such as these go, it would take me hours to quell my rage and leave me with a sense of unfinished business.

Later, I confessed this to him: I was beginning to see that my problem had always been that I was unable to remain calm and unaffected after a situation such as that.

He nodded. 'You see,' he continued, 'from a ninja point of view, we just want the person to do as we want. We're going beyond pride, beyond normal convention. So many people lose the situation to try to win status over the person.

'*Ninjutsu* is about winning the war, even if the opponent doesn't realise that you've won. Even if you make the opponent think he's won. Imagine that I'm in a bar. A guy approaches me wanting a fight. Maybe he knows about the martial-arts school and hits me.'

I nodded.

'Now what does he expect me to do? Hit him back, react and get angry? Here's one way that I can win the situation. I don't want to fight. I don't want to have to justify my actions to the police or risk arrest. Instead, I can feign injury – I can hold my mouth in pain, grimacing and whinging and walk out. And, you know, if he keeps on at me, I could just be honest. I could explain that no, actually, I don't want to fight. Sure, my pride may be hurt but I've got exactly what I want. So, it's just your pride that's getting in the way. Sometimes appearing to lose, or appearing not even to know that the guy is being aggressive, can be a far more powerful position.'

That had never occurred to me. He'd identified a chink in my armour. As part of my training in the earth element, I had to learn how to overcome my feelings of aggression and any inner ego or pride, which could ultimately trip me up. It was vital that I learnt how to keep a lid on them. In some cases, I could harness my feelings of aggression and be more productive as a result. By learning to ignore or beat my inner demons, I would be more powerful, have greater strength and eventually become a more balanced individual.

I understood exactly what Master Norris was trying to teach me but the idea of losing a fight deliberately was alien to me and I could barely imagine allowing myself to do such a thing. That was my first encounter not only with the creativity of *ninjutsu* strategy but also with manipulating my weaknesses to achieve my true aims. If I could learn to do that, so many situations in my life would improve. I felt I had started to turn the corner in my training. From that moment onwards, I could become earth in the mind, and my body would reflect it, becoming immovable both emotionally and physically. I was also finding myself better able to apply earth strategies in everyday situations.

James Norris's ability to know what I was thinking was starting to get rather spooky. How did he always know exactly what to say?

Then I sussed that it wasn't only James Norris who could second-guess me. When I thought back over the past few days, I discovered that most, if not all, the instructors had an intriguing habit of tapping into whichever area of *ninjutsu* I was either curious about or struggling with. Most students seemed oblivious to it, but on several occasions I found that if I had discussed a subject with someone before a private class, even though the instructor was not in the room, my questions would be answered in the next lesson. I deduced that some kind of Chinese Whispers operated behind the scenes at the *dojo*. If I mentioned something to one black belt in conversation pretty soon all the other black belts would know about it. While this was disconcerting, it made them amazing instructors. Their shared information allowed them to remain in tune with the students and adapt their lessons accordingly to help each of us. I once talked to Shane Stevens about bodybuilding and, within twenty-four hours, all the instructors I met started to use more 'physical' terminology, talked of muscle memory and making the technique part of the sinews. They were all advising me as though I had asked them the question.

With this knowledge under my belt, I was able to connect the dots and began to doubt the teaching methods less. In fact, I realised this mode of ninja behaviour was at the centre of what Stephen Hayes wanted to teach his students. Things seemed to make more sense and started to get easier and, at last, I could embrace the earth mind-set. Sure, it was hard and I knew it would take a lot of practice, but I was gradually able to improve my performance in class. Inside

I was becoming more solid, more resistant, more authoritative, unmoved by the opponent's aggression and emotions. I couldn't quite believe I'd finally grasped it – I began to feel quite in my element!

11

Water

> *Life is a series of natural and spontaneous changes. Don't resist them*
> *– that only creates sorrow. Let reality be reality. Let things flow natur-*
> *ally forward in whatever way they like.*
>
> Lao Tzu

We had a couple of days' rest before our next set of classes was to start: there was a public holiday after the weekend. Maybe I should have been embracing my free time and enjoying all America had to offer – many of my classmates were basking in the summer weather – but I couldn't seem to relax although I seriously needed to rest. I was worrying about the whereabouts of Stephen Hayes. Where was he? I really needed his expertise to help me progress. However, as if by some cosmic force and continuing the art of mind reading that members of the *dojo* seemed to have, the Griffin Family who seemed to always be in attendance, Bret and another guy appeared at the hotel and asked if I'd like to go to a cook-out at a local community pool. The mystery guest was soon introduced to me. His name was Rasmus and he had flown in from Denmark; the European contingent was growing. We all crammed into the Griffins' SUV and headed off into the searing heat; I hadn't acclimatised and was thanking God for air-con.

The lido was busy with families, all unloading huge cars full of food and drink for barbecues. Several of the students from the *dojo* were there and waved us over; the air was filled with the smell of carbonising burgers and just a hint of chlorine from the pool. I looked around at everyone enjoying the sun; the atmosphere was perfectly relaxed but no one seemed as preoccupied as I felt. Most of us were on the same quest so I decided to ask a few questions. As we discussed our progress, I noticed one very important difference between how I was approaching my training and how they were. Perhaps because of my previous martial-arts work, and the effective guidance I had received from the likes of Richard Roper and Bo, I had started to rely too heavily on the influence of my teachers at Dayton. I expected them to deliver answers to me and hadn't really embraced independence, like many of my fellow students. They were relying on themselves to make progress.

Suddenly I had a moment of clarity, one of those epiphanies. Perhaps Stephen Hayes, by his very absence, was teaching me how to be independent. Without him around I was learning – albeit slowly – to rely on myself.

I soon became tucked under the maternal but very feisty wing of veteran Quest Center member Cheryl Griffin and her clan; we spent a lot of the long weekend chatting about other aspects of the *dojo*. I began to relax. As we weren't sparring on mats or under the watchful eye of instructors, we could be far more informal. They began talking about Richard Sears, another instructor from the *dojo*. Apparently he had recently undertaken a pilgrimage to Japan and done lots of training in the style of the *yamabushi*, the mountain monks. My ears pricked up because I had heard that these monks practised incredible feats of endurance and mystical asceticism.

Cheryl was nodding as Rasmus recounted that Richard had told him he had even performed one of the hardest trials of standing beneath a freezing waterfall. 'Wow! I thought the *yamabushi* had all but died out.' But if a Dayton instructor had actually experienced such things for himself it must still exist.

Shaking his head, Rasmus carried on, 'You can become *yamabushi* by passing the trials – they hang you over a cliff!' That raised my eyebrows a bit but I was inwardly really excited.

The things Stephen Hayes talked about were actually still being practised and had been done by men I'd been taught by.

Next day, our classes based on the water element were due to begin.

I began the morning with my usual walk to the *dojo*; the police had given up hassling me by now and just gave me a one-fingered forehead touch salute as they cruised by. That morning I saw a lone figure coming over the crest of the hill towards me, waving. As I jogged closer, I saw a familiar thatch of blond hair and a rucksack perched on one shoulder. Rasmus.

'Yo!' He high-fived me. We'd bonded over a shared penchant for root beer and Taco Bell. He'd told me my *kamae* sucked.

We arrived, drenched from the walk in the stinging heat.

'OK!' Shane clapped his hands. 'Gather round, we're on to "water" techniques. These will teach you fluidity of movement and how they can overcome sheer strength. Watch carefully.'

Shane demonstrated *ichimonji no kamae* – the classic starting posture that allows you to slide back and dodge your attacker. It was the same stance that I'd failed to master in England during my 'robotic' fighting lesson. Here in Dayton it was performed in an upright and completely natural way. 'Rasmus, attack me.' In seconds, Rasmus had lunged forward, extending his right arm as if to grab Shane's chest. Equally swiftly, Shane had shifted stance and used his weight and momentum to pull Rasmus off balance by grabbing his hand and digging his elbow into his arm. Rasmus's face was a picture but Shane hadn't finished. He reversed his position into *ichimonji* stance on the opposite side, hugging Rasmus's wrist to his chest and twisting him into a wristlock. It was flowing, quick and devastatingly effective. We burst into a spontaneous round of applause and chuckled as a red-faced Rasmus extracted himself from Shane's grasp and joined us back on the mats.

I knew that now I had to discard earth and let my mind shift to work with my body to become less rigid and firm so I could impersonate water and flow through, past and over whomever I was fighting.

We began with some calming breathing exercises, inhaling and exhaling deeply and slowly letting our hands rise and fall. The object of this was to let oxygen circulate around the body, much like water flowing into us, stimulating our power of will and letting a feeling of wellbeing wash over us. Earth lessons had been about remaining fixed, strong and focused, while water classes taught us to be a powerful moving force that could be non-threatening, then instantly change into a force to be reckoned with.

I used the water element *kuji*, which involved linking the two ring fingers into interlocking rings. I imagined myself as a harmless stream trickling along until a storm turned it into an invincible force of nature. Once again, I took up the *ichimonji* position. I tried to remember my *tai chi* training and focus on the ability to be soft and receptive. We started to practise the water techniques and it was then I discovered it was easy to be calm, cool and water-like when you were with other calm people doing *tai chi*. However, when you have a simulated mugger shouting at you it was tricky. I found I couldn't move out of the way fast enough, so made up for it by jumping and being forceful, zigzagging in and out, like a lightning bolt rather than water flowing, a wave retreating or crashing breakers.

I found it far easier than the earth exercises but it still wasn't right. 'Martin, that's good but here is the next step. Fall, don't step.'

I had no idea what Master Norris meant.

'That's why the weight is all on your back leg.'

I looked at my back leg as if that would somehow give me the answer.

'If you just lift your leg, you will automatically move backwards.'

The principle worked in my mind – weight on back leg, body angled in a way that lifting back leg would cause an instant movement back-wards – but it seemed so artificial.

It took me a minute or two to get up the guts to try it.

I lifted my leg – not a step, just a lift. My whole body jumped back about a foot, while my front leg stretched out. I tried it again, this time using a slight push from the front foot to work with the actions. It worked. A fall was faster than any step as it just took a lift of the foot, and in this position I was propelled at exactly the right angle to avoid any blow. How to move faster than anyone else using body dynamics – ninja water magic!

I was flowing. I felt very 'water element' – cool, calm and calcu-lating, withdrawing like a wave and splashing back down upon the opponent. Shane Stephens and Master Norris watched and seemed to think there could be some improvement.

'Martin, what does it mean to win?' Master Norris asked an obviously rhetorical question. 'Part of ninja training is about re-examining what you see as winning. Imagine this. I'm in a bar and some guy walks up to me wanting trouble. He wants to show me up or to prove he's better than me.'

Shane Stephens played the part for him, puffing out his chest and giving him a shove.

'Most people respond by fighting back. It's an automatic response, but we don't want to be controlled by automatic responses when they don't serve us. Think about it. We're all trained martial artists and have a good chance of winning . . . but if we fought with him and won would we really be winning?'

Everyone stopped for a minute. I voiced what we were all thinking. 'If you fight, even if you win, you will probably get some injuries, problems with the law, reprisal from friends or revenge later.'

Rasmus added, 'And there's no prize for winning either.'

'Winning is when you get what *you* want, not when he gets what *he* wants.' Master Norris spoke but the voice sounded like that of Stephen Hayes.

'With water we out-think the opponent and use our ability to retreat or act calmly to get what we want. So, one option could be to simply leave at the first sign of trouble.'

'Before the fighting ritual starts . . .' Rasmus chimed in.

My God, they were right. There were times in the past when I could see that things were starting to go the wrong way and had carried on in the same vein until it had got to the pushing and shoving, threatening stage. If, as soon as I'd known there were going to be problems, I had pretended to go to the Gents but instead left the building, I would have avoided a whole lot of trouble. But why hadn't I?

'Or after . . .' Shane shrugged. 'Perhaps the guy has even hit you.' He play-acted taking the blow, turning his back on the opponent and walking away.

'Aww, man!'

He went out of an imaginary bar door.

'Let's face it, I've taken worse blows in the *dojo*!'

Rasmus was inspired. 'You give him what he wants so he leaves you alone?' He paused with a smile. 'You could burst into tears and say, "Don't hit me, big man. I'm scared," and run out. He might be laughing at you and feel proud but you're at home eating ice cream.'

I was stunned. How much conflict and pain were caused by thoughtless fighting? We were like animals who, when prodded, bit back without thought. But I had a worry. 'I understand what you're saying. He wants to fight, you don't, and if you fight, he gets what he wants. In truth, you just want him to go away. But what kind of lesson do you teach him by backing down or running away? Don't you think it's time someone taught him a lesson?'

I got a look back that pretty much said, 'You are not going to educate a thug who habitually fights in bars by fighting with him.'

'It's hard to not be controlled by your pride, anger and other emotions, and simply to let go of the situation and move on.'

Master Norris was right. In the few times that I had managed in the past to do as he suggested, I had been haunted by anger and thoughts of revenge for days afterwards.

In that moment I realised that although over the years I had accepted the principles of giving in to win, and using the opponent's forces against him to win, I had never developed it as a genuine strategy, as something I would use in real life. It had never been something I had emotionally connected with or learned how to use or that had become part of me.

As I continued to practise the water techniques, which involved strategies such as retreat, evasion, going with the flow and using the opponent's direction to your advantage, I felt something new inside me, as if I was discovering a part of myself I hadn't known was there. I was outside my comfort zone but it felt wonderful. It was authentic growth and self-development. Finally I was getting what I wanted. Not only was I learning to move faster and with more fluidity, inside I was learning to be flexible and recognising new options.

12

Fire

*We all have a box of matches in our hearts. It just sometimes takes
help from others to strike them.*

Today I was due to focus on fire, and James Norris was ready to
work. I had been feeling increasingly frustrated by the absence
of Stephen Hayes. I'd travelled halfway across the world, sunk my
savings into paying for tuition and hotels, yet here I was with Master
Norris again. I'd spent an hour on the phone to Pip the evening before,
pouring out all my angst and homesickness. Practical as always, she'd
reassured me that this was most likely one of two things: (a) Stephen
was genuinely busy and I'd just have to fit in with his schedule – 'After
all, you aren't his *only* student!'; or (b) he had my number and was
testing me to see what I was capable or not capable of. We'd eventually
parted yet again over thousands of miles of static, she sending me
some last droplets of love and reassurance and I feeling like my
superpowers were coming back a bit.

So, ironically, perhaps this lesson was all about harnessing aggression. Master Norris talked to me about fiercely pursuing my opponent,
explaining the point of using fire elements to overcome an adversary:
I was to use his actions to make my own movements stronger – 'The
more he struggles, the more powerful your blows become. It's like
you're a roaring fire: the more he struggles against you, the hotter
you get.'

My opponent should feel as though everything he does fans my flames,
making me hotter and brighter and harder to extinguish with each action.
I'd done some boxing in the past, so when Master Norris adopted crossed

arms over the torso and clenched fists in front of the face I recognised the classic 'protection' pose.

I felt as though I was learning about an element that came naturally to me. I had always been a ball of energy, very heated and passionate about things. Water and earth had been difficult elements for me to get to grips with. Now, studying fire, I was prepared to impress Master Norris and show him what fiery substance I was made of.

As soon as the drills started, I put all my energy into them. One key to the fire element was being able to react quickly, striking the opponent after he moves but before his attack lands. This requires restraint and watchfulness, precision and control. Previously my fire tactics had involved punching hard and as fast as possible.

Unfortunately, my energies didn't pay off. It appeared that my inner rage and fiery nature weren't what was needed. Instead of exploding at a situation, like a fireball of athleticism, I soon realised the fire element required a completely different strategy. I was supposed to be aiming well-judged punches and kicks – firing them off at speed – to harm my opponent, so my habit of letting my emotions erupt wasn't working. I had to be calm and focused, directing them like a laser beam, not exploding like a hand grenade – unlike my trademark flammable temper. The fire element was not about going crazy.

After an exhausting few hours, I was feeling disillusioned and decided to head back to the hotel for some much-needed rest.

As I got changed I reflected on my time in Dayton so far. As I reviewed each lesson, I cringed when I remembered the moments I had got something wrong or missed what was happening. Often the lessons during the day had only just sunk in when I'd got back to the hotel. Sometimes I had only understood what someone had meant two days after they'd said it. How could I be doing so badly? A lot of it still remained a mystery to me.

Rasmus, my fellow student from abroad, had had some thoughts on the matter and was about to deal me a swift reality check. As I came out of the changing room he was sitting there drinking soda, surrounded by other members of the *dojo*. I sat down to talk to him. He hadn't even been in Dayton a week but he informed me that everyone at the Quest

Center had grown tired of my loud boasting and considered me arrogant – most of them thought I was a liar too. 'You're so full of yourself, Martin. They just think you're talking crap.'

'Jeez, Rasmus, if you've got something to say just come out and say it. Don't hide it in parable and allegory!'

'Sure, OK. You're arrogant, you think everyone should bow down to you as if you're some huge expert. Most of the stuff you come out with is totally over the top . . .'

I waved my hand at him. 'Yeah, thanks, I get your point.' People were looking our way. I wanted to dig a hole and climb into it.

I was pretty devastated but, on reflection, he was right. I'd come in like a bull in a china shop, chest puffed up and full of my own bluster. I'd done everything I could to show everyone I met how amazing I thought I was and what wonderful things I'd done or was going to do. Most of my friends in the UK were used to me doing crazy things and being very vocal about everything, but with strangers in a different culture, outside my usual comfort zone, it had marked me out as an egocentric idiot. Contrary to cultural stereotypes, the Americans I had met had been courteous, gentle and understanding while I had been arrogant and boastful. Worst of all, I had not been able to match my words with my deeds. I had to swallow my pride and knuckle down now or risk looking like an even bigger fool. But Rasmus hadn't finished.

'Do you know why Stephen Hayes is not here? He's watching you to see if you're dangerous, a crazy man, and to see what you do without him around.'

I stood up to get another drink. It made perfect sense that Stephen and his team would test me in that way over the course of several weeks. I couldn't have been the first eager student to arrive wanting to spend time with Master Hayes. How many people had come here with problems or something to prove? With all my boasting and energy, were they worried I was a threat or was this really a way of seeing my true nature? I had to think about what I was doing there.

As I slammed open the changing-room door I came face to face with a familiar figure. Stephen Hayes was back.

I should have been relieved, happy, grateful, but instead I felt deflated.

Thanks to worry, I hadn't used my weekend off as well as I should have. While most of my classmates had slept and recharged, I had spent much of the time training and fretting. Now my body was paying for it. I was really tired: I had been training for seven hours a day for almost two weeks, living on junk food and caffeine, and I was exhausted in a way that I had never experienced before, despite my years of training. So far during my time in America, I'd wanted to soak up every drop of knowledge on offer so I hadn't skipped a class or stopped practising. All I had wanted to do was to show Stephen Hayes what I was capable of, and now he was back, I was knackered and dispirited.

Stephen seemed happy enough to see me and wanted to start a class immediately. I pulled myself together, hoping I would get a second wind.

Although he responded to my questions rather than driving the lesson, he kept me off balance and I never really understood whether he was testing or teaching me. A lot of things he was expressing I couldn't understand, and he changed direction frequently. He put me in different martial-arts positions or in different scenarios, almost as if to see what I would do. I wasn't reacting as I had hoped. I found myself confused and my mind was continually searching for the purpose of whatever we were covering in the lesson. He would demonstrate locks and holds, throws and sweeps, but moved on so quickly I had no idea what was going on. Was he just looking at my reactions? I was thinking too much, which stopped my body reacting as it should have. I don't know if it was the tiredness or whether this was a deliberate strategy but, whatever was happening, I wasn't succeeding in my attempt to impress him.

In retrospect, perhaps I wasn't the easiest student to deal with. Sometimes, when Stephen was trying to demonstrate a technique, I'd been doing my best to get out of it by trying to display my previous knowledge. I had wanted Stephen to see me as an experienced martial artist, but I think this started to create a barrier between us and prevented me absorbing what he was trying to give me. Instead of listening and considering, I was preoccupied with trying to deliver a good impression. Sooner or later, things came to a head. Stephen was demonstrating a technique but I, as usual, was resisting and trying to show him how much I already knew. The situation began to disintegrate into a form of playful combat. Well, for Stephen it was playful. For me, it was deadly serious.

I had done well in *kuk sool* tournaments and other competitions and was used to sparring with other martial artists. Stephen Hayes, however, was a completely new experience for me. I was extremely physically fit. I had trained for an hour and a half in the gym every single day for the last six years, and not many people had the kind of strength I thought I had. Meanwhile, Stephen was approaching sixty, so I didn't expect to have any problems when it came to overpowering him. But he had a different way of fighting, which I had never encountered before. Everything he did was powered by me and the results were completely unexpected. I decided to try to tackle him with a single-leg takedown. It's a move from wrestling and I'd also seen it used in Russian martial arts; it had never failed to work before. I grabbed Stephen's leg, threw my shoulder into the top of his thigh and put my entire weight into toppling him. I felt a leg buckle under me, and I knew that I had taken down the martial-arts legend, Stephen K. Hayes.

However, my satisfaction was short-lived. Suddenly a pain shot through both my arms leaving me trapped. Hayes had relaxed his entire body, allowing the leg I had been tackling to collapse, catching my right hand under his shin against the ground, my left hand between his thigh and lower leg. I was pretty much pinned to the floor, and the pain was in danger of incapacitating my arms. As I struggled to move my hands I marvelled at what Stephen had done – I'd never seen that move before. While I jostled and panted, Stephen remained calm, a look of serene curiosity on his face. For him this was not a contest: he was simply teaching me a few simple moves. I decided to change my approach.

While I had this exclusive one-on-one time with Stephen, it was the perfect opportunity to show him what I could do. I took hold of his arm to pull him into an arm lock that I knew anyone would struggle to escape from, much less a weaker man. I pulled his elbow right under my arm and I could see he was surprised by my action. To complete the move, I put all my body weight onto the arm and he started to fall towards the floor. I had won! He might have been able to get out of the tackle, but I had specialised in that arm bar since I was a young boy – the years of watching wrestling had paid off!

The smugness didn't last long. Stephen's arms seemingly melted away from beneath me, as though they had disappeared. He shifted his body in such a way that his whole weight was behind every movement, moving the arm I was clinging to with such force that it pulled me off my feet. This was just a simple move, but from my position on the floor it seemed like a supernatural power. My strike missed; my wrist hold no longer existed and I'd fallen off balance.

Any advantage I'd had disappeared but I stubbornly refused to let go of Stephen's wrist: my plan was to yank his hand and watch him crumple. But with another simple movement, Stephen pushed a point on one of my fingers that caused a giant crunch. My finger felt dislocated, but how had he done it? Despite my knowledge of pressure points, I had never witnessed such a move before. Stephen hadn't finished. He tried to get my wrist into a lock but I rolled out just in time. Then he surprised me – again. Using his leg, he jammed my arm and put me in a hammer lock. This was the type of thing I had used in choreographed fights – but never with a resistant opponent. I was too stunned to react. He had been play-fighting with me, while I had been using all my might and cunning to try to beat him. I looked at him in awe and realised Stephen Hayes was indeed unique. I had never met a martial artist like him before in my life.

Rubbing my aching muscles, I realised I was completely out-skilled. I'd thought I had a good knowledge of martial arts but I was clearly mistaken. Rasmus's words rang in my ears as I reflected on what had just happened. I felt foolish. I'd just proved to myself, Stephen and the rest of the instructors at Dayton that my skills were far from impressive. There was no doubt in my mind when I came to America that I would amaze everyone but my performance had been mediocre.

My confidence plummeted. I'd been so sure of what I wanted to accomplish but now I had to reconsider my ambitions. I was filled with doubt that I could ever achieve my aims. It was hard to switch off from this pattern of negative thinking and, given my damaged state from our last bout, I was dreading my next lesson with Stephen. I was miserable and incapable of doing much correctly. Even the most basic jabs and

THE AUTHOR WITH STEPHEN K HAYES

punches seemed impossible and the whole time I was aware of disappointing him. My co-ordination had always been razor sharp but today, in front of Stephen, I had as much technique as a beginner.

Sensing my low mood, Stephen tried to mix things up. He grinned at me. 'We should practise with a sword, just for fun.' Fun wasn't really on my radar and, as it happened, neither were sword skills. It was alien to me to feel so incapable. Even as a child in PE lessons I had been able to grasp things quickly. Physical skills had always come naturally to me – until today. The simplest things were impossible, proving to me that, ultimately, physical skill lies in our minds.

The next day, I walked into the *dojo* noticeably deflated. Rasmus and Bret were flicking bottle tops at each other in the seating area.

'Hey, dude, what's up?'

'Nothing. I'm fine. Got a class with An-shu Hayes – catch you later.' They tossed an enquiring glance at each other and shrugged. I didn't care.

'Hold up, it's a mixed-ability class today. We're coming too.' They scrabbled to get their gear together and followed me into the training area.

'Great . . .' I muttered, through gritted teeth.

I thought we were going to be learning more about the fire element but instead Stephen regaled us with a tale about a businessman he once knew who would often use his intellect to dominate other people. If the man's boss wasn't around, he would bully his colleagues. This happened a lot, but one day the boss arrived at the office unannounced; he paused and listened. Unsurprisingly he didn't like what he heard. To test his theory about the businessman, the boss planted a mole to ask a question and stayed hidden to hear the answer. As Stephen made clear, people who use their apparent intelligence to bully others and make them feel inadequate often don't know they're doing it.

He moved on with another story. A businessman once approached the Dalai Lama asking to buy enlightenment. The Dalai Lama quietly explained to the businessman that enlightenment couldn't be bought.

I'd been listening to all this, wondering what the point was, but as I glanced around the *dojo*, I caught the eyes of the other students and, slowly but sickeningly, I wondered if Stephen's stories were about me. A few days earlier, one of the instructors had asked me if I knew anything about the pictures on the wall of the *dojo*. I had been at great pains to illustrate my extensive knowledge and explained what I had learnt from James Norris in minute detail.

I glanced self-consciously around the room again. From the look on several people's faces I could see I wasn't the only one internally cursing myself. We had all made errors and shown ourselves up in our weeks at Dayton so I suppose they rang true for many of us. But I couldn't be sure. Once more, I couldn't tell if Stephen Hayes had done something deliberately or not. I could never pin him down and he constantly kept me guessing. I was dying to ask the question: had he really left the centre? Or had he impersonated the boss in his stories and observed from afar? Had he wanted to test me with our fight? I suppose he was exhibiting true ninja traits, which, I came to realise, was typical of him.

After the lesson Stephen took me to one side. 'Martin, one of the most important things for a ninja is to know oneself. In order to control others' emotions, you must first be able to control your own.' He went on, 'To do this, you must know what they're feeling. You can know how they would feel in any situation by putting yourself in a similar one.

'To find your true motives, I'd like you to contemplate this. If you were to win millions of pounds and never have to work again, what would you do with the money? Would you spend it to glorify yourself? Would you use it to party and have fun? Would you give some away to charity to help people?' His eyes held mine; he gave absolutely nothing away. With that he nodded and walked off to greet another student.

I pondered these questions, which made me realise something big. I had never stopped to contemplate what I was trying to do in life. I had never really focused on the big goal but had been making it up as I went along. It seemed very strange to think that the most important question of all was something no one normally asked of themselves or indeed others. In that moment I couldn't believe that in our society our main aim in life was something we didn't have as part of our school system or parenting. I was dumbfounded.

I realised that, before my experiences in America, I would probably have spent the money partly on self-glorification. Now I had changed my focus. I knew more about where I wanted to go and who I wanted to be. I would use the money for two purposes: I would try to do good but I would also spend money on my travels, seeking out the finest spiritual masters and learning from them in order to develop my spiritual, physical and mental self. I had redefined my purpose and my aims, which was surprisingly satisfying and strangely comforting.

When we next spoke Stephen could see this had had an impact on me. I think he was pleased.

'Martin, in all things you do, examine your motives and keep focused on the true goal behind your undertakings. In this lies the greatest power.' His words echoed those of Bo all those months ago: 'Keep the heart pure and correct.'

The penny had spectacularly dropped. My goal in visiting Dayton had been to study the ways and secrets of ninja, but to what end? I knew I wanted to improve myself and to reach my full potential but the rest had been sketchy. In a world obsessed with money, pleasure and power, we are all programmed to think in a certain way. Work hard, excel and conform to the goals given to you. People who hold back and take an easy, low-paid job in order to focus on other goals, like family or hobbies, are looked down on and judged not to have reached their full potential.

Considering my idea of an ideal life, I realised how little these goals meant to me. It was as if this questioning put things into a different perspective for me. When you take pride in a real, higher goal, material wealth dwindles and, eventually, its importance and power begin to lessen. It's almost as though by knowing your emotions, and understanding what you really want, you gain more control over their expression. Perhaps when you listen to them and are more aware of them, they become easier to deal with. It's no secret that people who are listened to don't need to shout. Perhaps it is the same with wants and emotions. With this knowledge, I was able to begin to control feelings of negativity and negative thoughts, and as the weeks passed, I felt different. My conversation with Stephen Hayes prompted me to look more carefully at my motivation for doing things and examine what I wanted from certain situations.

Never before had I stopped to question what I was doing with my life. It seemed so obvious, but it made me think of lyrics from *South Pacific*: 'You've gotta have a dream, if you don't have a dream, how you gonna have a dream come true?'

We lived in a world devoid of focus and direction, full of people moving from one immediate fulfilment to the next with no idea of a life goal. With some kind of insight into the big picture we could do so much more. With a sharpened focus, it is possible to aim for and achieve the things we most want. This all rang true with the type of *ninjutsu* taught at the Quest Center and with the aim of Stephen Hayes: rather than equip students with the skills to fight and punch, he wanted us to develop ourselves – as he had – and become part of a wider vision for the world.

So far, I had learnt the value of defending myself and holding my ground, thanks to my earth training. Water training had shown me how to dodge problems before they became larger issues. Fire, a strong and scary force, can be harnessed to do good. It's possible to use our skills to help others rather than set out along a personal path. This resonated with me. Given Stephen Hayes's previous work with the Dalai Lama, he was practised in protecting what we deem to be sacred. This was a skill he wanted others to learn for the good of the planet.

After many days of uncertainty, I had begun to feel more secure in myself again. I liked the concept of remaining hidden but having the skills to help or rescue others when necessary. I realised that I didn't need what I'd dreamt of as a child: the flattery or fame that came with being a public hero.

Now, as I was reaching the end of my trip, I had to reconsider why I had travelled all this way. I mulled it over as I ate breakfast. I had wanted enlightenment, respect and praise, but my experiences had proved to me that these were harder to obtain than I'd imagined. With all my showing off and trying too hard, I had made a spectacle of myself.

I continued to mull over my experiences as I watched another guest, who had got up to fetch a cup of coffee. He pressed the button on the machine but it failed to dispense any coffee. Impatient, he pressed it again and the coffee cup started to fill. But he wasn't really watching and pressed it a third time: scalding coffee spilt over his hand. The mug had been overflowing, but he was still trying to fill it. Suddenly I sat bolt upright, jolting the table and startling the other guests nearby. I had been doing the same as the impatient hotel guest. I was too full, continually trying to over-fill myself with everything. I now had to empty myself of all my preconceived thoughts and ideas and be ready to open my mind to something bigger.

13

Wind

Like vanishing dew,
a passing apparition
or the sudden flash
of lightning – already gone –
thus should one regard one's self.

Ikkyu

The following day, I arrived at my lesson and was greeted at the door by Stephen Hayes.

'Now, are you ready to learn?'

Fresh from my inner pep talk, with renewed vigour and an improved attitude, I nodded. I truly was. Once again, Stephen knew what was going on inside my head. Today, we were focusing on the element of wind. He began by describing a method of fighting, which, like the wind, would disarm my opponent, send him off balance and keep me moving all the time. This was all about judging what my enemy *might* do and using his own strength and skills against him.

'Under the influence of the wind, you fight like a whirlwind of force. Your focus is not on injuring him, but you use enough force to discourage without harshly punishing.'

I didn't really understand what this meant. In the past, using enough force simply to discourage someone hadn't been remotely on my radar and I couldn't see the point of it now. Would this not just make the attacker angry and leave you with a threat? Should you not take such a situation more seriously and immobilise him totally?

As a group, we worked on positions and stances, copying Stephen's posture. We also practised nifty footwork, using speedy movements to escape an opponent's reach. This all looked fairly straightforward but, as with much of what was taught at Dayton, I soon discerned these apparently effortless movements were quite the opposite: Stephen Hayes made a lot of things look easy. Compared to the other elements we had focused on – earth, fire and water – I found wind the most difficult to master. Just as with the physical element itself, wind could change direction, be harsh or gentle and disappear in a second.

After class, Stephen took me aside. A week ago, I would have been leaping up and down with excitement at this development but today I remained calm. Stephen began to talk. He explained to me how the exercises were only part of my development. To complete my overall growth, I had to understand and acknowledge the ninja way of regarding the body and its sensual capabilities. As a whole package, I could accomplish what I needed to, but before that happened, I had to learn how to fine-tune my senses and improve my consciousness.

Once again, we were talking about the five elements but this time in connection to our five senses. Each element corresponded to a sense, and once I had honed them all, my overall awareness would improve as my physical and sensual skills could combine. Stephen explained which elements and senses matched up: I learnt that earth corresponded with my sense of smell, water with taste; fire was connected to sight, wind to touch, and void with hearing.

Stephen guided me through several exercises, each designed to alert my senses and reawaken my awareness. I also learnt how to remain focused on what each sense was telling me. First, I learnt how to breathe passively and take in new smells as part of my connection with earth. For water, I had to become increasingly aware of every substance that passed over my tongue, even trying to determine the individual ingredients in each meal I ate.

Mastering the sense of sight was most effective when I woke in the morning. I learnt a technique whereby you expand your peripheral vision; they use this in high-performance sports to increase reaction time and reflexes. From taking in all I could see, to allowing the shapes before my eyes to form, with the light and colours they were composed of, I managed to look at familiar objects in a new way. Everything appeared different and I came to realise that I had been blindly seeing – not really observing – before.

The wind and touch combination allowed me to feel sensations in each of my limbs that I had previously been unaware of. And void? Well, hearing is the most vital sense to a ninja and I was aware of how sound could deliver information to me, whether it was approaching footsteps or a changing tone in somebody's voice.

I consciously practised the exercises. Instead of simply going through the motions, I found that they had an effect on *me*. I felt more in tune with my emotions, and awareness of my senses had reached a new peak. Since childhood, I had always heard how the loss of one sense strengthens the others, but I had never considered my ability to develop my senses like this. Every time I became fully aware of them, I was surprised by how much each allowed me to taste, see, smell, hear or feel; it was an exercise in mindfulness.

There was another sense that I hoped to learn about. Ninja were famed for their 'sixth sense' and the ability to pinpoint danger. According to Stephen Hayes, it was possible to sense an enemy and know when danger was upon you. I'd read that he swore by the awareness training he had learnt from his master, Masaaki Hatsumi. I'd assumed we would do many exercises that I would need to practise for hours but he surprised me.

'Awareness training is all about ensuring you are focusing your intentions. Every move you make, every strike you perform must be filled with intention. Then, not only will you believe in your actions but an opponent will sense how serious you are.' Stephen told me that any nervousness my opponent felt would show itself to me with his every move: I would sense and take advantage of it. By becoming more aware of my intentions and learning to focus on what I wanted to happen, he said I would become more in tune with my own actions and those of others. Eventually, my instincts would improve, and a strong instinct will always help you against an unseen enemy. Ancient ninja had always relied on instinct to avoid being surprised or poisoned by an enemy.

Becoming more aware of my senses and trying to hone my natural instincts wasn't enough, though. The next thing Stephen told me about was terrifying: the *sakki* test.

'Martin, the time will come when you will be tested. You will be blindfolded and a blade will be held over your head. Only you will be able to protect yourself and you will have to sense the intention of the person holding the sword as they raise it. You will have to sense if they are filled with the express intent to kill you.'

I'd heard of extreme tests before but this sounded barbaric. My reactions would have to save me. I would have to remain calm and resolute, not roll out of the way too early if the sword was held steady, or I would fail the test. But I should also be able to sense the strike so I could roll out of the way before the sword came into contact with me, seriously injuring me or perhaps worse. I gulped. I wasn't often afraid but this prospect was more than a little scary. I was told that, in modern times, this test was used only in the *bujinkan* system at *godan*, fifth *dan* grade, which, luckily for me, was not imminent.

I began to regard awareness skills and mastering others' intent as my sixth sense. During the course of the next few days, I concentrated, paid attention and noticed that I was continually observing things differently and in more and more detail. Situations became easier to read and I responded more confidently. I hoped this would help me as we progressed to learn more about the unpredictable wind element.

In class, my eyes were on An-shu Hayes more than ever before. He began our next lesson with a series of gestures and movements, which inexplicably shifted the energy of the entire room. I can't have been the only student to sense such a change in the atmosphere and I believed Stephen was making the 'nine magical cuts' or *kuji-kiri*: a series of cuts drawn in the air linked to the mystic hand gestures used in *shugendō*. When I saw it performed, I couldn't believe it: the routine I had read about so long ago involved using all the power of the *kuji-in* (the secret magical hand positions of the ninja). As we saw earlier, these positions were said to command an amazing array of powers, including invisibility, the ability to control people and read minds, superhuman strength and so on. This practice is protective, used with a mantra that translates as 'Here all the warriors are lined up boldly in front.' While you are intoning the mantra, you draw a grid in the air, using two fingers, as if cutting with a sword. Four cuts down and five cuts across. It's a way of creating a magical grid of protection in front of you and readying yourself inside to use all your abilities for what is about to come.

Without explanation, Stephen moved on to one of his well-practised meditation routines. For him, meditation was essential and our classes often focused on this spiritual aspect of *ninjutsu*. By then I was – and continue to be – a devotee of meditation. I practise daily and feel as though something is lacking if I miss a session, so much so that I haven't missed a day for fifteen years. Meditation is now so much a part of my life that I incorporate it into my daily routine. Each evening, I like to go for a run and complete my exercise with meditation while sitting in the peace and tranquillity of some nearby woodland. I enjoy the feeling of focusing on one thing in particular, and because it is essential to remain calm, meditation is a restful pursuit. The ability to remain calm, yet focused, is undoubtedly useful when it comes to martial arts so it stands to reason that Stephen Hayes teaches meditation alongside martial arts.

That day, we began with a meditation of purification. As a class, we were instructed to imagine a divine figure pouring cleansing liquids over us. This sounded simple enough but, despite my many years of practice, once again I let myself down at a vital moment. I was so tired from all the training that I couldn't help but be distracted. My muscles ached, making me lose focus repeatedly and I failed to meditate.

Afterwards I approached Stephen, thinking he might have some advice. Interestingly, he recommended having something to ignore during meditation. 'Use the situation to your advantage – you had a cramp in your leg, right? Put your mind on the focus of the meditation as a means to resist the distraction!'

I wasn't totally convinced, but that evening when I was back in my hotel room, I had ample time to practise Stephen's theory. I'd been for a swim straight after dinner, which had been a bad idea as it induced some serious leg and back pain due to tiredness. An attempt to sit in the lotus posture didn't improve matters, and halfway through I was broadsided by my calf muscle screaming. Here was the perfect opportunity to endure: by concentrating on relaxing the muscle, I found my focus deepened and my meditation was more successful. I decided to use the same technique when it came to my *ninjutsu* practice. I knew that instead of complaining when I got distracted, or allowing my lack of focus to affect my movements and attitude, I had to start accepting the situation I was in. Stephen Hayes had shown me that it was important to realise what was preoccupying your mind, to resolutely ignore it and continue with your practice – whether it was strikes, kicks or meditation.

The next day, after another long day's training, I left the *dojo*, planning to head back to my hotel for the evening. I was chatting to a few of the younger black-belt students, and as our conversation continued, we ended up at a local Chinese restaurant. I was relaxed and enjoying myself but, clearly, my awareness skills weren't yet good enough to predict a potentially challenging situation.

The students I was with were mostly teenagers, and although they were seemingly good kids, one took a particular interest in the story of my defeat at the hands of Stephen Hayes.

'So he totally took you out?' He leant over the table, making steady eye contact.

I had to laugh at his earnest little face. 'He certainly gave me a lesson I won't forget!'

More questions followed and I was happy to discuss this. After all, I felt I had turned a corner since my earlier days of boasting, and we were all there to learn. Over our meal I kept repeating how impressive Stephen Hayes's skills were, and how mine evidently did not match up. As we finished eating, the boy asked about my martial-arts qualifications so I told him. Not much more was said and we soon left the restaurant, but as we stepped outside, the teenage black belt's whole attitude changed. He became aggressive and said he wanted to fight me. I took a second to register this. Of course! That was why he had been so keen to hear about my failure in front of

Stephen Hayes – and why my martial-arts exams and experience were of so much interest.

Several possible reactions went through my mind. I didn't want to show him immediately what I was made of. He was clearly skilled but I had age and experience over that. In addition, the *to-shin do* code of conduct warned against using violence unnecessarily and this would be a fight for superficial reasons: he was a clear example of James Norris's 'little yapping dog'. I had to remain the larger dog and not stoop to his level.

The other black belts had formed a group, waiting to see how I would react. I knew I had to be careful. It was possible that this was another of the tests the senior instructors at Dayton had laid on for me. Nothing would surprise me.

I made my decision and walked away. I returned to my hotel knowing that, however much I wanted to show the kid the damage I was capable of, I would gain nothing from a fight. I would just revert to the character I had been when I landed in the USA.

But the incident bothered me on several levels. First, I was disappointed that I had trusted the lad. I had revealed things to him and shared details about my life. I had let my guard down. Second, I was upset with Stephen Hayes. I'd never know for sure if he'd had a hand in the evening's events but I suspected that, once again, An-shu had outsmarted me.

14

Void

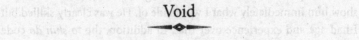

The way out is through the door. Why is it that no one will use this method?

Confucius

Stephen was unlike any other teacher I had worked with before. He hadn't responded to my actions or my behaviour as I had expected him to. These things seemed to wash over him as though he was focused on a much higher plain. He had lived up to every hope I had. He was the real deal, a true master of the arts of *ninjutsu*.

Now, as I spent my last few days in Ohio, I realised his air of detachment reflected his enlightenment. He didn't react suddenly, with his emotions, to anything I said or did – although some of my earlier actions must have been infuriating.

As I approached the *dojo* on my final day, I took advantage of the walk to reflect on what I had experienced. Something came over me. On one of my first days at the *dojo*, when I had been pestering James Norris with a multitude of questions, I had asked him how I could possibly understand the elements through meditation and study. I could almost laugh at myself now. I could see how patient he had been with me when he had told me that the only way to fully comprehend the elements was to immerse myself in them, to truly use them. Four short weeks ago, I had been looking to tick boxes off a list and find a shortcut, but there was no shortcut in *ninjutsu*. Since my first days in the *dojo*, I had meditated, studied, questioned and contemplated everything my teachers had told me. I had taken time out every evening to practise my *kuji-in* and really *become* the element. In the *dojo*, however, I had resisted learning any new elemental strategies because it had been uncomfortable; only when I had started to use them and stopped resisting had the other areas of study and effort become aids.

In life, we get stuck in what works for us. We might have found as a child that if we held on and were stubborn we gained what we wanted. If this happened, we became an *earth* person. If we found deception or misdirection effective, then *water* became our element. Perhaps we found arguing or avoidance the best method, in which case we may have become a *wind* person, while those who used aggression or connection may have adopted *fire* habits. Whatever the element, we develop a comfort zone and can find ourselves stuck in it. We use the tactic more and more. It's very hard to do something else. We do the same thing even when it's not working because we think it's right. The element becomes us and we it. To break free of it and be flexible is very hard.

At that moment, I knew something within me and about me had been transformed, perhaps something that can only be wholly understood if you have been through it yourself. In life, as in the *dojo*, people get stuck in one element or in one strategy and will do anything rather than change and adapt, even if that means failing constantly. The strategy *feels* right, so the world must be to blame if it does not work – 'I never get a break.' My unwillingness to change was a symptom of the pride and ego or emotional baggage I had arrived with – almost as though I'd packed an extra suitcase. Now it had disappeared. In its place was a far lighter feeling of strategy, adaptability and flexibility. I saw things and interpreted them in a completely new way, and I was capable of thinking things through, rather than wading in immediately. Thanks to my new grasp of the elements, my levels of understanding had increased: not only in understanding myself but also in reading others, their emotions, their motivations and what was really important. I felt as if I had shed a lot of weight, that I would walk away from Dayton feeling lighter, with much less baggage than when I had arrived.

Perhaps most importantly, my time with Stephen Hayes and his

talented staff made me disregard a few of my preconceived ideas about
ninja. I felt it was less about silent justice and cunning, like most
people believed, and more about identifying a goal and achieving it.
My absorption of the elements had changed my attitudes and thoughts.
Now I knew that *ninjutsu* was a tool with which I could obtain what
I needed but it didn't have to involve the force, violence or emotions
that would mark me out as weak. As I walked down the street, I could
see the whole of existence around me in terms of the elements.

The Five Elemental Manifestations

Chi – earth: a solid state, a natural posture
Sui – water: a liquid state, a defensive posture
Ka – fire: an energy-releasing state, an offensive posture
Fu – wind: a gaseous state, a receiving posture
Ku – void: subatomic energy, potential, the substance from which
things take form

Somehow the vision of these five elements had opened up in me
a different consciousness: an ability to see the big picture, to see the
forces at work and an ability to think through any circumstance
strategically.

Walking into the *dojo* I could see Stephen already sitting there. I
took my shoes off and walked up beside him.

'You made it then?' He smiled. I think it was obvious that the Ohio
heat was playing havoc with me.

'Last day here, An-shu.'

'Uh-huh.'

I still marvelled at his laid-back American drawl, which seemed
faintly incongruous in such a martial and spiritual master. Perhaps
his manner was useful for making people feel at ease in his company
or, more importantly, disarming those who might want something
more from him.

For a few moments we sat quietly. I was in a contemplative mood.
From my bubbling excitement when my flight had landed, to bull-
dozing my way through lessons that had led to my embarrassing

comeuppance at the hands of Master Hayes, then my realisations, it was fair to say I had been through all elements during my time there. Stephen agreed. He reassured me: what I had learnt about myself was natural; it was all a part of the essential journey as you progress through martial arts. He told me that my time in America had taken me out of my comfort zone and made me lose hold of three vital things: name, elements and void.

Now, finally, Stephen explained the importance of the void. He said it reflects our ideas of how things work and shows that the values we believed to be universal are not. As I had come to accept, different cultures have different ways of doing things.

At this point, I asked him a question: I wanted him to tell me how to master the void element. His answer seemed evasive: 'To master the void you really have to go beyond the other elements.'

I could understand how mastery of the elements could lead to a further fifth state of potential beyond the others but going *beyond* the elements sounded like letting go of the tools you had just gained.

'You know the *togakure-ryū** also used the elements to identify flaws and weaknesses in someone's character, Martin.'

Something about the change of pace or the feel of the conversation caught me off guard. When Stephen spoke, his voice seemed usually to come from the centre of his being, pre-thought and already digested. Now there was a note of urgency I had never heard before.

Stephen explained that the ninja would look at the needs of an adversary and, in so doing, find ways to manipulate and control them. The ninja could then be at the centre of activity yet remain hidden. I tried my best to listen and take it all in as he listed them in order.

'OK. We have the "Five Needs" and they correspond to the elements. First up is "purpose". This is the highest possible motive for a person. Genuine purpose, however, is truly very rare. Most people's actions are driven by one of the other motives or elements. However, we tend to hide our motives from ourselves and others on purpose. Make sense?'

---

* A historical tradition of *ninjutsu*, the 'School of the Hidden Door'.

I nodded, and he continued, ticking them off on his fingers.

'Social status. What do you reckon that corresponds with?' He looked at me slyly, stroking his beard. I knew this was a subtle dig at me.

I hazarded a guess: 'Wind?'

'Sure is. It corresponds to the verbal, social wind element. Wanting to look good in front of others and achieve high status in the pack. It's one heck of a motivator.

'Then we have "power"!' His voice changed, eyes penetrating, and he spread his arms as if embracing the entire world. 'Corresponds to the fire element, the urge to be in control and able to dictate what happens in the world around us.' He leant towards me. 'It dictates so many people's actions. It's why we push ourselves and fight hard for things.

'Number four is "sex", or our need for love – water element. Controls the sexual centre and is also a very powerful motivator. It drives us hard to win friends and to put ourselves into a position in which people want us. Finally, there's "security", earth element. Ultimately, fear is the motivator for security. This is also what is behind much of the motivation for possessions or money, wanting to protect ourselves against the world, to feel safe in our own little bubble.

'It seems to me that, in life, we all like to pretend we are moved primarily by the "spirit" or "void" element. That is to say, we always *claim* that we are acting for a higher purpose, a nobler cause . . . But the truth is the *four other elements* are more likely to be controlling our decisions. Earth, for example, would be about material possessions or the security that they bring. Water would be more about sexuality or the fulfilment of our emotions. Fire would be about ambition and power, and wind would be about social status and standing. These emotions, these aspects of our personality, are the ones that control us. By understanding the elements, we can strategically make people do what we want. *Ninjutsu* is about achieving this goal.'

He paused, and we regarded each other quietly. I was both inspired and confused. Had I just spent a month trying to master the elements, but now in order not to be manipulated or hoodwinked, I had to go past or eliminate them? 'So, to be able to do this, we first need to understand ourselves so that we can eliminate these emotions and ways of being?'

Stephen shook his head emphatically. 'No. You cannot eliminate them, Martin. We need to start with being honest about what we want and express those wants in a positive way that is under our control. Only then can we start to deceive, control and manipulate others. Of course, those are tools that we use for the higher good.'

It was certainly a lot to take in. It seemed to me that if you don't control the elements they control you, and that your ability to know yourself is directly connected with your ability to control this in others. I was not sure if I was getting into a muddle or had just got it. Stephen didn't give any clear answer. He just changed tack to a parable.

'Here's a fun example of how this philosophy could be applied. Imagine you're in seventeenth-century Japan. Let's think of someone who should be above those needs.' His eyes twinkled again. 'Let's say a Buddhist monk. Imagine you want to sell a piece of land to a nearby Buddhist monastery. When you approach the abbot in charge, you are probably tempted to use notions of "higher" purpose as the means to convince him. Now, *ninjutsu* teaches that, although the abbot would like to pretend that purpose is his ultimate motivation, it is probably better for you to appeal to one of the other emotions but dress them up with "purpose".

'You could say to him, "Listen, I really want to sell you this land and I think it would be very good for your monastery and Buddhism . . . but I want you to be aware that we have had other offers, including one from a Western Christian missionary who wants to buy the land to build a church here."

'Now this, on the earth level, would stir his fear of rival religions and alien things. It would allow him to believe he was purchasing the land out of the Buddhist noble doctrine. But, in fact, he is fearful of Christians moving in. If earth doesn't work, perhaps he is a water element kind of person. Perhaps you could appeal to something sexual. Of course, this is a monk who shouldn't have any of these feelings, but when you start to work with the elements you become rather cynical and see the true motives behind people's actions. So you could say to him something like this: "Perhaps it's about time there was a convent here, a Buddhist convent that perhaps could work in association with your monastery." Now this, on a very subconscious base level, may well appear to the abbot to be a possibility, as having close interaction with females is essentially a sublimation of his sexual urge. This could persuade him to purchase the land.

'Or you could use fire as a strategy and say to him, "Think of the power! Think of the influence you could have! Maybe you need your own special school, to be promoted as the head of a *new* monastery. Perhaps with this land you could increase your influence." This would appeal to him if he was fire personality.'

I had to laugh. Stephen's rendition of the story was like a one-man play with full-on flamboyant physical actions.

He continued: 'If he was a wind personality, you could say to him, "Think of the fame. You're *such* a good teacher that it's your duty to put yourself forward with this. It's *your* duty to have a big stage, a large school to spread Buddhism. But it's not for you, no, not for your own fame, not for your own ego, but because you have a *duty* – with the kind of skill that you have as a teacher – to do this for others!"'

He was right – totally right. One of those tactics couldn't fail to increase the chances of success. The whole power of his approach hit me hard.

'But,' he held up a warning hand, 'these are also connected with the "Five Weaknesses", which are confusion, anger/ambition, vanity, sympathy and fear. These, of course, are also connected with the person's needs. Someone looking for purpose shows confusion; a person looking for power shows anger and ambition – ambition is the urge to make things how you want them and anger is that, but amplified. Someone looking for social status shows vanity. The urge for love shows as sympathy, and the urge for security manifests from fear.'

In that moment, I realised something. We tend to think of emotions as good or bad – happiness is good, sadness is bad. Love is good, hate is bad. The truth is, how they are used makes a difference. We should all be sad if something bad happens and all hate the right things. Love can be destructive, as can misplaced sympathy.

I was not sure how but I felt this wisdom was somehow connected with the void or how to understand the void. It was, though, beyond me now. I needed time to reflect and digest. Things were changing inside me so quickly.

The time for me to fly home had arrived, and as I left the Quest Center for the final time, it was with sadness. *Ninjutsu* is not a common aim, so it had been wonderful to find a group of like-minded people. We all wanted to improve and to progress, not solely for our individual gains but to make the world a better place for others around us. I hoped I could start to apply on home turf what I had learnt.

Master Hayes had taught me about the emotions and how they relate to the elements and I realised that this had given me the ability to understand the emotions and use them on others.

I had let go of the childish image of the ninja as a silent assassin, and understood that he would do whatever was effective to achieve his goals. A lot of getting what you want is about making people do what you want by understanding what *they* want. Through my contemplation and study, my own vision of these needs started to manifest itself. What Stephen had predicted had happened. I had focused on the elements and on using the strategies, in the *dojo* and in the real world, to such a degree that a profound change had come over me.

This brand new outlook felt like a vital skill – something I have held on to. The elements and my understanding of them have meant I have been able to achieve success in several aspects of my life. For instance, I have become fitter, stronger and healthier than ever before. My professional life has improved immeasurably: I have gained several promotions and regard myself as successful at work. Now I cannot imagine life without the elements. They have become a part of me, of everything I do, and each day feels more successful than the last.

Through this elemental enlightenment, I began to know almost intuitively what kind of elemental person I was talking to. I found myself switching elemental strategy very easily. I also discovered my own real motives. I no longer hid them and lied to myself. Everything looked bigger and clearer to me, as if a divine vision of the world had opened up. I felt empowered; I felt stronger.

My vision of the elements was starting to develop slightly differently from others' and, indeed, from what I had initially been taught. That didn't worry me: to me it showed how genuine and powerful what had happened was. But, paradoxically, all this new elemental knowledge and experience made me suspicious. I wondered if there was something that Stephen Hayes was keeping secret from the world.

15

Planet Tokyo

❖

No matter how bad a state of mind you may get into, if you keep strong and hold out, eventually the floating clouds must vanish and the withering wind must cease.

Dōgen

I was on an aeroplane again, making another journey in my quest for ninja enlightenment, and this time I was off to the Far East. Most of my fellow passengers were Japanese. I couldn't hear a word of English being spoken but I let myself listen to the jumble of Japanese around me. After all, this would be my soundtrack for the next month. I should have been sleeping in preparation for the next leg of my journey, after we landed, but I couldn't seem to drift off. Instead, I let my mind reach back to an event a few weeks earlier, which had cemented my important decision to travel to Japan . . .

I was in London on business. Walking through Southwark on the way to an early breakfast meeting, I was still half asleep, a late night having put paid to feeling fresh for the day. Even the chill wind wasn't waking me up, and the only people I saw were a couple of street cleaners. Suddenly pain ripped through my right arm and I turned to see two teenagers, one of whom was trying to snatch my bag. He had attempted to grab and run, but feeling the tug on my arm I had naturally sunk into a low stance and gripped hard. This had stopped him in his tracks, almost throwing him off balance. Considering my earlier doziness, my body was already in action. My senses heightened and adrenaline pumped. Wham! My left hand hit his wrist with a hammer fist. I heard myself yell, 'Stop it!' several times. I punctuated each word with a swift punch to my would-be mugger's face; the crunch of nasal bone on fist was curiously satisfying.

Those two youths had bitten off far more than they could chew; rotten luck to attempt to steal a bag from a would-be ninja. However, I was perfectly aware that there were two of them and one of me, and as the second assailant stepped forward, I realised that things could definitely turn nasty if they had a blade with them. Quickly, I side-stepped so I was out of reach. Then they ran off. The whole thing had probably lasted under a minute and my body was shaking, adrenaline coursing through my veins. Despite my shock, I was pleased with myself. I'd done exactly what was taught by Stephen Hayes, a textbook *to-shin do* defence: verbal signals to distract, a low stance to gain strength, and I had executed each point perfectly without giving in to rage or exerting unnecessary force.

The problem came afterwards. I was shaken and unnerved by the attack. I couldn't remember much of the event or any detail about the appearance of anyone involved; I was haunted by it and paranoid for weeks. This was a wake-up call, with regard to my development. I knew I still had to do something to move things forwards.

That early-morning experience on a deserted London street had brought me to board another long-haul flight. I was flying to Tokyo, desperate to learn more. However, my visit wasn't entirely planned. I had written to the ninja grandmaster Masaaki Hatsumi, but I hadn't yet received a response.

Following my trip to the USA, and knowing the cultural differences that existed between East and West, I knew I would have to keep my enthusiasm in check. In America, my energy had been seen as ego and I couldn't risk the same thing happening in Japan. I had tried to be as prepared as possible: I had armed myself with the appropriate green belt and specialist boots (known as *tabi* boots) after doing my research into what ninja students in that part of the world wore. I wanted to look, seem and feel prepared, and I knew a respectful attitude was essential. I had also read as much as I could about Masaaki Hatsumi but, despite his evident knowledge, it was tricky to interpret his words. Maybe things got lost in translation. Or perhaps this visit was going to be harder than I imagined.

When we landed in Tokyo after thirteen hours of flying, the city was just starting to get going, and I was not looking forward to the stressful and confusing train ride ahead of me. My first experience of Tokyo was complete culture shock – if you've ever seen *Blade Runner*, well, that kind of sums up a Westerner's response to this frenetic city. It wasn't unpleasant, just a total shock to my senses. Imagine a city with around 12.5 million people, a quarter of whom live within commuting distance and most of whom were awake and on the move, like a colony of ants. After my sleepless hours in the sky, I felt as if I'd landed on a different planet and now, with all my dulled senses being forced into high energy, visual and auditory overload, I had to negotiate a train journey to Noda City, Chiba Prefecture, where I would be living for the duration of stay.

I suppose this first taste of Japan should have alerted me to what the next few weeks would hold. The noise, movement and frenetic nature of the train system in Japan were unlike anything I had seen before. It made the London Underground or the New York Subway look like sleepy village stations. 'OK, Martin,' I said aloud. 'Welcome to Shinjuku station.' I flicked through my travel guide: '"Shinjuku station serves as the main connecting hub for rail traffic between central Tokyo and its western suburbs on inter-city rail, commuter rail, and metro lines. The station is used by an average of 3.64 million people per day making it, by far, the world's busiest transport hub."'

I raised my head and looked around in total bemusement, then read on: '"The station has thirty-six platforms and, including an underground arcade, there are well over two hundred exits."'

'Bloody brilliant – thirty-six platforms and everything in pictograms. What does Chiba look like?' I slapped the book shut and swung round directly into the path of a tiny suit-clad female, who scowled venomously at me. 'Sorry!' I raised my hands in supplication, dropping the book and my rucksack on her feet.

She merely shook her head and sidestepped my chaos, muttering, '*Gaijin!*'

Ouch! My first insult – *gaijin* literally means 'outside person' or, I guess, 'alien', which was exactly how I felt!

I was hungry, thirsty and jet-lagged, and had to deal with the signs written in Japanese. As there were far more train lines than I had anticipated, it became an amusing game as I tried to identify which one I needed. I had visions of arriving in Osaka by mistake. Matters were further complicated by the booking and seat-reservation system. At first glance – with a jet-lagged brain – the Japanese Railway Network resembled an abstract tapestry.

After consulting guidebooks, noticeboards and endless signposts, I managed to purchase a train ticket and felt brave enough to step aboard a waiting train.

Bad move: the fuss and bother that ensued was enough to tell me I had made yet another stupid mistake. In the midst of all the exclamations and arm flapping, I noticed that, with the exception of myself, every other person in the carriage was a woman. I'd managed to get myself into the women-only carriage, and now that the train was moving I had little choice but to stay put. I must have looked like a right *gaijin*, frozen to the spot, clutching my luggage.

'*Sumimasen, sumimasen,*' I stuttered pathetically in my broken Japanese, and tried to look very sorry.

It worked: one of the women cracked a tiny smile and explained in halting English that it was clear I had made a mistake and, she gestured with her hand, I was welcome to stay in the carriage. I did my best to thank her and breathed a sigh of relief but, to be honest, there was not a lot I could have done other than a James Bond-style shimmy between connecting carriages.

This was all short-lived: I soon realised I had missed my stop. I had needed to catch a connecting train to Noda City but, during the carriage drama, we'd passed the station. My already complicated journey had just become even more difficult with the reluctance of the previously territorial females to let me get off: this time they didn't understand that I needed to change trains and were making amends for initially trying to hound me out. Eventually, I managed to extricate myself and got off at the next stop to catch a train travelling back towards Tokyo. Every move I made seemed to cause some form of international incident.

Back on a platform, I had to try to decipher the maps and signs to find the train that would enable me to catch a connection to Noda. My jet-lag was fast catching up with me and I cursed myself for not resting properly on the plane. I was getting hungry and nothing I could see around me offered me any familiarity or nourishment – the vending machines offered hot corn soup and energy drinks. The pangs of homesickness were beginning to kick in.

I sincerely hoped this trip, with all of its early challenges, would be worthwhile. I kept in my mind my determination to approach things differently: I had learnt my lesson in America. Instead of blindly throwing myself into situations and allowing others to make judgements of me, I vowed to keep a low profile and try to fit in.

I was swimming through tiredness by the time I finally reached Noda. Unable to relax, I had kept an eye on each station we passed through. Getting irretrievably lost in Japan was not on my to-do list, and I was very aware that the further away from Tokyo I ventured, the chances of finding anyone who spoke English diminished. When I left the confines of Noda City's station, I headed in what I hoped was the direction of my hotel. However, as my day had already mercilessly demonstrated, this wouldn't be straightforward. Whichever street I turned down, it was wrong. I was starting to panic.

A top tip that guidebooks and tourist websites offer is to have the name of your hotel, hostel or *ryokan* (traditional Japanese boarding house) written in Japanese, ready to show to anyone who looks friendly. I had forgotten to sort this out, so began an aimless wander around the area near Noda's station.

However, my luck seemed to be changing. I must have looked as desperate as I felt because a battered American car pulled up alongside me. It seemed completely out of place, and as I leant towards the window that rolled down, I saw that the driver was Western too. I'd been away from Europe for about twenty hours but the relief I felt at seeing someone who looked familiar was almost palpable. I grinned.

'You look like you might need some help.' He spoke English, he seemed sane, and as I explained that I was trying to track down a *ryokan* that didn't appear to exist, he motioned for me to get into the car. I gratefully slid into the passenger seat and off we went. The driver turned out to be American and introduced himself as Michael Pearce; by some bizarre coincidence, he happened to be a high-ranking student of Masaaki Hatsumi.

Despite his apparently easy-going manner, I wasn't prepared for how much Michael's teachings would clash ideologically with what I had been taught in Dayton. As I talked to him about *tengu* (the goblins that ninja were said to have evolved from) and *yamabushi*, he simply cut me off: 'Oh, Martin, goblins! I hate that rubbish.'

When I moved on to Stephen Hayes, the elements and *kuji-in*, he just let out a sigh that conveyed a thousand words. It could easily have said, 'I've been living in Japan, training under the grandmaster directly since I was a young man, and for decades I have met visitors with fantastical ideas and outrageous notions about my art. Let's just get back to the here and now and focus on training and improving ourselves.' This was an attitude I would later find Michael embodied in his actions.

Interpretations of ninja are subjective and everyone's view differs. However, Michael's and my views seemed at opposing ends of the scale. Where I was open to new ideas about *ninjutsu*, Michael had a firm position that only years of living in Japan and training with the grandmaster could bring, yet he didn't force his status or undoubted skill on me. He didn't care what I thought of him: he wasn't trying to prove anything to anyone. Later, I would find out just how different his methods were, but for now I was happy to make idle chat. I revealed my time spent being tutored by the myriad of *bujinkan* instructors, then outlined my trip to America and the wisdom of Stephen Hayes.

'Well, it seems that you're definitely following in Stephen Hayes's footsteps. The Azusa *ryokan* was where he first stayed!'

I felt comforted that, after my long day of travelling and taking wrong turns, something had gone to plan. Perhaps it was symbolic that Stephen Hayes had begun the Japanese chapter of his ninja studies in the same place as I was.

Throughout our conversation, I was mindful not to reveal too much about myself, as I had in America. I decided to glean information instead. 'So what brought you to Japan . . . Noda? Was it to train in *ninjutsu*?'

'Yeah, I came here to study under Hatsumi Sensei back in the eighties.'

He seemed nonchalant but I couldn't hide how impressed I was. It turned out Michael had been studying and training there for more than twenty years, since booking himself a one-way ticket and arriving in Japan from America when he was just a teenager. It had been his dream to learn from the ninja grandmaster and he'd made it his life's work to do so. He'd also been inspired by Stephen Hayes. Michael had seen an article in *Black Belt* magazine describing Hayes's adventures in Japan and decided that that was what he wanted to do. He then discovered that Hatsumi wasn't taking on any more students.

'Yeah, like that mattered – so I just booked a flight and got out here. I just figured that he'd take me!'

I had to laugh: it was a brash but awesome statement.

He was a twelfth belt. Twelfth! The skills of a twelfth *dan* extend far beyond the black belt made famous by ninja films and popular culture – it's pretty rare and requires a specialist degree of training and focus. I'd come to Noda to learn from specialist instructors with immense experience. I hadn't thought I would find one so soon. Jettisoning all plans to be aloof, I asked Michael if he would be willing to teach me. He agreed, but not before explaining just how tough my training would be. He also said I would need to be prepared to change aspects of my thinking and, ultimately, myself. Minutes later, we arrived where I would be staying for the next fortnight.

Initially, I had thought it exciting to stay in a *ryokan*. But, on first glance, I wished I had plumped for the stark anonymity of a Holiday Inn – if such places existed in Noda. Although I was keen to experience as many elements as possible of Japanese life, lodging at the *ryokan* might have been a step too far. I managed to offend the owners before I'd even shaken hands: I walked into the house with my shoes on. I could see Michael smirking as they gestured wildly to a pair of slippers just inside the door. Good grief! I'd known about this! I was just so tired that the one custom I should have remembered had evaded me. In Japan, they view wearing outdoor shoes indoors as very unhygienic so 'house slippers' are provided for guests.

The other thing that struck me was the stench of stale cigarette smoke. Western rules about not smoking in hotels clearly hadn't reached Noda. My heart sank further when I was shown to my room, which could only be described as shabby. It was covered with what appeared to be a layer of cigarette ash and was devoid of any large furniture. There were just a couple of straw mats on the floor, a table and a cushion; nothing else.

I turned to Michael and reinforced that I was in Japan to be challenged and to face tests. I wanted to show my dedication and prove myself. Michael simply nodded and smiled.

'OK. You've said that you'd like to be tested, and that you're here to develop your ninja skills to your highest ability. Well, here's your first test. You're going back to Tokyo to train with Master Hatsumi this evening.'

I was completely taken aback. Training? Now? I was not in any condition to walk, let alone train – I hadn't slept for more than twenty-four hours. It was almost five o'clock now, and I would still have to negotiate the complicated train network to get back to Tokyo. My face probably said all I was thinking. Michael shrugged. 'Better get changed and on that train.'

Clearly I had no choice. I kicked myself for having told Michael how much I wanted to be tested. Falling at the first hurdle was not an option. He gave me a map with some directions to get back to Noda station, then to the *dojo* I would be heading for in Tokyo – it was the famous Budokan Martial Arts Centre. Michael left, promising to pick me up the following morning. I got changed and prepared to head back to Tokyo; although I was excited, I was also afraid, and tiredness was beginning to overwhelm me.

I must have nodded off continually during the ninety-minute train journey, jolting awake at intervals to check which station we were passing through. Back in Tokyo, I clutched Michael's map, intent on finding the Budokan without being distracted by the sights and smells of the city.

My tiredness and the constant buzz of the city were overwhelming and I found a place to sit for five minutes while I got my bearings. I found it hard to compute that I was about to meet the great Masaaki Hatsumi, a living legend. He was reputed to know all the mystic arts. I'd seen the pictures – him doing *kuji-in* with his master, Takamatsu Sensei, whose father was rumoured to have been a *yamabushi*, one of the secretive mountain monks I had heard of in Dayton, who still held the key to ancient wisdom.

Was I about to meet a *tatsujin* – a fully actualised human being, a complete person? Thoughts rushed through my head. Would he have superhuman powers? I knew he was a doctor of traditional Japanese medicine, but would his skills in healing and fighting transfer to every other art or practice? I'd heard about his combat skills too. The story went that he had been involved in a fight that was brutal beyond compare: that one of his opponent's eyes had been lost in the combat and stood on. Then Hatsumi had had to put the remaining eye back in place. Rumour had it that he had sent the challenger a bill for his treatment.

I experienced a shiver of anticipation: Hatsumi was not a man to be messed with and, in a short time, I would be in his *dojo*. If he was as powerful as the stories maintained, would he be able to sense things about me, know my intentions or even read my mind? On the other hand, perhaps things more down to earth, as Michael's attitude had suggested.

The map was surprisingly easy to follow and after ten minutes I saw the Budokan from a few hundred yards away. The very sight of it was overwhelming. Less than a day into my quest in Japan and I had already experienced several 'pinch me' moments. It was clear I was in the right place: a gaggle of martial artists had gathered outside. Butterflies launched in my stomach. This was it. I was about to meet the grandmaster.

Luckily, I arrived at the Budokan minutes before classes started. I headed to the changing rooms about to change my shoes, only to be confronted with more slippers. I took all of this in as I put on my black *gi* and my indoor shoes. I then did several more removals of shoes and slippers before finally settling on a mat in the *dojo* . . . without wearing any slippers. The shoe business was a minefield!

Slowly, more students began to gather. Some seemed as nervous as I was, others more relaxed. I tried to calm myself, made a bit of small-talk and started doing some stretches. Suddenly, a prickling feeling on the back of my neck made me turn round. It was like something out of a movie: the hairs literally stood to attention and I had a sense of fear like a trickle of ice-cold sweat down my spine. There he was, the ninja grandmaster. I instantly recognised him from the photo in Stephen Hayes's office. Yet something seemed out of place. I was used to martial artists of rank dressing the part. The *kuk sool* grandmaster had always worn a golden martial-arts uniform and Stephen Hayes had had something similar, but nothing about Hatsumi Sensei struck me as showy or ostentatious. On the contrary, he was dressed in a lurid yellow shirt, his hair a wild shock of purple. Nevertheless, he seemed to exude power from every pore. Rather than joy, I felt fear. I had no doubt that this man could kill me very easily if he wanted to. It was like standing on the edge of a remote clifftop: you knew you were precariously close to danger but you couldn't resist the feeling of exhilaration. I have to admit that I'd come to Japan hoping to meet Yoda. What I got was Darth Vader.

I knelt with the other students, facing the front of the *dojo* with Hatsumi Sensei and his highest-ranking instructors. I was motioned to the back: we were sitting in grade order. We commenced with a short opening ceremony: palms raised above the head, then brought down together in front, and a moment of quiet contemplation.

'*Shiken haramitsu daikoumyo!*' the grandmaster barked. We repeated it. He clapped his hands twice, bowed, then clapped once and bowed again – we followed perfectly. I instantly recognised the phrase from the class in England. But what did it mean?

As if to answer the question, the grandmaster started to explain via a translator. The phrase *shiken haramitsu daikoumyo* encompasses a wealth of meaning – the *kanji* that represents it is 四拳 波羅蜜 大光明 and can be broken down into parts:

shi-ken 四拳 (*shi* – four; *ken*–heart/fist), 'four hearts': represents four perspectives of the heart:

The Merciful Heart: expresses love for everything.
The Sincere Heart: follows what is true.
The Attuned Heart: follows the natural order of things.
The Dedicated Heart: holds to the chosen pursuit.

ha-ra-mitsu 波羅蜜 (*ha* – wave; *ra* – gauze; *mitsu* – nectar): *paramita* or Buddha's *satori* or enlightened state. 波 means 'wave', a metaphor for instability – think ripples on a flat pond; 羅 means 'gauze' – a textured, interwoven fabric, a metaphor for cloudiness or obscurity of thought/ sight; 蜜 means 'nectar' – a sweet liquid, which may mean the sweet bliss of enlightenment, having a 'clear mind'. It is that happy 'aha' feeling you get when you suddenly understand. *Haramitsu* would seem to say that if you free your mind from life's clutter you will reach enlightenment.

dai-kou-myo 大光明 (*dai* – big/great; *kou* – light; *myo* – bright). This phrase effectively means 'big bright light' – so, the gaining of wisdom and enlightenment.

Put it together and we get something along the lines of 'to seek enlightenment by being pure of heart, clearing the mind of worldly clutter and persevering with dedication in the moment'. A Westerner whispered, 'It means every moment is a chance for enlightenment.' Hatsumi Sensei then faced the class, and his highest-ranking student said, '*Sensei, ni rei.*' This is a simple, humbling phrase, which roughly translates as 'thank you' to your teacher. *Sensei*, of course, is 'teacher' or 'guide', someone who has gone before in the teachings and who was once where you are now; *rei* can mean 'bow' but may also translate as 'spirit' or 'soul'. Therefore, for me, it is a phrase and action of gratitude to my guiding force, which comes from the seat of my spirit/soul (the *tan tien* – abdomen) in the form of a bow from the waist. After this, the rest of the class bowed as one and said, '*Onegai shimasu*' (literally, 'I humbly ask of you').

Hatsumi Sensei had a very specific way of teaching, which I discovered as the class began. He would begin by giving a eulogy of sorts to the class, subsequently translated for the non-Japanese among us. Today we were focusing on the concept of *sansin no kata* (form of the three hearts), designed to get our minds and bodies into the ideal state for combat, something all warriors should be able to summon.

I was partnered with two elderly Japanese men, both of whom were seasoned masters. I repeatedly copied the strike Sensei had shown the class – thankfully, it looked quite easy: raise hand in a flowing motion to strike your opponent in the face. However, my training partner looked at me in horror. To me, the technique seemed like a quick punch – nothing too complicated – but I was obviously doing something wrong and my partners were despairing of me. They gestured and barked at me in Japanese – I had no idea what they wanted from me and my blood pressure started to rise with anxiety.

When we got on to the next move, it was clear we weren't making any progress: their frustration with me didn't ease and now, I could tell, they were getting really annoyed. I was helpless, unable to communicate with either man. Every so often, we would stop and watch as Hatsumi demonstrated more techniques – one in particular where you end up pulling your opponent's arm, much like a length of rope. This was all about tying up your opposition without tying yourself in knots. I grasped that much.

Suddenly, he changed tack. Hatsumi was demonstrating a similar technique with rope – the opponent approached him, grabbed the rope; Hatsumi overpowered him and tied him up within seconds. They repeated a few of the exercises before Hatsumi turned to us students.

'*Ima anata wa asobu!*' he said. 'Now *you* play!'

Once again, I hadn't the faintest idea where to start and my training partners were again showing signs of annoyance and frustration. I panicked and probably hurt them – reverting to force to try to complete the move. This was not going according to plan. I was terrified that everyone would think me a terrible student on my very first day. I knew one of the instructors had a basic command of English so I tried to approach him. But after a few attempts, I could see that I was angering him too. I retreated after he barked, 'Too many questions. This is grandmaster's lesson!'

It was another custom I needed to observe: when in Japan, one does not question one's master. I didn't think things could deteriorate much more, but while I was being reprimanded by the instructor I had approached, I had missed the demonstration of the next technique. I turned away, dejected, and headed back towards my partner.

All of a sudden, I felt a blow to the face. Suddenly I couldn't see and my eyes were watering uncontrollably. By not paying attention, I had missed the demo for distracting an opponent. This was done simply by throwing or flicking an object off the floor (in this case a leather *shuriken*, or throwing star) into your assailant's face. I had seen throwing stars before in movies; the five-pointed metal stars used for blinding, cutting and distracting opponents were legendary but the idea of them being flipped up off the floor was completely new. Although I couldn't see, I soon realised everyone was laughing at me – my Japanese training partner had taken his revenge. While I had been feeling sorry for myself, he had decided to test my reactions by hurling the *shuriken* at me. Major fail.

As the class continued, it dawned on me that I was among some seriously talented martial artists. One by one, they approached the grandmaster to demonstrate what they could do and there were impressive skills on show. I was worried that I was totally out of my depth. The actions of my classmates combined with the complicated messages the grandmaster was giving us confused me. I couldn't follow any of the movements, and when the class ended I left quickly and quietly with my head down. I had to get back to Noda and reconsider everything.

Utterly exhausted, deflated and now about to embark on my third train journey of the day, I found myself standing on the platform with some Australians, who had joined the class later on. Like most Aussies, they were an amiable and positive bunch. We talked *ninjutsu* for a while, nothing deep, just easy-going chat about our various histories and where we had sought training. Naturally, my experiences in Dayton and with Stephen Hayes came up in conversation.

However, the next morning, it was made clear to me by the black belts when we were gathered in the *dojo* that I was not to mention Stephen's name. He had given great offence and disrespect to the grandmaster by going it alone. All traces of his time in Noda had been removed from the *dojo* and, rather chillingly, other students at the *dojo* had been told to cause Stephen Hayes great injury if they ever trained alongside him. I was rather shocked at this new aggressive side of Japanese ninja practitioners. Now, in Noda, the black belts were enquiring after Stephen's health but it wasn't out of courtesy.

I had never thought of Stephen being at risk or an enemy to anyone – he had worked for the Dalai Lama, for goodness' sake! Now things about my trip to America seemed clearer. James Norris had kept me apart from Stephen Hayes until he was sure of my intentions. Stephen had seemed distant and unpredictable but I guessed that his sudden appearances and disappearances were down to his being careful so he wasn't easy to trace.

I wasn't sure what to believe and what not to. I knew that Grandmaster Hatsumi focused on higher things so would not concern himself for long with another man's behaviour. It seemed also to me that his people skills and understanding of human nature meant that if he wanted to keep someone loyal he could, but as I listened, it became clear that many of his senior students had left and started their own organisations.

I also knew that Stephen followed the ninja path to help others, not for self-promotion.

After the class that morning, I was really not in the mood for any more confrontation but the group of black belts in the changing room were far from finished with me. They continued with their barrage of questions.

'Where do you live in England?'

Wearily I told them.

'We can have someone at your door in thirty minutes if you betray us.'

Now I was being threatened. Deep down I knew Japanese ninja had the power and capability to do a lot of damage if pushed, but surely they knew that I held no malice towards them. Nevertheless, if Stephen Hayes was such an enemy of the grandmaster then my talk about his training methods – in clear earshot of everyone in the *dojo* – had provoked a strong reaction. Which I might have guessed it would, if I hadn't been so busy chatting.

Clearly I wasn't about to scoff at the black belts. They had made a serious threat, but I also wondered if they knew that they were pawns in Hatsumi Sensei's game. It was a traditional ninja strategy to maintain fighting in the lower ranks to keep stability at the top. He had manipulated the black belts, who hadn't realised that if Hatsumi Sensei truly wanted harm to come to Stephen Hayes, he could cause it. *If* Hatsumi was the reason Stephen Hayes glanced over his shoulder, the reason he had relocated to remote Ohio and the reason he worked independently. This was ninja strategy at its best and, most impressive of all, even a black belt couldn't see it. I realised that not everybody could grasp *ninjutsu*. It functions and bubbles away beneath the surface: you have to look for it if you really want to find it.

I made my way back to the station, literally swimming through tiredness.

'Hey, mate, do you want a drink?' One of the Aussie guys held out a steaming cup he'd just bought from the vending machine. 'You *really* look like you could do with something!'

Taking the cup, I closed my eyes and inhaled the soothing scent of jasmine tea. The train swooshed into the station and my new companions pushed me on. I leant back in my seat – it was lovely to hear familiar accents again. As we chatted, I didn't get much out of them but, looking back, I gave away more about myself, as usual. Nevertheless, talking to them was really enjoyable and they happily pointed out which stop I needed to get off at.

I smiled to myself as I stepped off the train, holding the now lukewarm cup of tea. The grin soon vanished when I realised I'd got off at the wrong stop. Noda had two railway stations but this one was not where I needed to be. Had the seemingly friendly Aussies deliberately encouraged me to get off there? Was it another test? Even if it was, I had no way of tracking them down. I didn't even know their names while they knew pretty much everything about me: name, age, occupation, training background, where I was from, why I was in Japan – hell, I had probably even given them my bank details, considering how knackered I was. I felt so confused and dazed. The whole world shifted for a second and I found it hard to stand.

I looked at the cup in my hand and decided to tip away the contents. I couldn't trust anything about the people I had just met – what if they had tried to drug me? I was getting paranoid. Was I going mad – or just in need of sleep?

Alone in the darkness, in a place I didn't know, I couldn't see a soul – perfect for a ninja, but not for a chronically jet-lagged, miserable Westerner. I had no choice but to start walking and hope I was heading in the right direction. By now, the tiredness was almost making me delirious. All I could think of was Pip, my home and my comfortable bed in England.

I kept walking. The minutes ticked by and I let my mind wander. Maybe I would be abducted or attacked or simply vanish, and my poor wife would be worried sick about what had become of me. Eventually a taxi cruised up beside me. At this point, I didn't hold out much hope of making any sense to him – I still hadn't managed to get my *ryokan*'s address written in Japanese. However, the driver switched off the engine, got out of his cab and shook his bunch of keys at me. Oh, God, now what? I had no idea what was going to happen next. Then it dawned on me. Of course! The fob on the keys to the *ryokan*! I rummaged in my bag and thrust my room key at him. He glanced at the Japanese pictograms, bundled me into the car and gave me a lift back. He refused any payment, and my faith in humanity was restored.

I let myself in as quietly as possible and made my way stealthily to my room, not wanting to risk breaking any more rules. The room was bitterly cold, so I decided to put the heater on. It was fixed to the ceiling above my sleeping mat and had a long cord that I could pull from the comfort of the floor. I soon discovered there were two levels of heat available in the room: roasting or freezing. With the heater on, I could lie down, get second-degree burns and, thanks to the window that wouldn't close properly, be constantly hit with burning bugs falling on me *or*, with the heater off, shiver uncontrollably. After a few hours of this cycle, I opted for the latter and fell into an exhausted, miserable sleep.

16

The Ninja Grandmaster

❖

Where there are humans,
You'll find flies,
And Buddhas.

Kobayashi Issa

The next morning, after a fitful night of what I definitely wouldn't describe as rest, I was regretting my earlier desire to experience authentic Japanese culture. I woke up in a room full of burned flies. As I brushed them off, I realised that what I had previously thought was cigarette ash was actually cremated insects of various types.

I set off to find the bathroom. I had no idea what to expect but was soon greeted with the sound and sight of a dozen Japanese men going about their ablutions. Apparently, it was customary for us to share communal washing space and a big bathtub – and it seemed the norm to smoke in the tub too.

Undeterred, I stripped off and was about to start washing in one of the showers surrounding the oversized bath when I was aware of silence filling the bathroom. I glanced around and saw several men staring at me. This was not comforting. I hoped that they weren't interested in . . . Eventually I noticed that they were eyeing my tattoo. I have what I view as a perfectly tasteful lotus flower, done in the Japanese style, over my heart. I later found out that in Japan tattoos signify gang connections and can mark you out as Yakuza (the world's largest criminal organisation). So, in a matter of minutes, I had successfully cleared the entire washroom because everyone assumed I was a gangster.

In the breakfast room, though, I was greeted with friendly smiles. I like to pride myself on being a fairly easy-going chap when it comes to food and there are only three things I *really* dislike – Marmite, mushy peas and raw egg. Perfect: raw egg featured heavily on the breakfast menu and everything else looked unidentifiable, though I assumed some of it was rice. I soon learned that anything went for breakfast, from Western meatballs, spaghetti or cold cuts of unidentifiable meat to raw egg on rice, squid guts in tomato sauce, eels or fish. This was a million miles away from a boiled egg and toast soldiers! Nevertheless, as I was absolutely starving, I ate as much as I could and drank gallons of tea, knowing I would need my energy when I was 'tested' again and unsure when my next meal would be.

I returned to my room and unpacked my bag. Once again Pip had packed for me and she had included everything I would need but wouldn't have thought of packing – protein bars, thick insulated gloves, thermal underwear, a hat and, bless her, a tiny package that unfolded into a silver thermal blanket. I felt myself lurch with emotion: I could have done with that blanket last night and . . . I really missed my wife.

I was beginning to feel more human again and my natural optimism was kicking in. Despite my washroom encounters, I had to admit that Michael Pearce was right. As much as a whirlpool bath and a king-sized bed would have been welcome, I had indeed wanted to experience Japanese culture. So, comfort aside, I felt pretty pleased. I had finally arrived in Noda, I'd begun my training with the last ninja grandmaster, the world-renowned Masaaki Hatsumi, and, come what may, I was going to learn from this man and embrace Japan while I could.

The day before, Michael Pearce had told me to expect him in the morning, so now I waited outside in the cold for his recognisable car. It had snowed overnight and Noda was blanketed in a thick layer, although the streets were clear. When he arrived, I sat in the car and said very little. Michael, too, remained silent but eventually directed a question at me.

'In need of attitude adjustment?'

Obviously, he had heard about my unsuccessful class at the Budokan last night. It would appear news travelled fast round here.

'How did you know?' I asked.

Michael smiled thinly and shrugged. 'I could see it coming. You need to go see Noguchi Sensei.' He nodded to himself as if confirming his own thoughts. 'And then we need to go see some bonsai.'

Bonsai? What could bonsai have to do with *ninjutsu*? Maybe that was what Michael did for a living: perhaps he grew bonsai. He didn't look much like a gardener, but I'd learnt that things were not always as they seemed.

On the drive to see Noguchi Sensei – one of the senior instructors at the *dojo* – I looked out of the windows, wondering if any of the scenery would ever seem familiar to me. It was so different from home and made me yearn for the people and places I knew and loved. I felt confused, lost and distant, and was unusually quiet as I took in all the unfamiliar sights and scenes. My thoughts preoccupied me until we slowed to a stop. We had arrived at Noguchi Sensei's house and *dojo*.

Michael and I went inside, where Noguchi Sensei greeted us. He was older, but didn't terrify me in the way Masaaki Hatsumi had the day before. Like Hatsumi, Noguchi Sensei had a tangible energy about him but it was light and joyful, rather than scary and violent. It was just what I needed. Just being in his presence improved my mood immeasurably.

'*Ohayō!*'

He waved at us from where he was practising blowing darts at a piece of card with a person drawn on it. His shots were all spot on, hitting the sketched figure either between the eyes or straight through the heart. Noguchi gestured for me to have a go. Predictably, I wasn't very successful and we all laughed.

Michael took that as his cue to get down to business. 'Noguchi, I'm going to be teaching Martin the basics.'

A week ago, I'd have been insulted by these words – I'd years of training behind me – but after yesterday's dreadful class, the basics sounded ideal. I decided to keep my mouth shut.

We got started with a move that I felt at ease with: *kamae* – the same stance movements I had practised in Dayton and at home. It

MARTIN AND NOGUCHI SENSEI IN JAPAN

was refreshing to be taught by Noguchi Sensei: he was calm and patient and I felt my confidence rise again. I found that the stances we were working on were far lower than those I was used to, and even though he was in his sixties, Noguchi could keep his stance so low he almost touched the floor. We also did less footwork. This really was going back to basics but I was glad of the simplification. I realised that what I was learning didn't resemble my classes in the UK. I had always accepted what I had been taught at home but now I saw that I had been so absorbed during my training that I had never thought to question anything. After an hour in Noguchi's *dojo* my legs were shaking like jelly and ached from my exertions. Noguchi bade me farewell and disappeared into his house. But there was no rest.

Michael stepped forward: he was going to teach me to block and strike. We practised blocking for what seemed like hours. My legs were screaming with fatigue and could barely take my weight any longer but then we came to striking. I had to strike my opponent on the neck. I knew how to do this and was confident I wouldn't have any trouble against Michael.

'Hit me on the neck as hard as you can with a *shuto*,' he challenged me.

A *shuto* (knife-hand strike) is basically what most people know as a '*karate* chop', referring to a hand position that resembles the blade of a sword or knife, usually aimed towards the carotid artery and nerve, a classic key strike point, which will knock the opponent out, if successful.

I wasn't sure about this. Michael was egging me on but I knew the grave damage a misplaced *shuto* could do and worried I might injure him. The neck was precariously close to the spine.

He gestured with both hands. 'C'mon, hit me! Hit me as hard as you can!'

If he was so insistent, fine. I'd show him what I could do. Grabbing his arm with one hand, I landed an extremely hard strike with the other. I could tell I'd hurt him but he didn't react as I'd expected him to. He staggered back, and after he'd had a few minutes to recover, he explained how my strike hadn't worked as effectively as it might. Apparently, my force had been wrong, which had made the blow more like a push than the sharpness of a strike. Just then, as if to demonstrate, he struck my neck. A rushing noise filled my ears and my vision receded into a grey fog. Eventually the noise stopped and my eyes blinked back into focus. For a few moments, I had no idea where I was. I could just see something green in front of me and hear a strange noise, like bellows blowing a fire into life. After a minute or two, I realised the bellows noise was my breath and I was staring face down at the green mats. Michael Pearce had knocked me out!

I sat up slowly, waves of nausea washing over me. That tiny strike had floored me and I was pretty embarrassed. Michael presented me with a cup of tea, which I think was as close to an apology as I would get, then explained how I could master the strike myself.

'When most people think of the *shuto* strike, they imagine someone breaking boards in a demonstration, yeah? Even from my own observations, it seems this is the most common place that strike is used. Most people don't use strikes enough to make them a viable tool in their martial-arts practice.'

Michael went on – my dizziness had subsided – 'Here in Japan we use strikes extensively. I would even venture to say a *shuto* is the primary strike we use and from my experience is a devastating one – I've been and still do get hit with it often. Hatsumi Sensei has hit me so hard that my eyes have rolled up into the back of my head and I've been totally winded. It involves more than a punch.'

'What do you mean by "not using it enough"?'

'That although we *do* use it, we don't use it *effectively* or study how to use it. People, especially in the *bujinkan*, have taken it for granted that the *shuto* works without actually testing it.'

He explained that, often, we learn strikes without knowing how to implement them correctly or even what the effects would be. For example, hitting and breaking boards is completely different from hitting a person.

'What I have noticed, though, is that the old masters sure knew how to hit and still do. The guys here can drop you in a heartbeat with very little power. Lately, at seminars, I've told people to go and hit each other just as hard as they can in the neck with a *shuto* and see what happens – just like I made you do to me. I'd say that out of all the times I've told students to do that, there've probably been only five people that have actually fallen down from getting hit. Most just get pushed away.

'It's important to understand that in striking with the *shuto* it's a *strike* not a *push*. I've often observed that when someone tries to use the *shuto* the only visible effect is their training partner being pushed away or across the room. This is a weak push, not a strike. When Sensei or the expert instructors strike me, I fall down. I can't think of any one time when I was pushed away.'

Michael explained that two main factors stopped people like me performing an effective strike: 'One is the psychological. Let's say you're thirty years old and I tell you to hit someone as hard as you can. Now that someone is a training partner and probably a friend. The first thing you think is, I don't want to hurt my buddy. By the very nature of this thought, you'll not be able to, no matter how hard you try. Nor will it be an effective strike. The second factor I have found in my studies is this. Throughout our childhood we are told by our parents not to hit others. Society also tells us that it's wrong to fight or hit people. So now I come in and tell you to hit someone. After thirty years of that kind of conditioning, what chance do you have of breaking it within five minutes? None.'

He revealed more about his path to success at Noda. It was becoming clear that our attitudes were very different. Where I wanted to promote a positive view of ninja, Michael was the opposite. To him, the ninja was a hardened character who would employ trickery and deception to win, nothing more, nothing less. No big ideals, no sugar coating. While this was refreshing to see, because not many people are so openly antagonistic, I found Michael's behaviour odd. I knew I could learn much from him but I also knew that he was a very different man from Stephen Hayes.

Michael went on: 'I began to study my teachers and myself. I found that they were different in these areas. They tried to hit, not necessarily hard but always effectively. They trained as if every class was a real situation, so they were getting rid of the mentality that they were harming a friend every time they trained. I've realised this, so if and when they hit me hard, I'm not offended. In fact, I enjoy the chance to feel it and train with them. Remember, though, there's a difference between hitting hard and hitting with force and poor ability.'

I knew I would have to distance myself from any friends I made at Noda. I had to be more detached. By training and imagining each bout as a real fight, I would remove the filter of protecting my classmates. Hopefully my strikes would improve and become more effective. This might not have been my way of doing things but I had to admit that Michael knew his stuff.

Like a *shuto* metaphor, Michael kept hammering home his points. 'You have to study the whole body to understand how to make this strike truly devastating. You need to understand the best points of distance. Once you do, you'll be able to not only strike but also destroy an opponent with the *shuto*.'

Michael explained that, rather than just making contact, the *shuto* had to hit an artery on an opponent's neck. This would cause a massive increase in the blood pressure to the brain, which triggers a response whereby the opponent will collapse, like an emergency switch-off mechanism.

I nodded. It sounded brutal and I decided that I would use a true *shuto* only if my life were in danger: there was no way I wanted to mess with inflicting potential paralysis or brain damage on someone.

Thus ended my second lesson in Japan.

17

Bonsai

❖

According to Japanese tradition, the bonsai represents the three virtues or shin-zen-bi, *which translates into truth, goodness and beauty.*

Michael had told me that a visit to the bonsai farm was on the cards and he stuck to his word. On our way he took the opportunity to give me another talk. I was getting used to his lectures but I still hadn't fully warmed to him. This time, it was about something I'd never heard of before.

'*Budō* isn't something you can rush. It's something you work at. You chisel away at it, every year of your life, every day of every year of your life. *Budō* is a lifelong ambition. It's not something you can just charge at and master.'

I had never heard the term used before, and Michael must have picked up on my lack of comprehension. '*Bu*, meaning "war" or "martial", and *dō*, meaning "path" or "way". *Dō* signifies a "way of life". In the Japanese context it's a discipline cultivated through a given art form. Rather than being just a martial art it's a way of life, a path of self-development. In modern times *budō*'s only enemy is one's ego.'

He looked at me. I knew some choice words of wisdom were coming.

'The approach you're using is all wrong. You're burning yourself out in these tiny bursts of effort. It's time to show you a little bit about the Japanese culture. I used to work here.'

Learning about the intricacies of bonsai trees was not something I was particularly passionate about. Reluctantly, though, I admitted that learning something else about the Japanese culture might be a good idea, and it couldn't hurt to find out a bit more about Michael and what made him tick – even if it meant trailing around a farm.

It was interesting to see him handling those miniature wonders of nature. Usually, there was a sense of violence and strength about him – so different from Stephen Hayes. I suppose Michael was more like his own teacher, Hatsumi Sensei, a warrior spirit. But that afternoon, among the bonsai plants, he was totally different. He looked at me to check I was listening and began: 'Bonsai is an art that goes back thousands of years and it's not specific to Japan. We know that in the ancient Egyptian culture they also used to grow very small trees, ensuring that they didn't get to their full size by using a very similar process to that used by the Japanese now. The word "bonsai" is a Japanese pronunciation of a Chinese term *"penzai"*, which means a tray-contained pot plant. But, of course, now we just use it to mean undersized trees.'

As he spoke, I looked at some of the trees Michael said he had shaped and nurtured. I was impressed. They were beautiful and clearly demanded a lot of skill. He was explaining the process of making bonsai from seed to pruning; each stage is time-consuming and requires a lot of attention; the whole process takes many years. Michael showed me one of his trees – despite its unfinished state it was five years old.

'You see, bonsai is an ongoing process. The work is alive and therefore it never ends. You always have an opportunity to change, improve and maintain the shape of the bonsai.'

This, of course, wasn't just a tour of a bonsai farm. Michael was teaching me a further lesson. We'd been talking about attitude adjustment earlier and I had been taught to change my interpretation of the *kamae* stance by Noguchi Sensei. At the same time, ninja use the word 'attitude' to describe fighting positions. This was clearly no coincidence. I had to accept the dedication to years of work and the patience that ninja training required. Michael Pearce had taken me to the bonsai farm to illustrate this. I'd got the message. I knew then that this would be a long-term process, which might last the rest of my life.

We walked back to the car in near silence; the only sound was of the snow crunching underfoot. The farm looked stunning, tiny but perfectly formed trees decked in ice crystals, resembling one of the scale-model towns you can visit in the UK. The sun was magnified in its brightness, which, bouncing off the snow, gave a mystical feel to the environment.

He drove me back to the *ryokan* and said I was expected at the evening class at the Noda Street Hombu Dojo, the grandmaster's other training centre. As I watched him drive away, I had a sense of growing solidity, as if all the jigsaw pieces of an intricate puzzle were gently falling into place – I think I was finally starting to 'get' Japan.

As I had no transport, the owners of the *ryokan* showed me where I could rent a bicycle for the length of my stay. I hadn't ridden one since my teens but, as the old saying goes, 'You never forget how to ride a bike.' Cycling in snow is probably not my greatest skill and I was heartily relieved that I was in a small suburb, not a busy town. I had no idea about the rules of the road and didn't relish a 'crash' course.

I found my way to the Hombu Dojo quite easily and began to feel pleased with my new sense of direction. The *dojo* wasn't huge; inside, the floor was completely covered with the padded green mats universal to most martial-arts training halls. Row upon row of swords, staffs, chain weapons and a few kimonos lined the walls, plus a shelf of scrolls and a scattering of Japanese artworks, certificates and suits of samurai armour.

It was cold, too, and with my breath steaming in front of me, I contemplated another clash between the American and Japanese way of doing things. At Dayton, I had become accustomed to combining spirituality with physical training – meditation had frequently been part of our classes. At first, I'd been a bit disappointed with the Japanese way of doing things. Now I asked Michael Pearce about the choice to focus on purely physical, rather than spiritual, actions later. He answered simply, 'Every action presents a potential key to enlightenment.'

Instead of taking time to contemplate and meditate, this school of ninja believed that enlightenment came about through physical training. That explained the classes, which were far longer than any I had undertaken before.

Before the lesson got under way, I approached another of the English-speaking teachers. Since my teens, I'd had a shoulder injury that had never completely healed, thanks to some overly enthusiastic practice sessions. The muscles in question still got pretty tender, despite several years of physiotherapy, and some recent sparring work had made the old injury resurface, leaving me in quite a lot of pain. I thought it best to inform my instructor rather than risk greater damage. He was very understanding, reassuring me that the class would be gentle and cause me no harm.

As the class began a guy translated what was said into English – quite a few of us had little or no Japanese. We were learning about shoulder locks. The next two hours were a blur of pain. Everything we did or that was done to me caused me agony. I was confused: I had explained myself and been courteous. Why was I being punished? As we gathered our things to leave, the instructor addressed as all.

'Never show your weaknesses to anyone. This is an important lesson.' With that, he bowed and left the *dojo*.

Yep, it had been another test. By doing what I'd thought was polite I had caused myself further injury. I realised now that knowledge was power and, in future, I would keep what I knew to myself.

For the rest of the day I threw myself into classes. A few more differences between the Western ways of practice that I had learnt in America and the Japanese systems became evident. Nagato Sensei was a very strong, muscular man, whose presence was warm and friendly. I was told that he had been both a kick-boxing and judo champion in his youth. Now in his early fifties, he had the appearance of a thirty-year-old.

After we had bowed, he introduced the theme for the class. Nagato, who exuded the same calm and positivity as Noguchi Sensei, announced that we would be studying *sanshin no kata*. *Sanshin*, as described by Hatsumi Sensei at the first lesson, translates as 'three hearts'.

I listened carefully to ensure I would understand the *sensei*'s words.

Sanshin was apparently the awareness a ninja warrior must work towards in order to make himself battle-ready. We learned and performed a series of exercises and now I grasped how to strike more slowly and calmly, without the huge exertion of force I had previously been using. We moved on to hear about the *sanshin no kata's* connections with the five elements. At this point, my ears pricked up. This was the first mention of something that had been taught as central to the art in Dayton. The elements here – with their corresponding moves – sounded just like those I had practised repeatedly at the Quest Center in Ohio. I looked around but everyone else was completely focused, not a flicker of recognition in their eyes. Nagato Sensei continued with the lesson, explaining the importance of fluid and flowing movements. I couldn't believe it! This *was* just like the lessons I had taken part in a few months earlier in America.

We moved on to the techniques for the elemental strikes. The first was called . . . 'earth'. By now, I was convinced that this was the point where the American and Japanese arts crossed. The similarities didn't end there. When Nagato Sensei began each class, he would move his hands around in much the same way Stephen Hayes had when he performed his 'nine magical cuts' action to invoke a distinctive energy in the *dojo*.

Again, I felt as though I had stumbled on a discovery, but when I spoke to Michael Pearce, he dismissed what I said, brushing off the elements as a basic counting system and reiterating that, in Japan, things were different. He reminded me to forget about the elements. When I took a moment to reflect, I realised the strikes that had been performed might have been named after the elements but I couldn't see any connection with them; none of the movements exuded anything that was 'fiery' or 'watery'. Perhaps Michael was correct: they were just a simple counting method used in Japan and Stephen Hayes had grasped hold of them in a way that was never intended.

In Japan, I had to embrace a different system called *ten chi jin*. Translated, it means 'heaven', 'earth' and 'man'. I learnt that 'heaven' symbolises environmental factors, such as weather, but also represents the outlook and philosophy of those involved; 'earth' is the physical distance; 'man' represents social interactions and pressures upon an individual. In a combat situation, I would want to apply these principles. Heaven's part would involve positioning myself in the most favourable location, my back to the sun, avoiding slippery surfaces, out of the way of any snow or rain; earth would be represented by the size and stature of an opponent, then adjusting my distance accordingly. Man meant the other factors, which would influence and hopefully distract the opponent. This might mean fighting him in surroundings unnatural to him, where others might distract him or where he might be prompted to put a foot wrong. In theory, these principles could be applied in any situation, whether at work, with a financial problem or a relationship.

Just as I had embraced the elements in America, I now embraced *ten chi jin*. It gave me another set of tools that meant there was no situation I was not prepared for and no set of circumstances that I could not turn to my own advantage. It became clear to me that, despite what Michael Pearce had said, the elements were more than just a counting system: they embodied a state of mind. Sometimes the teachers would move in a way so consistent with an element that, to me, it was beyond doubt. Indeed, no matter what I was being told by others or what the outward teachings seemed to be, I was becoming convinced that secretly the elements were being used. I remember one day a teacher called Oguri was showing me a technique that involved standing on one leg, like a bird. He was jumping back and forwards as if he was weightless. Imagine a feeling of lightness and freedom, he explained. To me it seemed he was in a wind state of mind.

For several days, I threw myself into a demanding onslaught of martial-arts training. We would have four classes a day, often each one lasting up to two hours – more than I was used to. The concept of attacking and defending was blurred. We were supposed to do everything with purpose and conviction and keep working to deter an opponent. We were actively discouraged from freezing in combat because in a real situation you would not attack or defend but revert to freezing.

I found a lot about the Japanese martial arts very beautiful: they were designed to keep people balanced, and many of my instructors had arts interests, which they worked at alongside their studies, Michael and his bonsai trees being a good example. Michael had also immersed himself in traditional Japanese dance. However, contrary to popular belief, there was no intricate footwork involved in our practice. We were taught to defend and to attack – which has often been misunderstood when people become caught up with fancy arm work, making movements spectacular rather than effective.

My lessons were not without problems. Aside from the extended lengths of time we were training, I was also spending a lot of time with Michael outside the *dojo*. He was keen to debrief me at the end of each day and talk through any difficulties I had. His guidance was invaluable but our attitude to many things differed markedly. Instead of the large movements I was used to, the stances and postures I was taught at the *dojo* had to be much more subtle – sometimes moving my hands just a few centimetres. I found this hard to sustain, control and contain.

I was also trying to keep up with my meditation practice. I squeezed it in at the *ryokan* after training and before I went out to meet Michael. After several weeks of spending my days training – often grabbing just a few minutes to wolf some lunch – tiredness caught up with me. My evenings with Michael weren't as straightforward as a chat and an exchange of information. We indulged in regular curries at the smallest but most famous curry house in the area. It looked like a shed built on tarmac, one of the strangest places I had ever been to. When we talked, I sometimes tried to steer the conversation to less intense topics. I was tired and full of idle chit-chat, but he wasn't interested. He focused completely on his training with a total disregard for anything that could be considered a distraction. Other people and gossip were irrelevant to Michael. I realised this was a method of behaviour that he had adopted from the grandmaster. *Ninjutsu* was all he cared about; a Zen-like focus and way of being had made the grandmaster successful, Michael too.

'You need to have your mind completely on *budō*. You must have your mind on your own training. Even when you're teaching, you're there training for yourself. It's for the student to learn to be responsible for his own learning. You're just training with him. Always keep your focus on your own training. Never let it move to anything else. All this politics, this gossip, everything else around you, you have to ignore.'

So, instead of making small-talk, the deep conversations continued. They were matched by some large-scale drinking. I suppose it was the Japanese equivalent of going to the pub. We would drink beer or Michael would buy a bottle of whisky and we would both get drunk. None of this was relieving my exhaustion. I would try to make my excuses to head back to the *ryokan* for an early night but this rarely worked and a couple of hours' sleep were all I was getting. Michael, it appeared, didn't need to sleep.

Eventually after a few weeks of my intense schedule I found myself barely able to function in class. Because I was so run down, I hadn't been eating as much, which meant my body was weaker. Emotionally, I was less stable too. I desperately missed home, my wife and anything familiar.

Getting through lessons was a struggle. My legs ached and I could barely remain focused on what my instructors were saying. Typical, then, that during the one session being filmed, Noguchi Sensei picked me as an able volunteer to help him demonstrate an evasion technique. All I had to do was perform a simple kick but, instead of doing what was expected, I decided to confront Noguchi Sensei with a kick aimed at his head, from kick-boxing: a high roundhouse-style movement. No one in Japan appeared to kick so high and I was confident I would surprise everyone in the *dojo*, not least Michael – who was filming the whole thing – and Noguchi Sensei. I had judged things wrongly yet again. Noguchi Sensei simply stepped backwards avoiding my kick. He didn't even look surprised. I, on the other hand, must have looked really stupid: I ended up face down on the mats.

Next, we worked on darting movements. As luck would have it, my partner was an energetic and enthusiastic Japanese lad. I felt the opposite. We did the same drills repeatedly. I was by now so used to doing the same action without pause for hours at a time that it didn't ease my boredom. My aching legs and all-round tiredness meant that I was not functioning very well. I was making half-hearted moves when I should have been performing a decisive step. My partner was making mincemeat of me and all the time I was aware that this was being captured on camera, which made it even more embarrassing. I knew Michael had his eyes trained on me and watched me repeat the same mistakes. I heard a few words pass between him and another of the black belts, but in Japanese.

I didn't have to wait long for an explanation as my training partner chuckled and told me: 'He just said you can sleep now!'

I didn't know if I should be relieved, grateful or incensed. Michael had known exactly what he was doing to me and had denied me weeks of sleep. He had recognised my copious amounts of energy and had worked with the other instructors to push me to the limit. I'd been the victim of my own enthusiasm. It all made sense: the hours and hours of classes, the jam-packed evenings that hadn't given me a moment to rest.

It felt amazing finally sleeping for more than a few hours at a stretch and the mats in my room at the *ryokan* could have been the finest mattress on the most luxurious bed, given how easily I drifted off.

Once I was back at the *dojo*, feeling more awake, I started to look more carefully at the masters who were teaching me.

I continued to ask questions. I had already established that the Japanese didn't have much time for meditation and wondered whether stealth training had a place in Japanese ninja arts. Surprisingly, I was told that these skills were no longer taught or employed. It made sense: many stealth skills could be manipulated by others for a lower purpose and I supposed this had happened a long time ago. Ancient stealth skills included learning how to poison and sneak up on people, and the art of pickpocketing. Clearly, such skills had got into the wrong hands so now the Japanese preferred to pretend they didn't exist or couldn't be taught. This was underlined in class by something Masaaki Hatsumi had said: 'You need to steal their intention from them. You need to steal the combat.' He paused. '*Ninjutsu* is not anything you can be taught, or can be learnt. You have to steal *ninjutsu*.'

18

Stealing the Japanese Arts

◆

In a snowfall that covers the winter grass a white heron uses his own whiteness to disappear.

Dōgen

It became clear that no teacher in Noda was going to disclose stealth skills to me. I might not be taught them in a formal *dojo* setting but that didn't mean they weren't there for the taking.

I was aware that some of the instructors were keen to throw students like myself off the scent when we went looking for stealth-skill secrets. Michael Pearce had told me that when he had enquired about stealth and invisibility, as a much younger student, Masaaki Hatsumi had brushed his questions aside, telling him, 'That's just movie stuff.'

It's possible that our instructors were vague about stealth skills because our abilities were not at the right level. There's also a school of thought that suggests the Japanese are reticent about sharing skills of stealth with Westerners because with them comes a degree of responsibility, which, in the past, many Westerners have abused.

Stealing stealth knowledge was going to be tricky. As I had already learnt, asking too many questions was deemed disrespectful. I decided the best way to steal the stealth arts was to pretend I wanted to learn another skill.

Throwing stars, or *shuriken*, are the most iconic weapon of the ninja. The word '*shuriken*' literally translates as 'sword hidden in user's hand'. In films, they are depicted as deadly weapons covered with poison; in reality, they were discs of sharpened metal and carried as a distraction weapon. During my first lesson at the *dojo*, I had seen leather practice versions used briefly in a demonstration so I knew they had the equipment to teach the actual throwing of the stars. I just needed a way to make this happen. My direct requests had been met with refusal. I was told they didn't teach that any more. I had to be more ninja and find a way of getting them to do what I wanted.

I had got into the habit of turning up hours early for class and it was this that allowed me to prepare my plan. As our lessons got under way we would often be told to 'play' so I wanted to exploit the playful nature of the group. Two younger Japanese students always attended a particular class so when they turned up I started chucking throwing stars in their general direction, laughing all the time. They joined in immediately and battle began. A few minutes later, the instructor walked into the chaos I had created. He could react either in one of two ways. Thankfully, he took in the scene and grinned. Now came the vital part of the plan. Don't ask how to throw stars: ask how to dodge them.

It worked!

He joined in with our horseplay, instructing us on how best to dodge the stars and even catch them in mid-air before they struck. As he did, I made careful note of his body position. He stood in the same positions as we did but holding the stars in one hand then grabbing and throwing them with the other. There was force and power behind each throw, which came with an exhalation; this was similar to the strike of the *sanshin no kata* I had learnt earlier. I watched each throwing method, mentally connecting it with its equivalent strike. As he was about to throw, I saw him hold the star in his hand as a hidden weapon. He made a gesture as if to cut the wrist of one of the boys and, in that moment, it all fell into place. I remembered the techniques I was trying to learn at the lesson in England – the techniques I had seen as confusing 'robot' fighting when they were aiming for the wrist. It all made sense now. The neck and wrist were targets not because they were areas left uncovered by armour but because the ninja were armed. They had hidden blades, the throwing stars, in their hands and were using them to cut the wrists and neck: a single strike to either, and their opponent would die. That was why, in this art, they held their hand in a slightly bent manner when performing the *shuto* or 'sword hands' (rather than in a normal *karate*-chop formation). I got it. I now knew how to throw *and* strike with *shuriken*. I just needed to practise. More importantly, I was now completely convinced the art was real. This was exactly how a ninja would fight, using small, concealed weapons to distract or cut in a deadly way, if disturbed on a stealth mission. The fact that this was hidden, and that perhaps some of the practitioners had not made this connection, reinforced my conviction that this was the real deal: an art genuinely passed down from medieval Japanese *shinobi*. Just as important, however, my ninja skills were improving.

I'd learnt a skill by stealth and was filled with confidence, but I knew that extracting some of the other stealth skills wouldn't be as easy. I'd have to employ my knowledge of the elements and also the 'heaven', 'earth' and 'man' strategies to achieve what I wanted. I'd have to get inside the mind of my teacher and selecting the right one to work on was the key to success. I formulated a plan.

A key element in a ninja's arsenal is the ability to be unseen and silent. Indeed, even to this day, in fiction, the trademark of a ninja is silent walking and invisible movement. I *knew* they had this skill, and was told repeatedly that it was no longer taught. But I wanted to know. I had come all the way to Japan to train with the source of Japanese *ninjutsu* and must do everything I could to learn it from them. But could I find a way to get them to teach me this skill, as I had with the throwing stars?

In the next lesson, I had armed myself with packets of fine loose-leaf English tea. I knew that if I offered them to our teacher as a gift it would encourage him to give us a longer-than-usual break halfway through the class. We often stopped for tea but this break would be longer because my teacher would feel impolite if he didn't try his gift. I had also brought with me copies of historical ninja texts, which I hoped would provoke discussion about stealth skills. I enlisted a few bilingual students in case certain things required translation. I knew that the teacher would love this, as he was fascinated by old texts.

Before the lesson began, I was nervous. The class formed and I took a deep breath. Could I subtly steer them in the direction I wanted and gain education in subjects I was told were no longer taught? It was essential that I got the teacher on side and this needed to seem natural.

I practised hard and tried to keep my focus on the job in hand. When the break came, I sprang into action and my plan unfolded exactly as I had hoped. The teacher was overjoyed at his 'English' tea and even more overjoyed to see the *Bansenshukai*, a classic *ninjutsu* text from seventeenth-century Japan. With a sense of childlike wonder, we went through every step, every detail and every phrase of terminology. I demonstrated what I thought the walking methods in the text were, and something amazing happened: he started to correct and teach me.

'It's hard to practise these ancient skills. We need to be like a child and learn how to walk again.' He started walking around the *dojo* in a gentle, almost rolling gait, using the whole of the foot in an exaggerated heel–toe motion – it's like a normal walk but in slow motion. 'We use traditional walking methods. Don't try to be completely silent at first. Just copy us.'

Someone coughed and he suddenly crouched. 'In all stealth training, if you hear a noise, drop and freeze like an animal in the wood.' He waited for a few seconds, then started walking again. 'You need to get the hang of using these methods silently and with agility in a variety of places.' He moved to a very low stance and started a new, very deep step, crossing his rear leg over the front in a very slow toe-to-heel motion. 'Keep under the horizon – lower stance, Martin, lower!'

Whenever any of us made a noise, we would all freeze and crouch. It felt a bit like when I was at infant school and we played 'What's the time, Mr Wolf?' You had to creep up on someone, who would, at any moment, turn round and growl. Anyone still moving would be 'eaten'.

'As you walk, be calm and patient, breathing quietly and slowly through your nose. Never hold your breath.'

I'd been doing exactly that and exhaled loudly: everyone crouched mid-step, which made us all descend into mirth.

As we continued round the hall, he went through each walking method in turn, explaining to us the advice the 'ancient manuscripts gave on the subject'. 'To train in stealth, the best method possible is to make normal walking your training and your main method of stealth. The ninja called this *suri ashi* or "normal walking technique".

'It helps us understand one of the most important principles of *ninjutsu*. Nature is our greatest teacher and our most powerful ally. The natural way is always the correct way, and we should always make sure our movements are natural, not artificial or stiff. The first method of stealth walking taught to new students is natural walking. It is also the last method of the great masters.'

We glanced at each other. The exercise had started as a game but had become a serious philosophical and tactical lesson.

'Time to talk – OK, so let's walk,' our instructor's translator corrected himself.

He then listened for a long time to some very fast Japanese, with gestures and many heel–toe movements.

'The most important principle here is slowing the whole thing down – ninety per cent of stealth is to do with patience. You need to move extremely slowly in order to be silent. For this type of walking, I find it useful to lift the toes and to make a small but more exaggerated heel–toe movement. It helps if you imagine your feet as a curved shape, rolling through from heel to toe in a slight exaggeration. This walking method is usually better if you are wearing normal shoes. The rubber of the heel makes the point of heel contact softer.'

We all did as we were told.

'Take natural silence training into everything in your life. When you walk in daily life, make it gentle and soft. When you open doors or put objects down, try to be silent.

'Natural walking makes you fit in if someone sees you. It gives away nothing about what you are doing. Most people look obvious when trying to be quiet.'

He made an exaggerated tiptoe movement to demonstrate how easy it was to detect someone trying to be stealthy normally.

'If you are natural no one will think anything of you if you are seen. They will think you are supposed to be there. This method of walking is extremely effective on tarmac or concrete, but should be avoided on gravel. If using this method indoors on squeaky floorboards, it is important to find where the floorboard is attached to the supporting beams underneath. Then you can walk along this line silently. When practising this method start out with hard surfaces, like pavements and car parks, then learn how to be silent on moving ground, like sand and gravel. When you can do that, you are ready to practise indoors on *tatami* and floorboards. Also, if it's really dark, make sure you move your arms in time with your step so you touch any objects in front of you.'

He made a kind of gesture, like an octopus moving its tentacles out in front of it. Then without warning, he dropped into an exaggerated *ichimonji stance*. It is well known to anyone practising *ninjutsu*: it involves the body being side on, with the feet at a right angle and the knees bent. One arm he held parallel to the floor at shoulder height and the other hand rested on his heart.

'Sometimes, if you need to keep low and near to objects, you can walk like this using a cross step.'

I had an 'aha' moment. The reason we held our arms out ahead of us in this position was so we could feel for obstacles in the dark. I tried my best but I couldn't get my body as low as his.

He started to walk very slowly, crossing his rear leg over the other, all the time remaining in a low crouch.

I was impressed: the man was in his seventies, yet he achieved it with such balance and poise.

'With this step keep low under the horizon and touch your feet down *very* gently, one at a time.' He placed his foot down in a kind of sliding toe to heel movement that would have made a ballet dancer proud. 'Always keep *zanshin* while making each step!'

I knew that *zanshin* was a state of 'relaxed alertness' in which you are very aware of the environment around you. The meaning was reiterated to me by the way my teacher had been looking all around as he moved.

'Be very gentle. Slowly lower your foot and be ready to lift it if the ground is not firm or makes a noise.' He made a gesture as if standing on a twig and having to withdraw his foot quickly. 'As with the other steps, make sure you reach around you with your arms as you walk.' With this he started to move his arms in time with his feet, crossing them as the rear leg crossed the front and opening them out so that one was in front and the other behind with each step from the front leg.

Having said all this he stopped moving his arms, backed up against the wall of the *dojo*, and continued the step with his whole body close to the wall. 'Do this if you hear a noise!' He demonstrated responding to the risk of discovery by putting his whole body flat against the wall so as not to be seen. The whole class stood transfixed: we were completely in awe at how quiet he was. You could have heard a pin drop.

We all practised. My legs shook and shook. I couldn't keep up the depth of the crouch. Just as I was about to get a major cramp in my thigh, our teacher glanced at the clock, looked at the pages of the manuscript I had brought and said, 'Only one more method is needed.' He gestured with his index finger as if pointing at the sky. '*Ko-ashi* – crane walk!'

He stood on one leg, like Oguri had done in his lesson. I knew this position to be called *hitcho no kamae*, meaning 'flying bird'.

Something about his body was lighter and different, and as I watched him hop from one leg to the other, he truly seemed to have a bird-like quality.

'Walking in water silently, to do this you need to step high.'

He started making steps, which involved an exaggerated lift of the foot, then gently lowering it to the ground, the toes pointed as if dipping into a stream. I could instantly see how this would work if you were wading in water, to prevent any splashing or rapid water movement. He carried on for a while, as if stepping over an assault course of invisible boxes. None of us imitated him, we just watched in silence.

'Keep the foot pointed when raising the leg. This is also good for walking through long grass.'

We came to the end of the lesson. I knew there were more stepping methods, even ones involving crawling, but I could see that the three most important were the ones we had covered and that the principles and training methods could be applied to any stealth movement. By the end, I had managed to learn all of the traditional lessons in stealth from one of the longest-standing students of the last ninja on earth. I had been successful. I had also shown how powerful my strategic training had been!

Then something amazing happened. My Japanese instructor gave me something that would change my whole life.

'Martin, this business card is from a collector of old Japanese writing, in Tokyo.'

I took the card. It was in Japanese but had a picture of a Buddhist deity smiling on it.

'He has many texts written by ninja. Perhaps you should have them translated for your own use.'

19

Seeking a Purpose

◆

Everything is dependent on everything else,
everything is connected, nothing is separate.
Therefore everything is going in the only way it can go.
If people were different everything would be different.
They are what they are, so everything is as it is . . . Man is asleep.

George Gurdjieff

As I sat on the train, ready to catch another connection to fly back to the UK, where I would catch yet more trains and eventually drive home, I found myself in a meditative mood. Unlike my fellow passengers, I couldn't focus on reading or concentrate on watching a film. Instead, I reflected on what had been a tough yet enlightening month of experiences. I found myself thinking of the saying at the start of each class in Japan: *Shikin haramitsu daikomyo.*

'Every action presents a potential key to enlightenment,' as Michael Pearce had put it.

Then it struck me like a thunderbolt. The true meaning of the phrase appeared from nowhere. The ninja interprets everything in life as part of his training; he has been a ninja since birth, so everything he does is *ninjutsu.* We are all following the way of enduring and overcoming. Every event that happens in life is something we should learn from, and I had found a way of making this happen, whether the event had been bad or whether it had been of value. I had always been able to see the positive side of a situation and this hadn't changed as I had got older.

I found myself reflecting on the things I was good at and those where I was lacking. Why did I sometimes not try when doing something old or new? Why didn't I pay attention in some classes even when I wanted to learn what was being taught? Why did I deliberately rebel against success or effort in some areas? If I was not going to apply my disciplines and abilities to real life, what was the point? Events flashed through my mind – times when I had asked for directions, then made no effort to remember those I was given. Times when I had offended people deliberately even when it meant I would lose out or cause problems. Silly things when I had made the same mistake repeatedly. What did all this mean?

Then I woke up to the concept 'It's always your go'!

They used to say that in Stephen Hayes's class. I had been taking everything so literally it had been staring me in the face; it meant the same as *Shikin haramitsu daikoumyo*.

They didn't just mean you should try, no matter what role you were taking in a martial-arts class. They were saying that you should be 'awake' and trying for every moment of your life.

It's hard to put in words but at that moment something changed for me. I realised I had been wasting a large portion of my life by not engaging. I had done so many things grudgingly, without involvement, and never realised that if I was going to learn to be disciplined and focused I had to learn to apply myself 'in the now', not put it off for the future. Everything I did was a chance to learn and better myself. It just took a change of attitude. I needed to treat everyday tasks in a new way: make my normal writing my calligraphy class, my cooking my knife lesson, my conversation my psychology instruction. Something inside me had woken up and I was glad because I was going to need this new insight.

Ninjutsu is about continuing, no matter what, and as I returned to England, I could see a huge challenge in front of me. I had a terrible sense of divided loyalty. I'd trained under two great masters, who taught differently and had their own ideas about the ninja arts. I felt great respect for both and, because of their differences, I had gained more than I could ever have hoped for than by training with just one school. Their apparent questioning of each other's philosophies had helped me decide what was of value to me. Each layer of teaching had held such value to me that I couldn't bear the idea of discounting or rejecting any of it.

In America, I'd found people whom I related to and who had really cared for me; I'd learnt invaluable skills from Stephen Hayes, and I'd bonded with the community at Dayton. In Japan they thought that Stephen Hayes had betrayed the ninja grandmaster and I was starting to form an idea as to how. Could he have grasped something he wasn't meant to? Had he learned more than was expected, metaphorically wandered into a room that the ninja grandmaster hadn't wanted him to? Had he taken that secret knowledge to America and forced his teacher into the open?

This dichotomy confused me. In a sense, Stephen was able to take the *ninjutsu* skills and philosophy beyond the locked-in traditional Japanese mind-set. It would show misunderstanding not to, as *ninjutsu* was and is the art of adaption; yet this had involved betraying his teacher by going beyond his authority. Yet he would not have been true to his teacher if he had balked at applying the teaching to his true ability. The paradox was driving me crazy.

For me, one way or another, the true mind-set of the ninja was hidden in the elements of earth, water, fire, wind and void. That may be seen as a simple classification or counting system by the Japanese but Stephen Hayes, a Westerner, had discovered the truth: he had looked beyond the counting and taken a step further than he was ever expected to. With a flood of new students, Hatsumi needed to be more on his guard, to adapt and readjust what he was doing. He had had to go under cover to some degree and stop teaching stealth, mystical arts and the like.

In America the real stuff is presented openly; indeed, learning at the *to-shin do* school, you are part of a team. Your teacher is as excited about your progress as you are. Not so in Japan: you have to learn the hard way. I was fed a diet of lengthy and physically demanding martial-arts classes. If you want to understand the whole art, you have to contemplate *everything* your teacher says and take full personal responsibility for your learning. I suspect the whole thing had been set up deliberately like that to ensure that only those who are absolutely willing to fight for the art get the true teachings. The instructors are focused on their *budō*. To learn the whole art of *ninjutsu* you would have to go in with everything you had and steal the art. If anyone says you can no longer learn genuine *ninjutsu* in Japan, they are wrong, but if you want it, you'll have to fight for it every step of the way, or you will simply learn self-defence, nothing more.

I was lucky I had found Michael Pearce, Noguchi Sensei and other instructors who made the experience extremely valuable to me. Without them, I wouldn't have gained any of the specialist knowledge and understanding. Most of all, I would never have had that moment of awakening that made every moment of my life important and focused. I would have been another anonymous person attending martial-arts classes. In fact, I believe that the vast majority of people visiting Japan don't learn a fraction of what I did, thanks to the guidance I received.

I decided I would have to ignore all politics and pursue the art. That, after all, is what Hatsumi did. I had to focus on the effectiveness of my methods, whether the ninja world approved or not, to continue my ninja training and gravitate to whoever could teach me most efficiently the real and effective art.

The changes to my life and being began to take place in the months after I had been in Japan. *Ninjutsu* was changing for me. *Shiken haramitsu daikoumyo* had now become part of me; a valuable and insistent part that reminded me whenever I drifted off or didn't make an effort. As my ability to understand things started to open up, so my strategic thinking improved. My perception of the world changed. Not all of a sudden, but I had moments of revelation as to the true motives behind my actions and those of others. It was as if an illusion was slowly drifting away. People around me seemed asleep and unaware; they floated through life, able to hold on to an aim for just a few moments before their emotions redirected them and they became distracted. It was as though they couldn't see beyond the surface of things. I had been the same.

I began to appreciate how being a ninja was about being able to make something inside endure and to remain focused on a true goal. It is knowing your purpose in life and living for that purpose, just as the ninja keeps focused on his mission and does not let emotions, distractions or hardships get in the way. In Japan, they embrace this and encourage a firm state of immovability. Clearly, as I had come to learn, the ability to be honest with oneself is a skill. Inevitably, as you practise and get better at it, the more powerful and focused you become. However, although I had begun to feel surer of my actions and increasingly secure in myself, things started to change in other ways.

One evening I went out to a jazz club with friends. We laughed at the cabaret act's name: Kitty la Roar and Nick of Time. I'd never been to any music clubs before and this one was not impressive for a first-timer. It was small, cramped, and the stench of urine mingled with that of the various alcoholic beverages on offer. The music, however, was transfixing and I was hooked. As the evening continued, my friends deserted me but I just sat there, enjoying the show. It was like a trip into the past. The elegant Kitty held the room with her voice and Nick played like Nat King Cole. They were performing old-time jazz numbers and I just relaxed and listened – 'Mack The Knife', 'Ain't Misbehavin'' and bluesy tunes I'd never really liked before. As the evening wore on, they moved away from the old favourites and started to play free-form jazz, a genre of music I had never heard before in which everyone improvises.

Drifting off in reverie, I had another epiphany, not merely in an intellectual sense but on a deep emotional level, and I started to understand the hidden message. Watching the two skilled musicians reacting and adapting to each other seamlessly took me back to Hatsumi Sensei in Japan. When he'd said, 'It's like outliving jazz,' he was trying to explain how ninja combat strategy is about an emotive and adaptive response to the flow and beat of the events around you. I'd never really been a fan of jazz, but I knew for my ninja training that to pick up the feel of the art I would have to see someone performing and observe them as they practised it. If I had learnt anything from my training, it was that you had to learn from 'doing'. I started going to that jazz club every week, just enjoying it, and there was the key I had not noticed before. To be fully in tune with the world, to feel the rhythm and flow, you need to connect, and that connection is through enjoyment and interest.

True to the principle of *Shiken haramitsu daikoumyo*, I started to take the lessons of enjoyment, rhythm and timing into my training. As I practised, I experienced a new level of emotion and sudden outbursts of creativity from my connection with things around me. I could see opportunities now where I never had before. I would become inspired, like an artist or musician, and the master plan would flow. This was something I had never felt before, something strong and powerful inside. It was the final lesson I needed to complete my strategic training.

It entered all aspects of my exercises. During stealth training, I found I could tell when a person would step, a car would change gear or just where a noise was coming from. When training with other martial artists, I found they had a 'beat' to them. After we'd sparred for a few minutes, I could feel when they were about to strike, sense the beat of my opponent's attacks. Once I could 'feel the music' and know when to counter, my mind was not in my way. Like improvisational jazz, I just responded. Something would grab me with a sudden burst of artistic inspiration, and I knew how I could bring about the destruction of my enemy. Likewise, in life, stealth and other undertakings, if I could feel the beat of life and play the next note, all would be fine.

Don't get me wrong. This is not the answer to supreme strategic or martial power. It's just one of the elements. Alone it is quite weak, like having a can of petrol but no car – you can cause a lot of light and heat but can't go anywhere. Combining the elements, the *tenchijin*, the ability to recognise the pattern behind events and being inspired by the flow, is the key to amazing power. I began to achieve incredible success in everything I did. Six months after my time in Japan, the single phrase Hatsumi Sensei used in the class suddenly made sense.

I started to realise how people around me were out of step with their own mortality and unaware of how precious every moment of life is. The Russian mystic George Gurdjieff said, 'Man is asleep,' and this was how I felt about my fellow creatures! I felt as though they were letting opportunities go as life flowed right past them but they did nothing: they were slaves to themselves. I was already an avid reader of texts on all religions and traditions, and the idea that humankind had become less aware and more focused on base instincts really made me sit up and think. Gurdjieff's mid-twentieth-century teachings were coldly predictive of my own revelations:

> The crowd neither wants nor seeks knowledge, and the leaders of the crowd, in their own interests, try to strengthen its fear and dislike of everything new and unknown. The slavery in which mankind lives is based upon this fear. One thing alone is certain, that man's slavery grows and increases. Man is becoming a willing slave. He no longer needs chains. He begins to grow fond of his slavery, to be proud of it. And this is the most terrible thing that can happen to a man.

I began to feel the urge to save people from this 'slumber'. All around me, I saw people with dreams and goals but their every action would cause them to fail. I could see couples living together with completely different goals, neither of them realising how one would go to their deathbed with their dreams shattered, and both were unwilling to face the conflict. Everything began to seem like a tragedy. I was consumed with the most tremendous feelings of love and compassion, *and* the most terrible feelings of mourning and sadness.

I started helping my friends and people I met in my spare time. With my new skills I could see ways of making things happen that others couldn't. As this continued, I found myself getting tired and hurt. It seemed that many people didn't want their dreams to come true. When presented with it, they would reject it or subconsciously sabotage things. Often, anger would be the result of their actions. The urge to help others, to be a hero, which had prompted my quest, had now become a debilitating weakness. I was losing my own strength and expending my power on every lame duck I met. Sympathy was controlling me. I had to take hold of myself and start focusing on those who really wanted help, people who were willing to fight for their goals or were in grave danger. It was difficult: I had been gaining a lot from these quests and it pained me to let go of this behaviour but I had to focus on the big picture and put my skills to the best use.

The truth is that most of our problems in life are of our own making and we can solve them by working out why we keep causing them to happen. That view is supported by the ancient ninja texts, which my contact in Japan was translating for me page by page.

The first was the best known: the 'ninja bible' is entitled *Bansenshukai* (万川集海), which translates as 'Sea of Myriad Rivers Merging'. My contact was also sending me fragments of other texts and planning to move on to two rival smaller ones called *Ninpiden* and *Shoninki*, as well as many fragments of documents and *yamabushi* texts.

A DEPICTION OF THE NINJA FROM THE 1800S

Ninja teachers had penned these writings for their students and I was, as far as I could make out, the first Westerner to study them like this. I was so excited to be able finally to get into the mind-set of the true ninja, which Hatsumi Sensei had said was the most important secret a ninja had.

As the chapter list for *Bansenshukai* came through, I realised I was about to receive instruction from the most complete ninja text of all time, authentic without doubt. I was slowly learning from a collection of ninja knowledge widely regarded as being a complete culmination of ninja philosophy, military strategy, astrology and weapons. Although the translation was rough, I could grasp the meaning behind it.

Isolated in England, with no kindred spirit nearby, I decided it was time to apply these teachings and to focus on the stealth arts I had learnt in Japan. It was time to study everything in the texts – lock-picking, crossing water, throwing stars, blinding powders, caltrops, smoke bombs, escape and evasion, and so on. In short, I would study all eighteen of the traditional ninja arts. I would solve my conflict and divided loyalties by going it alone. My new teachers would be the greatest of all: the original ninja from the past.

I started to practise my *taijutsu* every night. I focused on making my movement relaxed, flowing and natural, continuing to test myself against the elements, both internal and external, inspired by the texts I was reading, written by the *yamabushi* monks in Japan. They advised using weather as a test and learning to endure all temperatures with equanimity. This fitted perfectly with my nightly stealth training.

I acquired the habit of developing a new, more relaxed natural focus, which I put into action in every aspect of my life – I no longer had to remind myself quite as much to do my best to learn and perform every action with mindfulness. In the evenings, I would challenge nature by attempting to travel silently across all types of terrain and to approach animals and people without being detected. For example, if I heard an owl hooting I would do my best to see it as closely as I could without disturbing it. If I knew of a badger sett or some fox cubs, I would visit every night and stake out the area until I saw them. These very real tests of stealth taught me far more than the texts themselves. During my daily life, I watched how the elements tested me and fought to overcome them, keeping my equilibrium at all costs. It is the duty of a ninja to use all the power he has at his disposal to keep his inner calm intact.

I saw a distinct change in my efforts and everything started to flow. I found that when one skill improved, so did the others. A ninja's training would traditionally cover many areas – climbing, running, even forms of weightlifting – all skills needed to infiltrate a medieval Japanese castle. I was doing it all and I had some surprising results. The extreme focus needed for lock-picking, for example, improved other areas of my life, like writing emails in noisy railway stations. To run long distances you need a certain mental toughness to keep running when your body says it's time to stop and rest. This discipline was not one-way: with this new attitude, I was learning to do better everything I did. I was focused and improving, and it was amazing how normal daily tasks transformed to training opportunities. When cutting vegetables, I could practise knife skills with both hands; when talking to the next-door neighbour, I learnt how to build loyalty and get information from what the ninja texts called 'local spies'.

A development or insight in one skill would lead to similar advances in another. I began to develop an inner resilience I had never felt before. I started to lose many of the feelings that had held me back in the past, such as fear of failure or authority. The challenge was now between nature and me; the opinions and thoughts of other people lost relevance and importance. Nature had become my guide. I was no longer practising *ninjutsu*: I *was* a ninja. The art was in everything I did.

On my return from Japan, I couldn't settle into any martial-arts class. None of them matched up. I suppose they had a hard act to follow and, besides, as I had found before, my *ninjutsu* was not many other people's *ninjutsu*. To me, it is about challenging yourself and pushing the boundaries, about overcoming your limitations and realising your hidden potential. For me, the world of ninja training has become stiff and limited, like *karate* or any other martial art. For me, the true process was about finding your inner potential and seeking the most direct way of achieving your goals without being misdirected by internal or external shortcomings.

The culmination of this process hit me one day. I was performing meditation in some woods when the lightning bolt struck. Just as my perception of how things worked and how to do things had held me back in the past, so, too, had my perception of who I am. Perhaps to be the total master of your own mind you simply had to believe yourself to be so.

I once heard that when the ancient ninja first appeared in Japan they shocked the world by attacking and escaping through the walls of the houses. In those times, the walls were made of paper, but people had never thought of attacking through them. The ninja, with his new ability to see things differently, had shocked the world by simply jumping through them. I have found that almost all our limitations were like those paper walls: it's possible to break through them if we realise that they are not real limitations but simply things put in place to make borders for our own comfort.

I also wondered whether we are guilty of holding ourselves back from achieving our true potential because we are not willing to take responsibility for our actions. It's a human trait to hold on to our faults and weaknesses because we enjoy them. They give us drama and, in a way, we are addicted to them. If we let go of them we will have to take responsibility for everything.

It is my belief that all the tools we have evolved to improve ourselves are really just there to help us gain confidence and come to terms with our inherent power. We are all enlightened and the masters of our own minds; we struggle with accepting that state. Leading from this insight, I found that if I acted the part of the person I'd always dreamt of being, reality shifted rapidly in that direction.

It was time to test myself.

20

Bansenshukai

Bansenshukai *translates as 'a thousand rivers meet the sea'. It's the most comprehensive of the ancient ninja manuals written in the 1600s as a training manual for ninja of the time. Its name summarises the ninja's attitude of drawing whatever works from wherever you can find it without judgement or prejudice.*

The rain was pelting down as I entered the grounds. It would have been almost impossible to see someone creeping through the shadows but I made sure I evaded the two security guards and cameras, using the weather to my advantage. I had predicted that it would make the guards hide inside and, sure enough, I was right. I could see them, feet up in the warmth of the office to one side of the estate. The rain also made lots of noise in which I could move undetected. It obscured visibility and provided a cover for anything I wanted to do. A TV flickered in the corner of the office and now I could make out one of the men walking around with a mug cupped in his hands.

It was time to get back what was rightfully mine: my translation of a rare and ancient text. Unfortunately, the person I had lent it to was not someone to be messed with. A respected historian, he and his family came from a very tough culture. I had considered him a friend, but he was unpredictable and suffered from severe depression. During a relapse of his illness, our friendship had turned sour and he had made it clear that I would have to get the document back through stealth. I never knew if he really intended me to undertake this test or if he was just being awkward for the sake of it. Either way, the gauntlet had been thrown down.

As I edged towards the big house, I saw a member of the family through the main bay window. The light it cast illuminated the manicured lawns. The rain began to slow, and I decided to move past the window to a better vantage-point. I took a step and a length of old barbed wire caught my leg. It twanged loudly and, instead of remaining still, I tried to yank my leg free. The light from the room had destroyed my night vision and crucially my focus.

The rattle of the wire would not have been a problem: no one notices something like that from inside a house. But I'd disturbed a roosting pheasant, which let out an unearthly shriek as it flew out from the branches of a tree beside me, wings flapping. I was now no more than six feet from the window; suddenly I was lit up. I saw movement towards the glass, the curtain at the side pulled back, and fear overcame me. I should have frozen, but instead I ran for cover.

The person had obviously spotted me, so I leapt and rolled under a thick evergreen. I would try to blend with the shadow and contours of the land. I lay there with my heart racing, my breathing out of control. My senses were so heightened I could hear the drip of the rain falling off the trees, almost taste the overwhelming scent of wet soil where my face was squashed into it. I could also hear what I thought were approaching footsteps – or was it just the rain? I struggled to hear over my heartbeat as my mind played tricks on me. For some moments, I felt as if I was going to have a heart attack. Suddenly there was a flash of a torch: they were looking for me. I spotted one man, then two more, all bearing torches and, more worryingly, one I thought was carrying a shotgun.

For the last fourteen months, I had focused my attention on traditional ninja texts from the sixteenth century, working through every single detail of each chapter, contemplating and applying everything in that text to my life and training. Nowadays I lived by books that had been barely known, until recently, in the Western world, including the *Shoniniki* (meaning 'shinobi guide'), *Ninpiden* (meaning 'ninja traditions'), and the *Bansenshukai* ('sea of myriad rivers merging') because they had never been made available to the public. I treated them with reverence. I also had a folder full of fragments of works that we don't even have names for, with mysterious diagrams of goblins with birds' beaks (*tengu*), demonstrating sword techniques, and tools for setting buildings on fire. I had entrusted several of these documents to someone I should not have – the owner of the house – and I would get them back only by applying the teachings.

From the original ninja texts, I'd discovered how to make a mask by wrapping a length of black material around the head and neck, so that all that was visible were the eyes. The mask could be unravelled if I needed to walk on it or use it for climbing. For this mission I was in a black tracksuit to get near to the house, traditional ninja mask for close quarters and *tabi* boots, which were perfect for stealth: they fit to your foot with the unique split toe, giving extra flexibility in movement.

I heard feet approaching. The rain had stopped but water was pouring off the trees. The hood of my tracksuit was flooded but I remained motionless.

They began to search the grounds, systematic, professional and thorough. I had no idea whether they had a radio or even if they were fit enough to chase me but I wasn't going to take any chances.

I rehearsed every scenario in my head. Should I come out, confess, and put my hands up? Should I make a break and run for it? I imagined myself at the police station, humiliated and distraught. I was bordering on panic: breathe, slow deep breaths – lie still, keep calm and pray!

The torch came closer. They were looking under my tree . . .

When you read the ancient manuscripts you discover something staggering: the ninja were samurai. The world has it wrong when it comes to ninja versus samurai. The honourable and impeccable samurai were sometimes ninja by night! Some of the books even use the term *shinobi no Samurai* meaning 'Samurai Ninja'. The *Bansenshukai* even says that the '*nin*' in *ninjutsu* means being brave and immovable as the result of obligation to one's lord (master). In addition, that his dedication to his lord should result from a calm sense of duty at all times. It recommends the use of *kuji-kiri* and the contemplation of one's duty to one's lord at times when one needs to be immovable. I, of course, had no lord, but it was my duty to protect and care for a number of people: my wife, daughter, family and friends. I reflected on the negative effect it would have on them if I were caught. I focused on my duty towards them and remained still. Keeping your mind on those you love and things you find important in life is an important samurai principle and a very practical one.

When I first started training outside at night, I soon discovered that my teacher in Japan had been correct: one of the most important disciplines for stealth is to get into the habit of instantly and silently falling into a crouch and freezing whenever you hear a noise or think you may be seen. If you think you are about to be discovered, your animal instinct to run, move and hide will kick in. If you do that you will give yourself away. Wait, keep still and be at one with your environment. The person who heard a noise or suspected your presence will soon decide that it was 'probably nothing' and you will be free to move again. The bigger and more human the noise you make, the longer you should wait.

As I felt the flashlight go over my skin, I held my breath. My mind was racing. I felt the urge to give myself up getting stronger by the minute. Under the scrutiny of a flashlight, most people would assume the game was over and just give up but I knew better. I reminded myself that most people see what they expect to see. I had learnt about the art of letting people see what they expect: to become part of the scenery.

When you first start to go out in darkness, especially when you are alone, you realise how scared of the dark you truly are. It takes a while to learn to function with minimal sight of what is around you. You start to learn to be able to see in the dark more effectively, and gradually realise how far shadows and other people's expectations can protect you. To do this when people are around takes guts. In fact, guts, patience and nerves of steel are really the most important elements in the ninja stealth skills. Often, as in this case, you have to hide near the person hunting for you or even lie flat on the ground at their feet.

My 'immovable heart' paid off. The searchers moved away from where I was trapped and were starting to give up. I would have to wait at least an hour before moving, as they would still be on the alert. I couldn't stay much longer than that, though, or the sun would rise and I would be exposed. I had to find a new way out that would be less risky than the way in.

Kuji-in NINJA MAGIC FEATURES IN MANY
TRADITIONAL TEXTS

Woods are the natural home of any ninja: when you are there you can hide in the dark and are effectively on the edge of society. The *Ninpiden* states that in *ninjutsu* you aim to be at one with nature.

When I was in the woods, the natural world was my training partner. When I noticed a fox, owl or even a deer, the challenge was to approach the animal without it noticing. It was amazing to see such animals within touching distance. In the darkness of the forest the plants and animals are your greatest allies and your greatest threat – the two greatest enemies to ninja are sleeping birds and thorns. When walking silently you must learn to be far quieter than man normally is, so silent that the birds in the trees do not wake up and make a racket. The ninja were reputed to be able to change form into different animals or to be able to control them, or people, with telepathy or hypnotism.

It was time for me to move from under my tree. The branches were so low that they would be hard to navigate. A slow exit could send them pinging. In night training I had learnt to flow around obstacles; not to break branches or try to push them away. I decided to climb the tree to see what was going on. I used the principle taught in the ninja texts. When climbing trees and cliffs, be aware of where your foot lands; try to place the toes and front padding of the foot between branches and on crevices of the cliff face. If you are forced to step in the middle of a branch or push up the side of the cliff, do it slowly and proceed with caution. A little force may dislodge a shower of debris or break a twig, making a noise. From a few steps up, I could see a clear way of stepping out of the tree without making a noise.

I could also see someone walking across the grass on the other side of the house about to head over the gravel to get into a car. Perfect.

Sometimes when I was training, a person would come into the woods. Treating them like a fox or deer, I would test my skills by seeing how close I could go undetected. To do this best, you should match the rhythm of the person you are following. When the person steps forward, you step. This will help mask any noise your feet may make. Remember that sound travels at about 340 metres per second (1116 feet per second) depending on the temperature and environment, so you might need to adjust your walk accordingly. Note the delay between the actual step and the sound of the step, and try to use the same delay for your steps, only the other way around: you must step slightly before the person you are following. Now, if I was lucky, he would start the car and I could dash, using 'lightning step', to get to the small area of woodland, then out via the tennis courts at the back.

Most of the art of stealth is using nature as your ally. This is the key to true stealth and *ninjutsu*. When practising stealth you learn to capitalise on external sources of noise – gusts of wind, other animal movement and passing traffic – to suppress or camouflage any noise

you make. Once you get the hang of it, you can time a quick burst
of lightning step when an ambulance, police car or even just a heavy
truck goes by. If a jogger passes, you have a chance to jog too. Normally,
untrained people do just the opposite. They see being outnumbered
as a disadvantage when it could be just the opportunity they need.
Blending in is a crucial skill and having more than one assailant is
perfect for using the art of misdirection. Once you acquire the mind-
set of the ninja, the whole world is your ally. The shadows hide you,
the birds are your lookouts and darkness is your armour.

He moved and so did I. As the engine started, I felt indestructible.
I could see there was a natural route through the woods used as a
short-cut by visitors to the house. I took it. One way to avoid obstacles
as you make your way through woods is to follow a route already used
by humans or animals because the ground is trampled down and will
be less likely to result in any noise. Soon I was through the woods and
out of direct sight but not clear: my way was barred by a large locked
gate leading into a second garden area. The fence was tall, blowing
backwards and forwards in the wind; too noisy to climb and too visible.

I took out my lock picks, eyed the padlock on the gate and decided
my lock-picking skills were up to it. I'd spent the last year without
using keys, simply using my lock picks and a copy of *The Complete
Guide to Lock Picking* by 'Eddie the Wire'. This was a Yale lock. The
basic pick I had in my hand would not do the job.

I brought a soft leather case out of my inside pocket that contained
a set of thin metal hooks, lock picks, rakes and a bit of sheet plastic
with the words 'For Issue to Locksmiths Only' written on it in bold
black letters. Ever seen those spy films where someone uses a credit
card to open a door? Well, this was the real thing. I removed a pick
of the right size and pulled the padlock so there was tension on the
mechanism, which would help it open if I got this right. If I went
through the outdoor tennis courts I would reach the training hall
where I knew the text would be kept.

Taking a deep breath, I started to explore the mechanism with one
pick after another. It was strangely meditative; after a few minutes or
so of fumbling, I began to be able to feel the pins in the mechanism.

The pins made a very slight 'tick' when released and combined with easing the pick back and forth I was able to get into a rhythmic flow.

So, with a gentle hand and patience – admittedly not previously two of my strong points – and gently, gently moving the pick with a minute rocking motion, I released one pin, then another. The literal clock was ticking and thankfully, after about ten minutes, I finally felt it click open. My back was aching and every muscle screamed from craning over the lock but I was really pleased that I'd actually managed to do it.

As I approached the training hall, my whole body felt as if it was being remotely controlled. I prised a window open and eased myself into the darkness. I had only my previous recollection of the layout of the room to guide me. I knew there was a long fitted cupboard on the back wall that housed equipment, but the top was used to store books and decorative scrolls. I felt my way through the room, crouched low in a stance Hatsumi Sensei would have been proud of. Reaching the cupboard, I felt along it, willing myself to recognise the folder I had put the documents in. If I remembered correctly, it had a distinct raised pattern. My fingers edged over piles of books and suddenly I found what I was searching for. With no emotion, I picked it up and left the way I had come in, my heartbeat loud in my ears. Pain tore through me when the latch on the window snagged my head as I dropped to the ground. Grasping the folder, I checked in the moonlight that I had got what I wanted. Luck was on my side.

I took a few moments to make sure I was the only person there, checking the surroundings with the 'night sight' moon scope, a clever little gadget that allows you to pick out shapes in the dark. In this case, there was no need. At the end of the field, there were houses with small walled gardens. I just needed to go through one of those gardens and then I was free.

The Big Cat Challenge

❖

Destiny places a person into the appropriate circumstances, society
and environment through which he may successfully improve himself.

Franz Bardon

After all these months, something had changed inside me. I felt more at one with the animals I saw at night, the foxes, bats and cats.

I realised that no one really 'owns' anything: the world was effectively my back garden. We like other animals mark our territory and divide it up in our pack. Our ownership is no more real than that of the tom cat marking its area or the mole building its network of tunnels. In some ways, we delude ourselves into believing that we have control – of people and the circumstances we find ourselves in. Buddhist teachings tell us that we are only in control of ourselves, our words and actions: everything else is a flowing river of circumstance with ripples big or small that we create for ourselves or that other people set in motion for us.

I found that if a fox was in the area I could smell it. They have a distinctive strong, musky odour; if the wind was in the right direction I could, using my stealth skills, get very close to it. With deer, I could even touch them before they knew I was there.

When you spend so many hours and nights in the dark, some of the darkness stays with you afterwards. The use of fear as a means to heighten my senses was having side effects. I was paranoid. The darkness opened up a childlike fear inside me and every noise became a being in the dark, potential danger. My wife was anxious about my nightly pursuits too. She would often stay awake until I returned, restless and on edge. Perhaps wartime skills from feudal Japan need to be moderated for application in the modern world but I was too addicted even to consider that. I wanted to see what I was capable of.

I shed aspects of life that most people would consider normal. I gave up watching TV, listening to the news or picking up a newspaper. Sometimes I'd miss whole chunks of world events because I had simply decided to tune out. It's amazing how much time you can save yourself when you stop allowing yourself to be distracted by what is happening in the media, on TV or even in your own street. I had few interests outside my goals and this afforded me much more time to practise my training and keep focused on my aims.

Training became my *only* focus. It felt like my destiny, my duty and my place. I discovered that the greatest power I had was in my faults. I have always been an attention-seeking, obsessive person, so I learnt to channel these two qualities like never before. I would set myself challenges, then do everything to achieve them. Through this approach my abilities began to progress. I would often video myself and play it back, learning from my own experience.

Through this method, I learnt acrobatics and amazingly accurate *shuriken* throwing. A video of me turning off a light switch with a throwing star was an instant internet hit. I learnt to climb trees using cat claws faster than anyone I had ever seen.

Despite all these accomplishments and the results of some very successful training, I still felt empty inside. Something was missing. I started to make my challenges public, which only Stephen Hayes had done in the past.

One day an American-based film company called Reality Entertainment approached me to demonstrate my ninja skills for transmission on Sky TV and several American cable channels. They asked me to prove that, with my years of ninja training, I was more silent than any living predator. Using the most sophisticated scientific equipment, the staff at Dartmoor Zoological Park would trigger the stealth response in a wolf, a tiger, a lion, and – the biggest challenge – in the most silent of big cats: a jaguar.

According to zoologists, the jaguar will walk slowly down forest paths, listening for and stalking prey before rushing or ambushing. They attack from cover with a quick pounce.

The sound level of the animal would be recorded and I would be challenged to cross the same area of land. How could I possibly win? The jaguar has many advantages over man: it walks on all fours, it's a born predator and has paws made for stealth. I was going to use my mind and *ninjutsu* to outdo the animal's innate abilities.

The first time we were booked for the challenge it was rained off. Gale-force winds forced the keepers to put the animals away: a fallen tree and damage to a perimeter fence could easily give them access to escape. The delay gave me an advantage: I was able to experiment with the recording equipment and find out which sounds stood out against background noise. I also got to see the environment that I would be challenged in and formulated my master plan. I decided I would move in time with any advantageous background noise or when the recording equipment was moved.

We were able to go ahead with the challenge on a really cold day – everyone was standing around stamping their feet and heading into the kitchens for cups of tea. As they tested every animal in turn, I did my best to cause problems for my unknowing rivals, including making sure that the jaguar took the challenge after being fed, so he was far less motivated. I watched the sound ratings on the screen as they came in. The jaguar was virtually silent. The only way I was going to win this was to be *totally* silent.

I took ten minutes to meditate and bring about a sense of total calm. I indicated to the crew that I was about to start and took a deep breath. One single twig or loose stone and I would let down every teacher I had ever had. I'd memorised the route of the jaguar during his test: he would know the best route in his own territory. However, I was surprised to see that he took a direct route to his prey over grass and mud. I decided to ignore this judgement and to take a route alongside the fence where there was a rim of concrete all the way along. This, I thought, would be the easy option.

The challenge was about noise, so I did not worry about my visibility and focused all my energy on silence. I was slow, very slow, and moved only when a car passed, someone coughed or when the staff holding the microphone lost concentration. I took advantage of every distraction, background noise, wolf's howl or lion's roar. I was patient and gentle, but it was stressful not knowing how I was doing or if I had failed. Then disaster struck. Pain rippled through me. I squatted instinctively and the pain stopped as I moved. It took me a few moments to realise that the fence was electrified and I had just made full contact with it: that was why the jaguar had avoided it. It was a wonder I had not been shocked the moment I started: you don't have to touch the fence for the electricity to jump to your body – a trickle of water or standing on wet foliage will do it.

Now I had to finish the test without changing route, with the dual focus of keeping silent *and* not getting too near the fence. By the end of the challenge I was exhausted and soaked with sweat.

As I started to peel off my ninja uniform, the director Phil Gardiner approached me. 'Congratulations! You're as stealthy as a jaguar.'

I had matched the best nature had to offer and proven a ninja skill.

22

Overthrowing Pharaoh

───◆───

Be a craftsman in speech that thou mayest be strong, for the strength
of one is the tongue, and speech is mightier than all fighting.

Maxims of Ptahhotep, 3400 BC

'**H**e wants to kill you.'

The man who'd just sold me some sticky sugar cane said it in jest but the thought had already skimmed through my mind as I looked at the one-eyed Egyptian cradling a long staff in the crook of his arm. His turban partially covered an empty eye socket, which gave him a terrifying aura. I'd already had a brief exchange of conversation with him via the English-speaking sweet seller.

Luxor Temple glowed golden in the evening light. The sun always takes its time to go down in Egypt but when it's ready it just slips from the sky, like a thief in the night. We'd wandered into the square just outside the temple after having supper at a nearby restaurant and, by a stroke of luck, we'd arrived just as they were setting up a stage to host the *tahtib* (stick fighting/dancing) championships. Men had flocked in from neighbouring towns and villages, some from Qena and others from further afield in the desert oasis regions of Kharga and Dakhla. Most were in the classic *baladi* dress of long *jalabiya*, turban, and a fetching combination of socks and Western slip-on shoes.

Tahtib is probably one of the oldest surviving martial skills from ancient Egypt, along with wrestling and fencing. It appears to have been used since pharaonic times sometimes as a dance or a mock-fight for processions, at religious or marriage ceremonies. You can see depictions of this form on the walls of temples and on fragments of *ostraca* (pieces of pottery often used for writing or drawing in ancient times) – one such carving can be found on the wall of Medinet Habu, the mortuary temple of Ramesses III. It is thought that *tahtib* was used as part of the training for Pharaoh's army rather than a battle technique; it resembles the many uses of stick or staff fighting seen today, such as *eskrima* (Filipino stick fighting), *capoiera* (a Brazilian Acrobatic Martial Art) and, of course, the short staff or *hanbo* used in *ninjutsu*.

'Can he show me the basic moves?' I glanced at the chap who had been translating. He relayed the message, then nodded enthusiastically. He thrust a stick into my hands and motioned for me to watch the one-eyed man.

The stick is around four feet long and is swung in elegant circles either over the head or in front of the body and used for striking blows, preferably to the head. I'd used staff and sticks before when I'd practised *kuk sool won* so the fluid movements came fairly naturally.

'Like this? Is that how it's done?'

The man nodded and smiled. 'Look!' He spoke his first word of English.

I was taken off guard by his sudden switch to my language and just managed to jump to the side as he brought the staff down in a two-handed overhead strike. It was like a perfect *men* strike from Japanese *kendo*.

'Wow, that's pretty good!' I laughed and made a mock ducking movement. He nodded vigorously again, chuckling to himself, probably entertaining amusing images of beating me, the infidel, senseless.

I asked about the rules and was assured that, aside from the basic strikes, blocks and flourishes, the only other thing to master was the fancy footwork. Whatever, it seemed to be a beautiful form that involved a dynamic energy, replete with stylistic movements and martial elements tempered by fluidity similar to *tai chi* 'push hands', with a counter-for-counter flow.*

---

* As one form of *tahtib* is executed on horseback (the stick would generally have been longer in that case, around twelve feet), one of the patterns of 'dance' is called 'horse-stepping'. The movements of the dance or fight would mimic the pattern of 'charge and attack' as used by those on horseback.

'Your name?' It seemed he knew a bit more English.

'Martin . . . and yours?'

He patted his chest proudly, 'Bomani! We fight!'

'OK!'

He whirled the stick in a series of figure-of-eight patterns so fast and with such force that the sudden displacement of air created a frantic whooshing sound. He also started to dance. I felt a shot of adrenaline. Do we actually fight or is it some form of ritualistic enactment, like morris dancing?

'Game on!' someone in the crowd shouted at me.

I gripped the stick firmly and spun it with a flourish.

Even though my opponent was older, he was skilled. I'd learn later that this martial art had been the way villagers once defended themselves or settled disputes with their neighbours, long before Kalashnikovs became *de rigueur*.

As the dance continued, a crowd of around twenty men gathered. As we danced he would perform a twirl, block or strike in the air and the crowd would roar. In turn I would be given a chance to do something intimidating, so I would perform something from the *kuk sool* sword form or from *ninjutsu hanbo*. All around me there were smiling faces, amused by a tourist taking part. I could see drinks and snacks being sold by small, barefoot boys. It was obviously just a dance, wasn't it?

By now, the sun had sunk beneath the West Bank and we were bathed in light from the floodlit temple. More men, now joined by women and children, jostled to see what would happen and I think many were hoping to see my head taken off. Music drifted across the square from where the orchestra were warming up for the official *tahtib* challenges and demonstrations that were due to take place that evening. A specific set of music is used for *tahtib*, which involves a double-sided drum called a *tabal*, worn with a shoulder strap and beaten with two sticks, and the *mizmar*, a double-reed instrument with a haunting sound. Several *fellaheen* women had gathered near the musicians and let out shrill ululations, a beautiful trilling sound made by rapid movement of the tongue within the mouth as they sing. It distracted me and, in that moment, his staff smashed my hand.

Instinctively I sucked my bleeding thumb, glaring at him for having taken advantage of my momentary lapse in concentration – or had that noise signalled the start of the fight? He was laughing, his gold teeth glinting. He gestured with his gnarled hand to carry on fighting – easy for him but my thumb was bleeding badly and I could barely hold the staff. However, gritting my teeth, I spun it around my head and we were off again.

He was too quick: blow after blow struck me – the back of the hand, my leg. I only had a moment to register the pain when another blow caught me off-guard. The crowd cheered happily and the 'dance' continued.

It was time to fight back but I was new to this game and needed to do something special, something unexpected. Should I throw my stick at him, poke him in the eye or give in and kick him in the head?

Whack! This time he missed my hand and hit the stick, which ricocheted painfully down my arm. A second blow was a direct thrust to the middle of my chest just below the sternum. Anger exploded from nowhere and I struck him hard directly to the face. I was too involved to see the result but it couldn't have hurt him much – he just carried on fighting. He raised his stick to block the blow but was too slow to prevent an almighty strike. He tried to back off but I was on him, striking again and again as hard as possible, holding his clothing with my other hand and pulling him about to try to break his balance. Each blow hit his stick as he managed to block them. I swung my stick and thrust it downwards, like a dagger, ready to stab him directly in the shoulder – he let out a yelp and we were separated for a moment. Eyes locked, we contemplated our next moves, but then the music ended and so did our fight. A group of women in flowing robes pushed past us to demonstrate a traditional peasant dance. Between the lines forming, I could see him looking back at me while holding his shoulder. The look on his face was firm but a hint of a smile gave something away. He nodded at me almost imperceptibly: I had gained his respect.

Then he pointed at the women with his stick and said something.

'He says women dance and men fight,' Mohamed, my interpreter, said to me as we walked away. 'But it should be the other way around.

Women should learn to fight and men learn to dance, so women can defend themselves and men can be more gentle.'

The old man chuckled to himself, then looked at me, his eye narrowed in seriousness.

'Have you ever used your skills to defend someone?' he asked.

Only a short time ago Rowan Mantell, a journalist from the *Eastern Daily Press*, had asked me the same question.

A few weeks earlier Pip and I had been shopping in Norwich. As we were walking home, we noticed a stocky man approaching two women, one a mother pushing a pram. He looked determined and pretty fired up; he shouted and gestured to the women.

'Here comes trouble,' murmured Pip.

Sure enough, within seconds the guy had pushed the mother away and grabbed at the pushchair, dragging it precariously back the way he'd come, the wheels spinning wildly against the kerb. The woman had slipped and fallen awkwardly, her friend screaming at him to stop.

'Oh, my God, he's trying to steal the child!' Pip yelled at me. 'I'll see to the woman and call the police. You get him!'

I didn't need to be told twice. I dropped my carrier bag and shot after the guy who was half running, half walking down the hill adjacent to the main road. Seeing me coming he began to run, the pushchair swinging from side to side and dangerously close to tipping the child out. I gave him no warning before I grabbed him around the neck in a chokehold. Instinctively his hands flew up to pull my arms off him, letting go of the pushchair. Great. Now I had to decide whether to choke out a furious, unpredictable male or rescue the child, who by now was rolling in the pushchair down the hill. I figured if I quickly got him to his knees, I could run for the kid.

I spied the unattended pram slowly drift towards the road. There was no question: I had to loosen my grip to protect the child. Moving quickly, I dragged him down, pushed him hard and scrambled after the pushchair. I grabbed at the handle and stopped it just before it bumped down the kerb into the road. Pausing to catch my breath, I was grabbed from behind and pulled over. I saw Pip running down the hill; I motioned her to grab the pram and tried to disentangle myself. He grabbed my T-shirt to pull me around. We both stumbled but I was back on my feet in a second; it's amazing how the *toshindo* 'defence against kicks from the floor' technique sinks in. I dug my keys out of my pocket and threw them into his face – score one for distraction techniques. I managed to punch him hard in the stomach, then in the face. My whole body shook as I hit him directly at the base of the jaw. I heard the wail of a siren in the distance and so did he: with that, he was off, running into the distance.

I gave chase but soon lost him. He obviously knew his way around the rabbit warren of flats. Sweaty and exasperated I headed back to where I had left Pip, who had been joined by the two women and several police officers. Luckily the child was OK.

The officers headed in the direction of the flats where the man had disappeared – they didn't wait to ask me a single question. Just a 'thank you' and that was it. I returned to the street, picked up my keys and shopping and left.

Bomani smiled at my story. 'I run a hotel for hurt woman,' he said. 'This is where we teach the martial arts to help them protect from husband and bad man.'

Our 'fight' was over. We shook hands and his parting words were 'You good man and she,' he pointed at Pip and his eyes twinkled, 'she good woman.' Not a bad compliment from a traditional Egyptian man.

We thanked him profusely and wandered over to Snack Time, one of our regular haunts, to have a cup of tea, use the Wi-Fi and look out over the *tahtib* competition. We got a prime position on the balcony overlooking Luxor Temple; around us youngsters were obviously on surreptitious dates, smoking or texting furiously. They eyed us warily; Pip's blonde hair, usually covered, was drawing attention as she'd relaxed and slipped off her scarf. We'd noticed the streets had seemed tense over the past few days but had shrugged it off. I decided to check my emails and turned to ask Pip if she could pass me the laptop from her bag – but she had frozen, a look of horror etched on her face.

'What's wrong?' I followed her line of vision towards the large TV silently commanding one corner of the room. The scrolling headline on Al Jazeera screamed, 'Egypt on the Edge.' Neither of us had had any inkling of this: we'd been Temple-hopping and chilling out beside the pool. Nevertheless, the images flickering on the screen showed Cairo on the edge of anarchy.

Poor Pip was incredulous. Her beloved Egypt was in turmoil. I tried to reassure her that everything would be OK, but judging by the reports, it most definitely was not. The people were calling for the resignation of the president, who had kept Egypt stable politically for thirty years. They were sick of corruption, sick of the perpetual 'state of emergency'. They wanted democracy and to be 'without rules'. This came from a young man sitting near us who, overhearing our general conversation, was answering our questions with the pseudo-worldly flourish that only the young, idealistic and naïve can carry off.

'I hate to burst your bubble,' said Pip, 'but democracy does *not* mean no rules. It merely means having the chance to vote for the political leaders you want.'

He waved his cigarette. 'No! We need no rules – Mubarak has to go, *inshallah!*'

'You're in for a shock,' Pip muttered under her breath. She re-arranged her scarf and turned back to the TV.

I sat for a while and looked out at the familiar scene. We'd come to Egypt so many times it seemed like a second home. But now the call to prayer, which usually soothed the soul, seemed faintly ominous. We decided to head back to the hotel but just as we started off along the main Luxor road, the Corniche, Pip put her hand on mine. 'Listen!'

There was a faint rumble, indistinct shouting and more honking of horns than usual. People were stopping to look back towards the station. We followed their gaze and saw a large group of about fifty men erupt from the souk. Bricks and stones were being thrown at shop windows, fragments flying dangerously across the square. Several men ran into the middle of the street, narrowly avoiding a taxi, which screeched to a halt. They swarmed around the car, banging loudly on the roof, shouting, 'Mubarak out!'

One guy stood there in a white T-shirt, covered with dust. His face was a mixture of anger and excitement and he swung what looked like a large hunting knife. The moment I saw it, I knew we should get away. In the distance, sirens blared and smoke plumed from some darkened buildings at the far end of the street. More and more crowds were gathering and I felt a hand on my shoulder. A waiter from the hotel was standing behind me and suggested that we should get back there.

Pip was already moving, pulling me towards the Corniche. Acrid smoke and dust filled the air. We saw another small group of tourists half running along the road, scarves clasped over their faces. We caught up with them and they turned to us, eyes streaming, as they gestured towards the hotels.

'Tear gas!' croaked one woman.

We felt the prickle of it in our throats as we picked our way along the now teeming street. What I had thought was smoke and dust had been canisters of gas fired by military police. We felt the first twinge of fear at being caught in what we now realised was a revolution. By now, smoke was pouring from a car that had been set alight. We headed towards a group of uniformed police, who were watching us with blank stares. I was about to ask one if he could escort us back when he snarled, 'Fuck you!' and leered into my face.

At that moment, a half-brick hit me on the chest and dusty smoke enveloped us all. Another missile hit the last two fingers of my left hand with a painful crunch. I yelped. They were broken for sure.

Eyes stinging, I was being tugged along by my other hand. Somehow Pip was herding us towards the main roundabout – only another quarter of a mile and we'd be back to the safety of our hotel.

When we got there, shaken and confused, the place was empty. All of the tourist police had left their posts – normally there were armed men at the entrance to the hotel. Even so, as we entered the lobby a feeling of safety washed over me. Everything seemed so normal. I tried to flex my fingers but they were too swollen. Pip regaled the staff with what had happened, partly to explain why we looked like vagrants. Meanwhile I watched the BBC news on the TV in the foyer.

Protests were common after morning prayers on a Friday but this time the touch-paper had been well and truly lit. We learnt that sit-in protests in Tahrir Square had turned violent and the military had retaliated. It had led to the looting of shops and cutting of power lines. The government had identified social media as a key tool of the rebels – who were mainly students – and tried to cut all internet and external telephone connections. Police and army were using tear gas and rubber bullets to control the crowds. Luckily for us, we had experienced only the former.

Inside our hotel room, we found a note from our travel agent explaining that an emergency flight was being arranged for UK nationals and that we should stay in the hotel until then; daily meetings in the lobby to update us had been scheduled.

Pip looked so sad for various reasons. She was sitting watching news reports of museums looted, mummies being beheaded and Egypt on the brink of revolution. She glanced at the note from the travel agent and tossed it aside. 'Not doing it.'

'Not doing what?'

'Not going to give in and sit in the hotel for the rest of the time here.'

'It's not safe out there.'

'It's fine. The Egyptian people just want to be able to live a normal life, not in poverty. They have nothing against us.'

'Some of them don't like us much at all,' I muttered, still rubbing my fingers gingerly.

'Martin, there are nutters everywhere.' She broke a small smile. 'Anyway, I'm not being sequestered to a hotel when there's a nice steak waiting for me at Maxime's!'

Boy, was she stubborn. Sometimes I wondered who had more guts in this relationship.

She slid open the balcony door and leant against the rails. 'You see all these people here with shops and restaurants and taxis?' She gestured outside to the street, which looked peaceful. 'They are going to starve if no one goes out of their hotels. There are no benefits here, nothing to fall back on, no one to help them.'

I sighed. These final days were hardly going to be relaxing. We sent a few texts to people to say we were safe but replies were sporadic and the next day all communications were down.

Over the next two days, I had a lesson in good old English stiff upper lip. While other tourists stayed in the hotel, we carried on as usual. The streets were deserted, shops closed, shutters drawn. Two men at the far end of the road were guarding their shop with knives taped to sticks – *tahtib* with menaces! Pip walked purposefully, deep in thought, I could see she was already contemplating an article or a book. As we passed one shop, an elderly man beckoned us over; he had a carrier bag and motioned for us to look inside. Pip took a look and recoiled instantly, wrinkling her nose in disgust.

'What is it?'

'Molotov cocktails! Phew, fumes . . .'

The man explained in broken English that last night had been bad: people had tried to steal from him. He and his son had slept on the floor with knives and his bag of goodies. Pip was commiserating with him, when we heard what sounded like another protest. This time she got no chance to object: we went back to the hotel.

I went to the gym, and Pip to sunbathe.

Later I arrived by the pool to find gaggles of tourists already there. They told me that last night the staff had secured and protected the hotel when an armed gang had tried to storm it to steal the ATM. We'd slept through the whole thing, which was probably just as well: Pip would probably have grabbed her camera, hoping to capture some action. Now she was reading and sipping tea; several people asked how she could be so relaxed when there was no guarantee that we were safe. She replied from behind her dark glasses that she would rather be killed relaxing and drinking tea in a place she loved than panicking and wasting time. She was giving a great example of what the ninja call *fudōshen*, the immovable heart.

The following day we were informed at breakfast that we would be flown home that evening.

The moment the crowded plane took off I relaxed. A tear rolled down Pip's cheek – I knew what she was thinking: Will we ever come back?

Halfway through the flight I heard a muffled bleep from my mobile phone. I rummaged through my bag and retrieved it. I must have forgotten to turn it off: with all the hoo-ha over communications being cut, it had been languishing with no signal until now.

I read out the text: 'Hi, Martin, I'm a researcher from *This Morning*. Could you contact me as soon as possible about coming on the show?'

Why on earth was I being invited onto a TV show?

23

The Norfolk Ninja

*People too weak to follow their own dreams will always find a way
to discourage yours.*

I pondered about the text message for a while. It was probably just
a hoax by my mates. Whatever, it would have to wait. I put the
phone in what I thought was flight-mode and read for the rest of
the journey.

As soon as we landed, the phone went mad. Damn it, text messages
were flooding in. As I attempted to open the first, the whole thing
crashed. There was no time to start messing around with it as we were
herded through Security. The benefit of travelling light is no bags to
pick up: one carry-on and that was it. I just wanted to get to the car
and drive home.

I spent the journey counting down the miles; Pip slept most of the
way. When we got home, I decided I'd unload the car later: it was
time for meditation, then bed.

The front door stuck as I tried to open it. A massive amount of
post had been delivered while we were away and had got caught in
the door. Pip looked puzzled and stepped over it. As I moved the pile,
I noticed a soft package among it. Inside was a black T-shirt with a
ninja on the front and a slogan declaring, 'I'm not the Norfolk Ninja!'
I looked closer. The picture was of me dressed in full ninja garb – one
taken from my website. I scooped the whole pile up and dumped it
on the table, then took out my phone and tried to start it. No good,
so I changed the battery and tried again. While I waited for it to
restart, I waved the T-shirt at Pip. 'Look at this!'

My phone suddenly came to life and more texts flooded in.

Martin a ninja, yes, but a vigilante???? Duncan

Can you call me urgently, Martin? I'm a reporter from the Sun *and we want to do an interview with you for the paper.* Phil Goodridge

Martin, have you seen the T-shirts they are selling about you on the market. I have put one through your door along with some newspapers. Josh

Martin, this is James Cavendish from the BBC. We left you a message. Can you call me?

I looked at the stream of messages in total disbelief and rising anxiety.

Hey buddy – you're in today's Metro!

Pip raised an eyebrow ruefully. 'I know you wanted to be a superhero when you were a kid but this is taking it a bit far.'

There was a text from the boss, one from our daughter, another from my mum and some from random people, who were frankly pretty abusive.

You're a disgrace to martial arts, an embarrassment, you w***er!

Hey ninjaa boy, fink your hard do you?

A newspaper was waved under my nose. 'I think you should look at this!' Pip held up a copy of the *Sun*, replete with a big blow-up picture of me taken from my website. 'My dad just dropped it off.'

'The Norfolk Ninja!!' the headline screamed.

I snatched the article out of her hand:

Humble publishing clerk by day, ninja vigilante superhero by night, Martin Faulks trained in Japan for five years to use his powers to fight crime!

It was a great article and I would have loved it if it had been about anyone else but me. My first thought was of Michael Pearce. When he had awarded me my black belt, he had more or less said, 'Don't be an idiot with this.' Sadly, he was about to witness new levels of failure.

I then listened to my voicemails. There were at least fifty from radio and breakfast TV stations, and newspapers all over the world, many from Japan.

As we sifted through the newspapers some national, many local, it didn't take us long to reconstruct what had happened. After talking to Rowan Mantell at the *Eastern Daily Press* about the 'Big Cat Challenge' and the incident in the street before our trip to Egypt, I had provoked quite a reaction in both local and national press. Suddenly everyone seemed to know who I was. Stories had been printed about my ninja training; pictures had been lifted from my website and I was being proclaimed as some kind of superhero or vigilante who roamed the streets of Norwich. Throughout my life I had been seeking attention. Now I had more attention than I could handle. Somewhere in the world several people I had trained with were laughing. I had no time to laugh. I knew this was going to be trouble. What would my employer think? How would my teachers respond?

I was tired but also really worked up. I sent a bulk text to everyone who cared, saying we were home safe, then practised my meditation and went to bed in an attempt to sleep. That didn't happen: I just worried all night. Tomorrow I had to focus on catching up at work. Should I wait for it to blow over? Could I go on the TV shows and say, 'I'm not a ninja vigilante'? No, that would only add to the whole thing. I decided I had better do what ninjas do best and disappear.

The next day was madness. People recognised me in the street, the martial-arts forums were buzzing and my website was full of comments. I had a flood of emails, and from the number of threats, I could tell that a fair few men wanted a fight with the 'Norfolk Ninja'.

While some of what happened was laughable – Russell Howard mocked me on national television – online it was much worse. I was ridiculed on a martial-arts forum and cyber-stalked by someone I suspected was linked with it. On the internet, I found Photo-shopped pictures of me in compromising situations with other men, and animations of Pip and me as Punch and Judy.

The modern world of social media and easy access to information also brought out a far darker element. On a daily basis, threats were made towards my family – my mother, my wife and my stepdaughter. It seemed that my media identity as the so-called 'Norfolk Ninja' made me a target and my family fair game.

My boss was less than impressed with the media coverage. Day after day, it was non-stop front-page headlines and radio commentary. Soon there were copycats appearing in the tabloids, such as the 'Ninja of Tunbridge Wells'. The martial-arts organisations I most admired turned their backs on me, dismissing me as a fraud. That hurt. For many years, I had dedicated my energies and time to mastering *ninjutsu*, to becoming the best martial artist I could be. I'd worked hard to develop myself physically and spiritually. To be denounced by the circles I most admired was galling.

In the midst of all this stress and turmoil, I had to employ new techniques to limit the damage that had already been caused. It was necessary for me to be careful everywhere I went. My stealth training became invaluable as I moved around undetected; I kept my house as secure as possible and I became used to dealing with aggression. I was channelling my ninja training more than ever.

This went on for days, then weeks. I couldn't let my guard down for a moment. Internet trolls continued to harass me, and I was always on high alert, as though life was one long midnight practice session. I had constantly to change my routine and to be suspicious of any new people. I was living on the edge and there was never any let-up. I didn't realise it at the time but this was the greatest ninja training of my life.

I wasn't made welcome in any martial-arts classes. If I turned up, other students would either challenge or mock me. I was worried that I would be cornered so, in private, I needed to do something to keep my reactions as sharp as possible: I went to boxing classes. This became the most beautiful refuge. The club was full of teenagers but I didn't care. We ran four miles to start with, did some skipping, bag work and then full contact sparring. It gave me a chance to release all the anger I had inside.

After months of harassment from the media, general public and martial-arts community, I was in pain. I had put my family at risk and been humiliated. The former was inexcusable, the latter much needed. During my travels I had found that, although instructors had different views and training methods, I had always felt at home with them, part of a team. Before the 'Norfolk Ninja' media explosion, much of my life *had* been directed towards finding fame and attention. Now I had got what I had wanted and didn't like it. I had been surprised by the aggressive nature of some of the exchanges I had received – including hate-mail and death threats. The discovery that the Japanese ninja organisations thought so little of me had been the hardest thing to shake off. I hadn't trained endlessly for years only to be rejected in Japan. Although I had promised Pip that my days of touring and studying abroad were over, I wanted now to revisit Japan: I had to show the men for whom I had ultimate respect that I *could* be a ninja according to their very high ideals.

Something worse dawned on me. All the invasions of privacy I had inflicted on others, the disdain I had felt towards them, looking down on them as unenlightened: that was now how I was being viewed and treated. Karma had come to collect. I thought of the philosophy I had been studying in the ninja scrolls I had had translated in Japan. I also pondered on the warnings in the texts that a bad heart would bring downfall. I had not heeded Bo's advice. I had allowed my heart to be corrupted by the art, and I had not properly understood the ancient ninja texts.

The *Bansenshukai* makes clear that a ninja should never use any ninja ability without a noble goal. You should not pursue power or fame for the sake of it. You should be there to serve your lord and a higher ideal or the gods will not bless you and your heart cannot hold divine blessing. To me, there was a deeper meaning. Our heart has four sections: two passive, two active; two receiving, two giving. They are the elements: earth, air, fire and water. If you lack pure intentions in all four elements or let your vices control you, things move out of balance and you are punished by your confused vision. I needed to seek help from people with the wisdom and understanding to find the source the original medieval ninja respected and turned to in times of need.

First, I had to make sure my family were safe. To do this I had to use my ninja skills to spy on the worst of my stalkers: a *ninjutsu* instructor, who spent hours every day harassing those close to me and trying to blacken my name. I needed to make sure that this would-be opponent didn't have teeth. That he was insecure but not totally mad . . . and dangerous.

It was not long before I found a chance to observe him with his class around him in public. I'd discovered via a forum that his *dojo* would be enjoying a social night at the gym where they trained. I decided to visit, undisguised and uninvited, and settled myself across the bar with a drink I barely touched and an open packet of crisps to pick at. They had obviously had a class earlier and were now chilling out by getting drunk and watching martial-arts films. One scene especially caught their eye: ninjas in an array of coloured suits were pouring into a castle settlement, the leader of their 'clan' wearing a pristine white outfit.

'When would a ninja dress in white?' the instructor bellowed. He laughed inanely, looking round his 'disciples' for approval. Asian music blared out of the TV; images of ninja with exotic weapons flashed on the screen.

The instructor held high rank in his organisation and had, no doubt, dedicated his life to the art. So much so that he now saw himself as a ninja kind of guy. I reckoned he would feel the need to destroy anything that challenged his sense of self.

His latest challenge had been the 'Norfolk Ninja'. To him this man represented everything bad about *ninjutsu*, someone with little or no knowledge cashing in on his beloved art and giving the world the wrong impression of it. For this reason, he had spent the last three months of his life putting a daily effort into harassing and destroying me.

I had visited to find out if he was a threat to those I love before I boarded my flight to Tokyo. I was satisfied that he was not: neither he nor his disciples had recognised me, sitting twenty feet across the room from them. His question, however, was more symbolic than he could imagine and I found it almost an omen of what was to come.

Because this ninja was about to don a white uniform to travel to Japan and, like the original ninja in time of challenge and doubt, was about to seek advice from the greatest of spiritual teachers there.

24

As the Crow Flies

*Method is more important than strength, when you wish to control
your enemies. By dropping golden beads near a snake, a crow once
managed to have a passer-by kill the snake for the beads.*

Henry Wadsworth Longfellow

A small, perfectly attired man appeared.

'You speak Japanese?' He studied my passport as if searching
for some secret code. 'You been here before?'

'Yes,' I began. 'Well, no, I don't speak Japanese but I have been here
once before.'

His look offered no emotion. 'Where you stay?'

I rubbed my face wearily. 'I'm going up a mountain, Mount Haguro,
the Crow Mountain.'

His eyes narrowed.

What could I say? 'I'm here to spend a month with the *yamabushi*
– to train in *shugendō*.' I didn't expect him to understand but he blinked
hard.

'Mountains are not for holiday! Dangerous for tourist, you get sick
– you in trouble. You need be tough man, no food on mountain.
Western people not good for climbing.' He jabbed his finger at my
chest as he made his points.

'I don't know what to tell you except that I'm here to get free of all
this . . .'

I gestured towards the window that overlooked the teeming
terminal building, mankind swarming in every direction, dragging
their belongings with them, stressed, frantic and unsmiling.

He hadn't finished. 'Lot of things those monks do has been outlawed because they are foolhardy!'

I didn't really know what to say. I'd had no idea *shugendō* was outlawed. It seemed to me that if extreme ascetic practices, such as fasting for weeks without food or water, were banned, extreme sports, like bungee-jumping and skydiving, should be too. And if they *were* banned, was I about to be sent back to England?

I handed him the address of the *shukubo* at the base of the mountain. 'This is the address of the teacher who will be my guide.'

At that point, it really struck home how important this whole trip was to me. I was there to get away from everything that no longer resonated with me: my urge for fame, my craving for money and attention, all the petty emotions that were holding me back. I desperately wanted to reach a point whereby I could transcend all that and strive for a life full of spiritual richness. I knew that the *yamabushi* could help me do it.

He took the address with him, closing the interview-room door behind him, and I was left alone. I took the time to reflect. I thought if I could just get to the mountains, I would be able to learn from the monks the secrets that would allow me to see beyond the material world into something distant, mysterious and maybe even divine.

When the ancient ninja were in trouble or needed advice, they would turn to the *yamabushi*, the warrior monks of the mountains in Japan, and don their white uniform to ascend the mountain in retreat. As I sat there for what seemed eternity, I took time to consider the challenges ahead. The mystical figure of the *yamabushi* is monk and master magician. Their path, *shugendō*, translates as 'magical powers through hardships'. They are reputed to be able to run miles over the mountains at superhuman speed, endure fire, stand under the waterfalls in winter, talk to the gods and control the elements. I knew they trained in extreme and very dangerous ways. They performed feats involving hanging on ropes over deadly mountain drops to overcome fear, and climbed ladders of sharp swords. They ran through fire, took drugs that made you hallucinate your worst nightmare, and even fought with wild animals. The idea of what might await me was terrifying.

The *yamabushi* are so synonymous with the ninja that some ancient texts confuse the two. In popular tales, ninja earned their stripes through *yamabushi* training. So, here I was, after years of research and communication, about to be the first Westerner to visit the lesser known Haguro sect. I had chosen this obscure school after reading in *A Religious Study of The Mount Haguro Sect of* Shugendō: *An Example of Japanese Mountain Religion*, that this was the only group of *yamabushi* to be totally dedicated to the Shinto religion. They had remained unbroken by any bans or religious persecutions and, more importantly, were associated so strongly during the sixteenth century with *ninjutsu* that it was said the monks themselves could be hired for missions. If all that was true, I was about to visit a sect whose ninja training was historically verified as unbroken.

As these thoughts went through my mind, I realised what a fool I had been. How could I not have noticed it before? The word 'ninja' means 'to endure'. '*Shugendō*' means 'to gain powers through hardship'. It was so obvious now that the paths were one.

The immigration officer returned, looked at me pointedly, then walked away without saying anything. No one came back: they just left me sitting on the other side of the gate. Did the look and the open door say, 'You can go'? I decided to rely on my gut instinct and leave. After all, he had given me the stamps I needed in my passport.

I stood at the Nippon railway line entrance at the airport and took a deep breath. A small elderly man was at my side. He seemed to be doing the same as me: psyching himself up for the journey. I knew it was going to be a stamina job. I had at least seven hours of train time ahead of me, after a twelve-hour flight, which had left my shoulder and back really sore. Let the hardships begin!

As I got on the super-fast train, I looked around the carriage. It was full of schoolgirls playing with phones or Gameboys. They looked at me from beneath their lashes, heads lowered and hands smothering giggles. This was not going to be the quiet, relaxing journey I was yearning for. One of the bolder girls edged closer.

'Where you from?' She made it sound like an accusation and the question drew a crescendo of giggles.

'I'm from England.' Even more giggles.

'Do you like cats?'

'Yes, I do – I have a cat.' A flurry of hands flew up simultaneously to their mouths, leaving a row of wide eyes – and then a communal squeal. Japanese girls love cats almost as much as they love fashion.

Suddenly I was bombarded with questions from all angles.

'What colour?' Tabby.

'Boy or girl?' Girl.

'What's its name?' Mouse.

This last bit of information caused peals of laughter, much mouth-covering and bouncing up and down. I felt as if everything was getting a bit surreal and smiled wanly. Yes, the cat really was called 'Mouse' (another wave of mirth) and, yes, I had a picture on my phone (huge rush to see image of slightly overweight tabby) and, yes, I had a daughter, who actually owned the cat and had given her that name.

They eventually got over the cat thing and settled down a bit. But then I got another question, 'Are you married?' Here we go again. Yes, I am married: here's a picture of my wife – more squeals. Yes, she has lovely blonde hair and is very pretty . . .

Luckily, they all bundled off at the next station, waving and giggling. I leant back and sleep slid gently over me.

Eventually the train slowed to a halt and I stepped off at a virtually deserted rural station. We'd left the city and prefectures long behind, and now I was deep in the countryside; totally different from Noda City where I had stayed on my last trip to Japan. I settled on a bench, which was surprisingly rough and unpleasant. I had a new companion, an old peasant woman; she smelt a bit funny and seemed as puzzled by my presence as I was by the crate of chickens on her lap. Why give the birds holes to poke their heads through if you're going to spend your time constantly pushing them back inside? Let them look around a little.

I couldn't find a timetable but my questions fell on deaf ears. So, after an hour, I jumped on the first train heading in the right direction. Train followed train. I dug deep on my reserves, as my body strained against the pain of so much enforced sitting. I tried to read or learn more Japanese but was just too tired. Then I was there, Tsuruoka station. It was the closest I could get by rail to my destination and I was going to have to take a taxi to the mountains.

As I got off the train and sniffed the air, I was reminded of somewhere I had been before but I couldn't put my finger on it. The station was ugly, big shells of concrete, all the shops closed, and it was getting dark. Buses came and went but I didn't know where to. The timetable, of course, was in Japanese, and faded, and in the half-light I couldn't make anything out.

'Can you be helped?'

A taxi driver waiting near the entrance had got out of his car. The others were all poking their heads out of their windows, like the chickens on the bench.

'I would like to go to the Daishin-bo Shukubo and Haguro-san.'

The driver jumped. He had obviously thought I was English-speaking from my appearance, but I'd startled him with my very English response. Words evaded us but, using my map and the address of the *shukubo* in Japanese, we were close to an understanding. However, there was a problem: the mountain was closed. How do you close a mountain? After some discussion, it was a case of 'What the hell, let's just drive!'

As we passed through the town of Tsuruoka it dawned on me . . . Lowestoft! It reminded me of the cold, flat greyness of a seaside town in Norfolk, England. Luckily as we got away from the town, the scenery became far more beautiful. It was dusk but the bucolic countryside rolled by and I could just make out the mountain in the distance, sheathed in cloud and looking suitably mysterious. The motorway passed through a large red 'shrine' gate, indicating that we had now entered sacred ground.

In the sixteenth century, the original ninja had turned to the *yamabushi* for their spiritual guidance. True to form, I was doing the same.

In preparation for the trip, I had read everything I could about the *yamabushi* and their traditions. From this, I was convinced that the lessons taught in *ninjutsu* of facing the elements came directly from this *yamabushi* tradition.

The word *yamabushi* means 'one who lies in the mountains'. As we have seen, these mystical and enigmatic monks were known for following a path known as *shugendō*. This translates as 'attaining magical powers through hardship'. The *yamabushi* were mountain ascetics, hermits or holy men. Because of their reputed mystical or magical powers, they were highly respected and sought out to heal or prophesy for pilgrims or folk from nearby towns and villages.*

In their isolation of the mountains, they studied various martial arts, seen in Japan as a means of improving oneself mentally, spiritually and physically. This would also mean that, like the samurai, they could be called upon as 'warrior monks' when needed by the local lords.

The group of monks I was visiting were Shinto, which translates as 'the way of the gods' and is the pagan, nature-worshipping religion of Japan. All I could find were some details on their rituals and that they clothed themselves only in white robes. I also knew that the *yamabushi* brand of meditation is designed to allow followers to overcome even the strongest of elements: legend has it that a well-trained *yamabushi* was able to sit under powerful waterfalls even in the most freezing conditions. The same folklore told me a *yamabushi* could walk through flames and over burning coals without acquiring blisters. Where most men would fear extreme heights, a *yamabushi* could run along clifftops and mountain ridges. Unbelievably, *yamabushi* were also thought to

---

* Alongside their *shugendō* practices, most *yamabushi* sects tended towards the teachings of Tendai or Shingon Buddhism. Shingon is the primary sect of Esoteric Buddhism or *mikkyo*, whereby enlightenment is believed to be gained through isolation in nature, contemplation of oneself and the use of mandalas. Unlike other branches of Buddhism, this school also practises mystical and magical techniques of achieving enlightenment.

be able to survive being buried alive for at least a day, without succumbing to fear, panic or any of their inner demons.

I woke from a contemplative doze as the taxi went over a bump. I could see the first of the sacred mountains before me, the smallest, known as Haguro-san or 'the Crow Mountain'. I knew it was sacred to Kannon or, in Western terms, a personification of compassion. It was said to have been discovered by Prince Hachiko, the eldest son of the thirty-second emperor, Sushan, after a three-legged crow came to him in a vision during his meditation.

As I got out of the taxi, the scent and noise were overwhelming. The breeze brought a waft of sweet pine: fresh and light, a delicate warm balm to the senses after the stuffiness of the taxi. The whole street resounded with the noise of what I suspected was insects. It sounded like someone playing a kazoo, a deep whirring burr coming from the bushes and trees around me.

The neighbourhood was a bizarre mismatch of styles: some houses looked basic, rough and cheap, yet they were interspersed with stunning structures – pagoda-like layer cakes of dark wood and white plaster – that seemed to be from another era. It felt strangely like being on a film set. I stood outside the *shukubo* (the temple lodging), which was to be my home in the mountians. Its entrance was marked by a rope covered with 'thunderbolts' made of white paper – they resembled a stylised lightning flash, the paper folded into zigzags; I later learned that they were called *shide*. In front there was a beautiful garden, a sacred moat trickling from a fountain, flanked with bonsai and ancient statues.

The taxi had disappeared around the last bend in the road but I stood in indecision. Should I follow my heart up the Crow Mountain, or do the sensible thing and go inside? It was almost completely dark but I was prepared to do exactly what I knew I shouldn't. I was tired, hungry and thirsty but it wasn't far to the mountain path, maybe eight hundred metres, and I would be in the forest. I stashed my rucksack behind a large bush just inside the entrance to the *shukubo* and headed off.

For once, the signs were easy to follow. The road meandered, and I passed what appeared to be a small museum. I recognised a temple by its red gate and paper thunderbolts, fluttering eerily like startled birds. There was not another soul in the whole village; the only sounds were the incessant crickets and a persistent barking dog. I began to feel I was in a ghost town.

The imposing gate to the forest path was covered with paper thunderbolts. I knew the Shinto used them to signify the presence of *kami*, the nature spirits. The thunderbolts are placed around objects or in areas where the spirits are said to be present. It is said to be both a mark of respect and a warning of the power held there. As soon as I entered through the gates I was in front of one such object: a large stone with a rope around it, covered with the thunderbolts. I wondered if there was a spirit in the stone and took a few moments to see if I could sense something. Disappointingly, I couldn't.

Then it came home to me that I was actually standing at the foot of the first of the three sacred mountains, which were initially made sacred by En no Gyōja, the legendary founder of *shugendō*. A pilgrimage across the three sacred mountains was said to lead one to gain the magical powers of this tradition and I was about to embark on such a mission.

Something caught my eye: a glow in the dark, something that appeared unnatural in the forest. My heart raced. I felt like a frightened animal – I was exhausted, jet-lagged. Remember, fear is your friend, I told myself. It keeps you on your mettle and energises you. I peered past the trees, willing whatever it was to come into focus; from where I was standing it looked like a shimmering disc. I paused for a moment or two, then slowly made my way towards the apparition. As I got closer, I saw it was an illuminated sign on a narrow footpath, highlighting a map of the mountain, in Japanese and pidgin English:

Enter that Dewa Sanzan mountain, in fact the oldest sites of mountain worship in Japan. Mountains first open as religious center over 1400 years in 593 by Hachiko, Prince who was the first-born son of Emperor Sushun, 32nd emperor of Japan and reigning emperor at time.

Prince Hachiko looked like an Indian monk or yogi.

Prince Hachiko arrive 593 after flee the Soga clan upon the assassination of father. He devoted rest of his life to, eventually enduring difficult ascetic Shugendō exercises which led to his direct spiritual contact with Haguro Gongen, the deity of the mountain.

Following this, the prince began to stay at the Gassan (Moon) and Yudono (forbidden) mountains, establishing them as the centre of worship.

I decided to move forwards. By now it was pitch dark and before me was a winding flight of narrow slate steps. As I walked up them, I passed small wooden shrines with bells in them and what looked like gravestones adorned with Japanese writing. At the bottom of the stairs something felt different: the air was heavy and my heart started to beat faster. I walked forwards. What was the noise I was hearing aside from my heartbeat? Rushing water.

The air trembled with a tangible feeling of something powerful. As I took another step, it was before me looming out of the darkness: a tree of giant proportions, bigger than anything I had seen before in my entire life. Round its trunk there was a rope covered with thunderbolts. I stepped forwards to touch the sacred tree.

25

Over the Moon

◆

> *The moon is one, but on agitated water it produces many reflections.*
> *Similarly ultimate reality is one, yet it appears to be many in a mind*
> *agitated by thoughts.*
>
> Maharamayana

A monstrous sound, like a tree being felled by a thunderbolt, rico-cheted through my dreams and I sat bolt upright, heart pounding and breath coming in ragged gasps.

What was that noise – and where was I? It was very dark and I didn't have any idea how I'd got there.

More noises, this time coming from just outside – a shrill, keening yowl.

My whole body shuddered with a mixture of cold and fear but my eyes were beginning to adjust to the moonlit room. I could now see that I was on a very thin futon mattress placed on a *tatami* mat floor, the walls rice paper and bamboo. So, my brain clicked, I was in the temple lodgings, but how had I got there? I remembered being next to the tree on the mountain but nothing else. I shuffled forwards on my knees and reached out. Eventually I found a light switch.

Sitting on the floor, I gathered my thoughts: now I could remember a Japanese upset with me for walking into her house with my shoes still on and two young men in white martial-arts outfits. Had I walked all the way back from the mountain on autopilot, or was I just so jet-lagged that I had not woken up completely?

The scary noises had stopped but I felt ill and confused. I found myself beginning to cry but didn't know why. Maybe the high altitude or mountain air had something to do with it. More memories were slowly coming back. I wandered into the bathroom. It was three a.m. I remembered I *had* walked back, into a temple lodgings belonging to a family of Japanese dressed in white martial-arts uniforms. I had forgotten to take off my shoes, which, needless to say, had horrified them. The two younger men had seemed sinister and threatening.

I couldn't remember what had happened at the tree or how I had got to the room.

Tossing and turning on a thin mat on the floor, I could find no position that let me sleep. Sleep, though, wasn't on the agenda. A trumpet sound echoed through the room. The walls shook and I scrambled to my feet as a monk, clothed in white, appeared at the door. He was carrying a pile of white robes and a piece of paper, holding it at an angle so it was hard to read. It appeared to have some English phrases on it.

'Aremova uou cloving.'

I blinked hard, confused and disoriented. I had no idea what he'd just said. He repeated the phrase. I did nothing. 'Aremova uou cloving!' He was clearly exasperated. He pointed at me, then gestured to the robes in his hands.

Ah. He wanted me to remove my clothing.

I stripped to my underpants.

'Aremova uou cloving.' His expression didn't change a jot as he pointed at my pants.

I walked forwards to see what was written on the paper. 'Remove your clothing' was indeed the first phrase. Did I really have to be completely naked? It seemed so.

I was given a flap of white material (apparently my underwear) on a piece of string and shown how to tie it on, threading the material to make something that resembled sumo pants. Then he showed me how to put on various layers of ill-fitting clothing. The *hakama*, or trousers, came to just under the knee to meet a pair of sock-like items that tied on the calves. The jacket sleeves ended in something akin to arm warmers that tied just past the elbow. I added a pair of white *tabi* boots, then a type of bandana, tied in a complicated way that made me look as if I had devil's horns or, after my inept attempt at tying it, floppy rabbit's ears.

I was then fit to go. We walked through the *shukubo*. It was four a.m. and I was led to join a group of four other identically dressed people. I had been promised, via some very confused communication with the temple, that another person who spoke English would be attending the retreat, an academic from Tokyo who was studying the *yamabushi*. The group was all male, but the academic was a woman.

As I stood among the stern-looking men, I had never felt so out of place. No one smiled, and I had no idea what to do.

Suddenly there was a stirring within the group and everyone stood in line. Something was said loudly and I glimpsed a monk or priest at the front. I recognised him as the old man I had met at the *shukubo* who was obviously the head of the family at the temple. He was dressed just like us but with a larger, pointed headdress, and a kind of breastplate with four purple pompoms attached to the front. The other monks responded with an equally loud shout back – '*Okidamo!*' – and we started to march down the road.

It was only when I arrived at the foot of the imposing mountain that I realised how difficult this challenge might prove to be. Haguro-san is the first of the three mountains of Dewa Sanzan and at its summit stands Haguro-san Shrine, which holds the deities from all the mountains, making it the most important of the three. Although Haguro was the smallest of the mountains it was a marathon to me: I had jet-lag still and hadn't eaten for more than fourteen hours.

A group of us formed there, shuffling and blinking in the hazy dawn light. I was the only Westerner and the others looked curiously at me, some with a smile of surprise. Now there was a definite sense of unity or common purpose: each of us was clearly seeking to find something up the mountain or within ourselves. I took a moment to gather my thoughts and breathe in the refreshing mountain air – I was in Japan and this was it: if not the road to enlightenment, it was a damn good start.

A small stocky figure with a big smile stood up on a small grassy mound; behind him, through the trees, I could see a bright red temple.

He seemed very young – perhaps the son of the high priest I was staying with – but in the early-morning haze, with the headdress pulled low on his forehead, I couldn't be sure. The headdress looked like a pointed white hat with thunderbolts coming off it. Out of nowhere, a beautiful Japanese woman appeared next to me. She introduced herself with a smile.

'I am Jasmine. I am here to translate for you. It's . . . very early.'

I was about to sympathise when one of our group shouted something loud and unintelligible.

My translator whispered in my ear, 'Everything he says, do, and say, "*Okidamo*." OK?'

'What's *okidamo*?'

'Old Japanese. It means, "It will be done without question."'

Before I could respond, the priest at the front bellowed again.

'*OKIDAMO!*'

Everyone sat down and I hastily followed suit.

The master started to talk. My translator whispered to me what was being said. Insects continued their incessant whirr in an attempt to prevent me hearing.

'He says . . . it's a very hard thing to get the essence of *shugendō* . . .'

'OK.'

'He says . . . it's very hard to teach the art in such a limited time.'

I nodded.

'He says . . . perhaps you will sense something in the mountains.'

Pause.

'He talks about this being harder than Buddhist meditation.'

He spoke more, rapidly and forcefully, occasionally gesturing with the staff in his hand. Jasmine's eyes widened and she glanced sideways at me, with what looked like apprehension. 'He talk lots!'

Yep, he did indeed. The things buzzed and whirred.

She looked at me fearfully. 'Nature is your teacher – oh, this is going to be hard.'

'*Okidamo!*'

We all stood up and started walking. I wondered what he had said that took so long and was summarised in so few words.

As we started to climb the mountains, I tried to control my body and its responses so I could keep walking at the pace set for us. A man carrying a large staff with rings on it was at the front of the line, and at the back, a man with a bell. I was hungry, tired and shivering as we started walking up the steps I had explored the night before. Passing the tree was strange: once again, I felt a ripple of energy, a bit like the buzzing sensation you get from an electrical appliance that isn't sufficiently earthed. No one glanced or stopped to look at it but Jasmine remarked, 'Tree is over five hundred year old. Has a spirit in it.'

Well, that pretty much summed up what I had already felt. There was definitely a *kami* in residence.

We crossed a stone bridge with a stream running peacefully under it, beautiful in the morning light. Beyond, I could see a small waterfall with what looked like knives, blades and farming implements lying on the stones under the water. I peered closer: a ferocious figure with sharp teeth looked back at me. It resembled something from *Lord of the Rings*.

'Fudō-myōō,' a quiet voice whispered behind me. It belonged to one of the few women on the retreat other than my translator. She nodded in the direction of the brooding statue that was destined to be eternally beset by the beating of the waterfall. The statue was the one I had seen in the photograph in the book Bo had shown me all those years ago. Here I was again staring into the demonic eyes of Fudō-myōō, known as Acala in Sanskrit. His face expresses extreme wrath: he is frowning, left eye squinting or looking askance, lower teeth biting the upper lip. He has the physique of a corpulent child. He bears a *vajra* sword in his right hand, and a lariat or noose in the left. He is engulfed in flame, and seated on a huge rock base. His Sanskrit name literally translates as 'immovable wisdom king'. He originated from the Hindu deity Acalanātha ('immovable protector') and was absorbed into Chinese, then Japanese Buddhism, adopted, I guess, by the *yamabushi* within *shugendō*. The monks often carry a small representation of Fudō-myōō to use as a focus for contemplation.

We continued to climb, passing a teahouse further up the never-ending stone steps. I was desperate for a cup of steaming green tea but (a) the teahouse was closed and (b) there was no way we were stopping for tea. As we trudged onwards I noticed strange carvings on the stairs: some resembled *tengu* or goblins, others just Japanese pictograms; occasionally there were depictions of bread, *sake* or a bowl of rice – these, no doubt, were offerings or protective symbols. I whispered to Jasmine and she told me that along the way thirty-three figures were carved into the stone steps; they bring prosperity to anyone who can find them all. I wasn't sure if I had found any and at that moment I'd have settled for a bowl of rice.

We were all walking in silence. Suddenly, as if from nowhere, the monk who had instructed us appeared at my side.

Jasmine talked quickly, slightly out of breath. 'This Jonin Ekken. He will be your instructor. You need to imitate his example in all things.' As soon as she had finished talking, he was gone. Not even a handshake.

I could still hear the incessant chirping. I kept looking for a noisy bird or a giant cricket but could see nothing.

The steps went on and on and on. I could see Jasmine was struggling, and so were the couple in front of me. They seemed to be in their sixties, both short and rotund. They wheezed and coughed as they struggled over uneven stones and steps. Looks of disapproval from the austere monks at the front rippled back to us as the duo smiled at each other, pointed at sights and fiddled with each other's clothing – they were like a retired English couple hiking through the Lake District. Ahead, I could see a bald-headed boy or small woman, his or her scalp covered with scars, who seemed to glide over everything.

After what seemed like eternity, the route levelled out and the usual slabs of stone steps turned to giant cobbles, which were incredibly uncomfortable to walk on. I found myself going into a kind of trance with the pain and remembered Stephen Hayes's advice during medita-tion class in Dayton about having something to ignore when we are suffering or attempting to focus. Finally we stopped. I looked up and there it was, rising like a giant in the forest, the most beautiful wooden pagoda. It was the famous Gojū-tō, a five-storey structure. I was on one of the three sacred mountains, following a path of 2,466 stone steps to the summit of Haguro-san and now sitting among six-hundred-year-old sugi trees that soared more than two hundred feet to the canopy above. God knows what else I would experience along the way but I knew that we would eventually reach the Sanzan-Gosai-den Temple at the very top of the three peaks, which venerates the spirits of the collective mountains.

THE SACRED PAGODA

Before I could reflect more on the surreal nature of my situation, something was shouted both at the front and back of the line.

'*Okidamo!*'

Jonin and the head monks sat; we followed suit, getting into a meditative position.

'You sit still, look at the pagoda, think of the five levels.'

Everyone sat still. The cobbles were the size of dinner plates and dug in, making you uncomfortable in places you hadn't known existed. At the front of the group were four venerable *yamabushi*, Jonin in the centre. As they sat there, the wind blowing the trees behind them, they looked like statues.

Two of the younger monks on the outside of the four started to light lanterns and incense, which seemed to have appeared from nowhere. Everything seemed thought-out and precise. When they walked each footstep was gentle and perfectly placed. It took me a moment to realise that they were totally silent, gliding in their *tabi* boots with a lightness that reminded me of the jaguar at the zoo.

They looked perfectly relaxed, while we were all in discomfort. Almost all of us: just in front of me and to the right, the woman who had spoken to me earlier sat bolt upright, her eyes half closed and her body at rest. From my new vantage point, I noticed that, beneath the edges of her newly placed white headscarf, thick scars criss-crossed the base of her skull. I was intrigued. I knew I should be meditating but she was such a vision of abiding stillness.

I decided that I would follow the example set before me and focus on the mission, rather than just sit there suffering. I was going to focus on the pagoda and clear my mind of all other thoughts. I pushed my mind in that direction but extreme discomfort kept dragging me back. My body ached with hunger and tiredness. Gradually, though, the smell of pine, the distant sound of the waterfall and even the whirring things added to the mood and I managed to focus. The pagoda was all there was for me. Carved intricately, like the tiny versions I had seen made from cork in my grandparents' house, gathered from their travels to China and Malaya before the Second World War, it rose out of the forest like a daintily balanced layer cake. Each storey represents one of the five elements and their eventual unity. I inwardly contemplated earth, air, fire and wind, then drew them together to create the fifth, void.

A deep, haunting sound flooded the area and my eyes opened to see Jonin blowing into a giant conch shell. I had heard of these horns but never seen one before. I felt grounded and restored: the five levels had been balanced in me too.

The priest at the front gestured for us to stand and we followed him for a while to another teahouse. This time it was open and there was the distinct scent of rice cooking. Absolutely famished, we all lined up ready to eat.

'You can have bowl of rice, one of miso soup and two pickles.'

It didn't sound like a feast. I was feeling a bit irritable by the time I was just four people from the front of the queue, and my blood sugar had plummeted to the base of the mountain. That damn noise was really getting to me too. Finally I turned to Jasmine: 'What on earth *is* making that noise?'

'What noise?'

'The buzzing, whirring kind of noise all around us.' I did an impression.

'Ah!' She laughed, clapping her hands in delight at my bizarre rendition. 'That's beetle, *cicada*, drinks sap – might bite!' She giggled like one of the schoolgirls I had met on the train, covering her mouth, eyes wide like an anime cartoon.

That was that sorted then.

I was handed a bowl wrapped in white material with two chopsticks tied to it in a nice bow. I was informed that this package was going to be mine for the duration but I had the feeling there was no way it was ever going to look so pretty again under my care. I lined up and got a scoop of rice and a bowl of miso soup. Then I chose two pickles, both of which were red and tasted of vinegar mixed with bubble gum or rubber – but it was food and I was grateful. Everyone ate silently while looking at the view.

One of the group was not doing as well as the rest of us. He seemed ill and ate slowly. I asked Jasmine if he was OK. She told me she had met him the day before and that he was called Akira. 'He come from Tokyo and he's here because ninja training and *yamabushi* are close.'

Wow! An authentic Japanese ninja enthusiast! I had to find a way to talk to him.

Then the horn went again.

'Okidamo!'

We stood and lined up. Just one small flight of those 2,466 steps and there we were, at the top of Haguro-san. I felt like I was on top of the world.

Before us was the most beautiful temple housing the Shinto shrine of Gassai-den, inhabited by the deities of the three mountains, Tsukiyomi-no-Mikoto, Oyamatsumi-no-Mikoto, and Ideha-no-Mikoto. Flanked by two enormous statues of lion dogs, the building was captivating – I particularly liked the giant bell, which was about the size of a transit van with a battering ram set up to ring it. We gathered around to be instructed how ritually to wash our hands and mouth from a giant urn, before entering the temple for prayer.

Many of the locals and handfuls of tourists had come up by bus and gathered there. They seemed taken aback to see a Westerner dressed in *yamabushi* robes. Most of them laughed; some pointed.

Soon everyone began chanting. They all knew the words but me, so I just knelt and drank in the experience. I would quiz Jasmine later.

After the ceremony, Jonin Ekken stood up. Now that I had some blood sugar circulating, my memory had come online and I remembered 'Jonin' meant 'head' or 'boss' so it was not his first name. He talked, then Jasmine translated: 'We visit the pool now, sacred pool, has over five hundred bronze mirrors put into it from ancient times. It very important place.'

We were given a tour of the temple complex. Jasmine didn't translate a single word as it was all so fast.

As we approached the sacred pool, I noticed two statues of *yamabushi*, one wearing the white pilgrim robes like us and one in the full *yamabushi* uniform, which consisted of a blue and white chequered robe, with four purple pom-poms attached to the front. Bizarrely, they looked like me – a Westernised man with short-cut hair. The resemblance was uncanny, if not slightly comical. I was not the only one to notice: the woman with the shaved head also looked at the statues and made the comparison.

We then stood in front of the sacred pool and did nothing. My shoulder hurt and I felt faintly ill. I thought I knew how Akira from

Tokyo must be feeling. I looked at the shining water and a huge wave of nausea washed over me.

A tangible ripple went through the group: a *yamabushi* in full regalia appeared on the horizon, chequered robes and bright purple pom-poms, along with the sacred headwear that looks like a lacquered wooden bowl and contains the scriptures. He blew a conch horn three times.

Jasmine turned to me, fear in her eyes. 'It time for the trials of the four elements.'

26

Forbidden Knowledge

Prefer to be defeated in the presence of the wise than to excel among fools.

Dōgen

The thin rope flipped from side to side as we made our way along the narrow walkway. When it flipped, we flipped with it. Sections of the rope had been retied where it had previously snapped; some joins were wrapped with what looked like electrical tape. This was madness. It was tempting to look at the sheer drop to my left. Spiders as large as my palm crouched ominously in large, densely spun webs lodged in the foliage on the rock-face. Luckily, I didn't have a problem with spiders but, judging by the petrified look on her face, this was not Jasmine's favourite part of the journey so far. We were all soaked in dew and covered with webs from continual contact with ferns that unfurled and sprang from the mountainside. I had to adjust my position continually as we clambered over fallen trees. It was half mountain, half woodland, hard terrain to cover, and everyone was struggling. I even saw Jonin Ekken slip a couple of times.

On this kind of trek your body is on autopilot while the brain just registers the obstacles in the way. My mind drifted to my wife and daughter. What if I fell to my death?

Suddenly I recognised a noise on the edge of my hearing, a roar like machinery, an engine . . . Then it became a rushing torrent. A stream? No. It was a waterfall – our first trial. I'd known this was coming and I'd practised waterfall training in the mountains of Wales. I knew what to expect, but I was at such a low ebb that I found myself dreading it.

The waterfall is the most famous of all *yamabushi* trials and the one most associated with the ninja; in Japanese legend, and in modern fiction, you become a ninja through waterfall training. I also knew this had been part of the training of Takamatsu Sensei, the teacher of Masaaki Hatsumi, and that the black belts under Stephen Hayes valued it as a tool of self-improvement. As soon as I got a glimpse of the waterfall I knew this was going to be hard.

The flow was a giant, thin cascade of water – forty feet of pure power crashing onto a tiny platform, the violent rush of water at the top moving gravel and soil with it. I shivered. We travelled downwards and the waterfall shifted out of sight. As we manoeuvred the steep decline, sodden clods of earth fell away. The thin rope strained precariously as it was bearing the weight of us all and I'm sure we were all convinced it was going to snap.

We finally arrived at the basin and waded through the river to the base of the waterfall in all its glory. I realised I might have bitten off more than I could chew: the force of the water in the river alone was unbelievable, the people in front of me constantly backing out of the down-pouring tidal wave. I again found myself thinking of Hatsumi Sensei's teacher, Takamatsu. Legend had it that at one point he had found waterfall training so hard he had passed out and floated down the river.

The water foamed white and the roar was monumental, so much so that we couldn't hear each other speak. My translator tapped me on the shoulder – her headdress seemed to have washed away.

'Women go into back to change. Men, you go down to just underwear.'

Just underwear. Great. I was about to stand in a waterfall in front of loads of women with a small see-through flap of thin white material over my groin. This was going to be bad and, besides, how was I going to get out of this complicated uniform, never mind put it all back on?

I could still hear the whirr of the cicadas as I stripped down to what was effectively a see-through facecloth. As I was bigger than everyone else, it looked really silly.

I was about to focus on the challenge in hand when I had another worry: my tattoo. During my last visit to Japan at the bathhouse in the *ryokan* in Noda, I'd discovered that tattoos were frowned upon. What would the *yamabushi* think of the lotus flower on my chest? The women reappeared in white swimming costumes with big robes. The girl with the shaved head and scars came up to me. I realised she had only one hand. She frowned, pointed at my chest and said something. I asked Jasmine to tell her that tattoos didn't have the same connotation in England, that I wasn't a Yakuza and that the lotus flower was on my chest to remind me to keep my heart pure, no matter what.

Jasmine relayed all this to her.'

'Did that reassure her?'

Jasmine gave the hand-over-mouth giggle and shook her head. 'Martin, she didn't mention your tattoo. She was saying you had sunburn and was worried!'

Her name was Meyoke, and she was a Buddhist nun. Meyoke spoke to me in her best English: 'Like in English. Me,' she pointed at herself, 'you,' she pointed at me, 'key!' This was followed by a key-turning gesture.

'Pleased to meet you, Meyoke. I'm Martin.'

Jasmine turned to her. 'Martin-san.'

She bowed. So did I, then she did again. Then the horn blew.

I watched as, one at a time, those in the row before me took the test. Arguably it didn't appear that much of a 'test' at first: they just jumped in and equally quickly stepped out. However, they were then 'encouraged' back in by our guide and his friends. This continued with each person until they were exhausted. The real masters stood in the plunging cascade and then sat down . . . for ages. When you are devoid of clocks and phones, time becomes increasingly hard to estimate.

My turn came and my body tensed in anticipation. Standing in front of the waterfall, preparing myself mentally, I felt that it represented everything negative that stood in my way, everything that pushed me away from my spiritual calling and prevented me from living my life as I wanted to. I thought of the frustrating situations I had been caught up in and resolved to overcome them. I would stay in the flow; the water element would not defeat me. I would become a force of pure fire and the waterfall would be nothing compared to my heat. I performed the ninja hand gesture I'd been taught in Dayton by Stephen Hayes, the full fire *kuji* combined with visualisation. I imagined myself as a being of pure, unstoppable fire, heat and flame; a brightly burning god of combustion.

I opened my eyes for a moment and then, quite literally, took the plunge. The first thing I experienced was the sheer slicing cold, then the pressure. I gasped, the air forced from my lungs as the water beat and slapped against me like a hundred paddles. It felt as though a thousand little needles were firing into me and I had to sit down as my legs started to give way. I kept performing the fire *kuji*, held the visualisation in my mind and kept the hand grasped with the middle fingers joined as two circles. For a while, I just felt pressure. I had expected it to feel constant, like a giant hose, but instead it came in waves, like thousands of hands slapping on my back. All of a sudden, a big slap would knock me sidewise and some hit so hard that they forced my eyelids open. I broke my grip and stopped my visualisation to put my hands over my eyes and protect them. In an instant, I was cold; so cold that it felt like pain.

WATERFALL TRAINING

The slapping feeling was relentless and stung horribly. I struggled to breathe but there was no space between my face and the water, so I lowered my head to a pocket of air, which meant the water was breaking on the back of my head. My eyes stung and everything hurt; my entire body was shouting at me to get out of the water. I continued to resist and found myself counting the movements of my arms as I mastered the fire *kuji* again, imagining my body getting hotter, my blood flowing like lava and my whole being radiating heat. My mind became completely focused on the idea of channelling fire.

I don't know why, but at this point my eyes opened and right before me a rainbow formed. A feeling of calm realisation spread over me and I was reminded that the ninja is he 'who endures': this training, to the Japanese, obviously makes you a ninja because you learn to endure the waterfall.

Then a voice and a hand pulled me from my meditation. 'Martin-san, time to come out.'

I staggered out of the freezing channels and lay on the rocks, too tired and cold to move, but I had overcome the waterfall.

As I lay there, dazed, I heard peals of laughter and splashing. I turned my head to see what all the commotion was and witnessed something amazing. Meyoke was taking her test, but she was doing it with a giant smile, jumping in and out of the icy torrent like a little girl playing with a hosepipe. Smiling, splashing and just having fun.

There was I, so proud of my ability to stay under the waterfall without giving in, that I had forgotten: why endure when you can enjoy?

The horn sounded and one '*okidamo*' later we were on the go, this time taking a different route. It circled tree after tree until it led us back to the top in no time at all.

At the end of the path we found a small straw shack and a stand with drinking water. The hut was a kind of medieval bivouac with a solid thatch but a modern door that looked completely out of place. It had a sign on it in Japanese but I was more interested in getting something to drink. I made no move to ask but instead tried to jostle towards the front of the queue but failed as everyone else had had the same idea. It's a really strange feeling being soaked and thirsty at the same time.

Without a word everyone started to shuffle into the hut, this time no horn, instruction or bellowed '*okidamo*', just a mass shuffling, heads down in a resigned and sad manner. It was as if a microchip had been activated in everyone's head. Maybe I was still reeling from being assaulted by huge volumes of freezing water but there was a distinctly surreal feel to it all.

The masters sat down on a little wooden stage at the back of the hut while the rest of us sat on the soil floor.

'Fire trial,' Akira mouthed at me, as we collapsed next to each other.

I looked around. I couldn't see how this was going to work. I'd read that for the fire trial the *yamabushi* walked on flames or lit a circular fire and sat in the centre to learn how to endure the heat – in a sense the reverse of the waterfall trial. Once they had mastered this, they would make bigger fires and run through the flames.

So, were they going to set fire to us all? I was beginning to get a bit nervous and it was certainly getting warmer. I could hear the sound of fire crackling but could see nothing. Thick white smoke started to fill the room, coming from the front. Maybe it was incense. It smelt a bit like pine needles burning but everything smelt of pine here.

Then it hit me and, by the groaning and coughing, it had hit everyone else at the exact same time. I had an inkling it was chilli smoke because my eyes were burning. If you've ever accidentally rubbed your eye while cooking with chillies you'll understand how I felt. Everyone was coughing and choking, crumpling their robes in front of their faces in an attempt to shield themselves from the pungent, almost noxious fumes. Tears were streaming down everyone's faces, yet the masters at the front sat in total calm. The temperature in the room started to rocket and a fierce crackling broke out as the fire took hold. My skin itched as the smoke mixed with the damp. I started to sweat. All the sensitive parts of the body started to respond as if chilli was being rubbed on them, but the worst pain was on my back. It was as if a river of chilli lava was flowing down my spine. The heat reached a new intensity, I began to feel a new level of pain – sweat, water and chilli equalled that of a moderate acid bath.

Without thinking, I found myself using the *kuji* for wind. I imagined myself as a creature of the air, surrounded by pure oxygen and able to breathe freely.

I stopped struggling and sat in a state of serenity as my contemporaries had to remove themselves from the hut. To me there was only a breeze and a calm, light feeling. I could smell the chilli but it no longer hurt me. In the end, only the masters and I remained in the room as the chilli burnt itself out.

After our trial by chilli, everything stopped. Other members of the group were either sitting down or lying on the floor. I had no idea why we were just hanging around or what was going on. Jasmine lay with her eyes shut; she had taken part in both trials. In the end, I gave in and rested. Everything still stung from the chilli. I found myself rubbing my nose with leaves or grass to try to stop the pain. The edges of my mouth and deep in my ears itched painfully. Soon, however, the silence and gentle breeze allowed me to slip into a state of peace.

Then, unexpectedly, the horn sounded again and we were off.

'*Okidamo!*'

'It's time to go!' Jasmine yelled.

I'd just started to drift off and jerked awake.

We stood up, groaning, like zombies coming to life in a graveyard. We were exhausted, hungry and didn't smell too sweet; the sour odour of fasting sweat made me feel faintly nauseous.

We continued our trek up the mountain and I reflected on the methods I had used. The element that had helped me in each trial was not the element the trial was connected with: fire to heat water, wind to blow out fire. Was I cheating? Should I have used water to cool fire? We were headed for the second peak. I knew that this was going to involve the 'wind' test and that this mountain was viewed as even more holy than the previous one.

By this time, the day was getting on. I had no way of telling the exact time but I could see the sun was low in the sky.

We walked along a short pathway to an area of grassland with large stones, on which Japanese poems were written.

I tried to talk to Meyoke and Akira but they wanted to trudge along in a kind of walking sleep. So that was what we all did, just walked and itched, covered with sweat, chilli smoke and dirt. The pain and fatigue were such that I had to distract myself to keep going. I counted my steps, urging myself to 'just do another hundred'. I tried to remember things from school, poems and song lyrics. Pushing myself to take another step, to go another few rocks ahead, to think about how close we must be.

As we walked along increasingly tough terrain, with sheer drops that loomed at the side, I was apprehensive. The wind trial tradition-ally practised by the *yamabushi* involves hanging upside down from a rope on the side of a cliff while confessing your sins. Alternatively, you can sit on the very edge of a sheer drop and face the fear of death. Remembering the rope used in the woodland climbing range near the waterfall, I was worried about the safety of the whole thing.

The sun had dropped beneath the mountain and it was getting dark; I really wanted to sleep. It seemed like for ever before the line finally stopped. The rest of my fellow travellers were in some kind of trance, stretching body parts that had been subjected to freezing cold water, then almost roasted in a chilli-infused sweat lodge. Yawning, we shuffled towards an area of incongruous black tarmac in the middle of a wooded area.

Ekken shouted very loudly: 'We play *tengu sumo* and then we sleep.' Jasmine made a hand-clapping movement while standing like an American football player.

'*OKIDAMO!*'

Everyone moved with speed. I suspect many needed a 'comfort break' but I needed sleep.

It was now completely dark and, as usual, the cicadas were going mad, whirring and chirruping deep in the surrounding foliage. We were outside a large concrete room, like a training hall on the edge of the mountain. We were led inside to be greeted by a ring made of very thick rope. It looked just like the sumo wrestling rings I had seen on TV. I really didn't want to do any wrestling and had no idea what *tengu sumo* was, although, of course, *tengu* were goblin creatures with beaks like crows, and were said to be vain, selfish, capricious tricksters. Legend has it that ninja evolved from *tengu* or that *tengu* trained ninja. Sumo, of course, is a form of wrestling we all know well – giant fat men push each other outside a ring made of rope. I didn't know the rules but could see that something similar was about to happen.

TENGU

We were instructed to sit in meditation in the hall. White dust surrounded the area and the whole place smelt strongly of freshly cut grass. We all sat as if to meditate but I was too far gone. I was itchy and tired, so I just sat and suffered while I could see balls of rice being unpacked at the back of the hall. I didn't want to fight anyone: I ached all over.

The horn was blown and a *yamabushi* in full robes appeared and stood in the ring. He spoke.

Jasmine appeared next to me and hissed, 'He says because we are all dead we have to fight demons to get back to the material world.'

'The rules are, you need to push, throw or slap the person out of the ring. To get a rice ball for dinner you have to win a match. The grand champion will get a prize. The champion gets a special *yama-bushi* bag, a pilgrim's bell and a fish meal.' Jasmine bounced excitedly.

I blinked. Where on earth had she got a second wind from? She gave me a nervous smile and a blink back. I did not want to do this. In total, there were twenty or more of us. The tournament would go on for ever.

We sat in a circle around the ring. The head *yamabushi*, whom I didn't recognise, stood in the middle. Beside me sat the couple who were on the retreat together, I looked at them and re-estimated their age. They must have been fifty-something, yet both had almost permanent fixed cheeky smiles. The husband had positioned his *yamabushi* headdress to make it look like goats' or large devil's horns, which they obviously found faintly hilarious because the wife kept readjusting it and giggling wildly.

The master started to choose one person at a time, starting with the men. His first choice was a very old man indeed, who must have been in his late seventies or early eighties. He was paired, rather unfairly, against a younger man who was a bit overweight. The elderly man's hair hung like a limp mop and his slim frame strained as he stood and made his way to the ring. Nevertheless, they bowed perfunctorily to each other and salt was thrown in the air. The match was on.

I was shocked by the pure fighting spirit displayed. It seemed that a seventy-year-old Japanese man, who is starved, tired and thirsty, fights like an angry wolverine. From my viewpoint, there was very little slapping going on but lots of shoving, throwing and general argy-bargy.

I had no idea how the score was kept but those who won had to fight again and those who lost were matched against another loser for a second go. I just sat back in a sense of awe. The old guy had fought like a firework going off, just like the seventeen-year-old lads at the Lowestoft boxing club. Soon, though, in my famished state, it all became a bit of a blur and I must have dozed off for a while, only coming to when I heard my name being called. Adrenaline kept me awake.

'Martin-san!'

I hauled myself to my feet, dizzy with hunger and thirst, but the thought of getting through this bout and one step closer to supper spurred me on to win. My companions gave a rousing cheer, which also had a sound of foreboding. I lift weights every day and they could see I was bigger than most other people were.

A Japanese man of about forty with a small moustache stood before me, perfectly upright and stoic. The horn blew. I picked him up by his left leg, lifted him off the floor and slammed him to the ground. I was instantly declared the winner and asked to sit down – game definitely on!

As the matches continued, they got increasingly vicious. People really started slapping each other and an elite started to form.

A very tall Japanese man, who looked like Lurch from the *Addams Family* films, won every match he fought, simply by hugging his opponent and walking him back out of the ring. The devil-horns man, who sat next to me, was a crazy contestant: he ran away from his opponent and jumped around the room, continually cracking jokes; after a prolonged chase his opponent slipped up and set his foot outside the ring. Clearly there was method in Devil Man's madness. Then there was Akira, who simply slapped the living daylights out of everyone.

The matches continued far longer than I had hoped. It seemed that everyone had to fight *everyone*. Luckily, it didn't turn out like that, and Jasmine, Meyoke and the more elderly members of the group were exempt from the competition.

I continued using my winning tactic of what the wrestlers call a 'groin pick', which involves diving down towards the opponent's leg with my head on the outside and wrapping my arms around the top of the person's leg. Then with one powerful lift from the legs, I would bring them off their feet and lift high in the air, slamming them hard into the ground. The others, seeing this, were suitably filled with fear and that certainly helped my mission to win.

Four of us ended up in a kind of knock-out match. We'd all fought so many times we could hardly function. When you play a game like this you pick up injuries that are often unnoticeable at the time but later make themselves known. My left hand had been crushed at one point and my face had what looked like a carpet burn from the rough fabric of a robe. None of the four of us had lost; we all had our own unique tactics. Lurch bear-hugged, Akira slapped, 'Devil Man' dodged and ran circles round us and I slammed!

The burning question now was, who would win?

29

The Heart Sutra

❖

Gone, gone, gone beyond, gone completely beyond, awakened, so be it!

The Heart Sutra

The four of us stood solemnly in the ring. The rest watched with the fascination of those who know that, after a hard day, they don't have to fight any more. In retrospect, I think they were also reanimated by the knowledge that they would be fed when the fight was over. I looked at them as I stood awaiting my next opponent. I really wanted to win. Not just to prove something or gain respect, but for two very important other reasons: the winning of the tournament would represent a triumph over my inner demons and would symbolically show mastery of myself. More than that, though, something drove me to put it all on the line: I was really, really hungry and I wanted that fish supper!

Suddenly, the rest of the pilgrims were chanting and clapping. As the four of us stood in the ring and bowed to each other, a command was given and, to my utter incredulity, rice balls with mushrooms and other vegetables were handed out and everyone started munching happily – everyone but us finalists. Next to me I heard Lurch's stomach rumble.

The first match was me against Akira. I was prepared to be slapped. I looked at him and he stared back, madly and aggressively.

'Okidamo!'

The match started and all hell broke loose. I was too slow to do my normal 'grab the leg' routine and was hit with a resounding slap on the ear that knocked me for six. I grabbed at his arm instinctively to stop the slapping but he slapped my hand so hard that I let go. He delivered a flurry of slaps so hard and fast that I instinctively backed off. I couldn't believe I was ducking down and covering up at the same time, seriously on the run. I was going to lose.

I grabbed at him but failed, merely shoved him away, which only gave him space to hit me more. His finger or thumb jabbed me in the eye. Pain and tears blinded me. I wanted to back out and lose because I was sick of the fight but then something came over me. Rage! Total uncontrolled killer rage. I saw red in a way I never had before in my life – it was like a dream or possession. I pulled myself up, arms arced, and shouted in pure anger. The Incredible Hulk had nothing on me at that moment. It was so primeval that Akira stopped in his tracks and looked on in complete shock. In that moment I gave him the most solid slap I could muster, thrown with the whole body, like a claymore swinging to take someone's head off. I finished it with the heel of my hand to the side of his jaw.

Akira was stunned. The crowd was silent and I took the opportunity to pick him up by his left leg and slammed him into the ground.

Everyone went crazy – a 'Japanese wave' broke out, arms flailing in all directions and excited chatter that rivalled the incessant whirring of the cicada, which carried on regardless of our mortal combat.

We were both checked for injury, then sat down to watch the next match.

Next up was 'Devil Man' vs 'Lurch'. I did my best to discover their real names when they were called up but the Japanese was way too fast.

As they stood facing one another it dawned on me that I would have to face the winner. Lurch was tall and heavy. After the sudden anger in the last match, I felt totally spent, nothing left. It was late and I was beyond hungry and thirsty. 'Please win, Devil Man. I don't think I can lift Lurch.' I repeated this like a mantra.

'*Okidamo!*'

Match on and Devil Man looked older than I'd first thought but he cracked a huge smile, made a convoluted clapping motion and shouted something in Japanese.

Jasmine called to me from across the room: 'This is a playground joke. It means he distract him to get away or play a trick on him.' I nodded but saw concern flash across her face, her eyes scrolling down me. My robes were ripped and I had only one arm left on my tunic.

I heard a roar from the crowd, and when I looked back, my heart sank. Devil Man was in some kind of bear hug but upside down. With a big grin, he was trying to grab at the legs of his giant opponent. He made a mock tickling motion and walked a bit on his hands before he was carried and unceremoniously dumped out of the ring.

Oh, God . . .

I ran my hand wearily over my face. Why the hell had I signed up for this?

As we were called up, I found myself almost vibrating with fear. The man looked like a monster and I was shaking; I wasn't sure if it was just fear, lack of blood sugar or sheer exhaustion, probably a deadly combination of all three, and now I had to fight something that resembled one of the six-hundred-year-old trees we'd passed.

My hands were shaking so much that it must have been plainly visible to everyone. I felt embarrassed and that didn't help either. Sometimes when you're under pressure, inner demons come to attack you and a horrible one reared its head. Was I about to wet myself, or worse, in front of the whole group? I felt dizzy. My heart was pounding, and bile was rising in my throat.

'*Okidamo!*'

I heard the command to fight through an increasingly disorienting ringing in my ears. I shouted unconsciously and lunged at his leg. What was I doing? I would never lift him. There was no way I could do it normally, let alone when I was so tired. It was as if my whole body was on autopilot. As I thought about letting go and shoving him, I felt myself lift with all my might, as if he was a rag doll in my arms. His hips were at my head level; he kicked and struggled in an attempt to get free and I felt a stinging blow to my head. As I slammed him to the floor, my arm crumpled under him and a nauseating, ripping and popping tore through my shoulder. I rolled to the side and used what was left of my already depleted strength to pull my arm away.

I moved the shoulder to see if it was still working and there was a sickening crunch as it slotted back into place. I stood up and people crowded round Lurch to make sure he was OK. I'd won. I was the *yama-bushi tengu sumo* champion! I smiled inside. I was going to get a fish to eat and a special champion bag. I felt like a kid at a school tournament.

Jasmine summoned me to stand next to her. The head *yamabushi* was speaking, 'The winner due to knee touching floor is Yamamoto Hung!' The crowd roared and Lurch, or Yamamoto, raised his enormous tree-branch arms in jubilation. What? I was incredulous. I'd won fair and square . . . or so I'd thought.

Jasmine tapped my arm and whispered, 'Rules say your knees can't hit floor and your knee did when you picked him up.'

I was confused. Had I just been cheated? Could they not stand the idea of me winning? And I was *so* hungry. The 'champion' was given his ball of rice and bag but no fish dinner I could see. I got a ball of rice.

Then something horrible happened. The *yamabushi* called Jasmine up and as he spoke she translated: 'Four champions come forth.'

The other two finalists stood up.

'We have four people who didn't win a match. They are hungry.'

They went to Yamamoto. It was clear they were asking him if he would sacrifice his meal for someone else. He looked as if he was about to break down in tears and, to be honest, I felt like joining him.

'*Hai*.' He handed his rice ball to one of the older men.

I sighed as they turned to me. 'Will you give so your strength helps the weak and unlucky?'

'*Hai!*' My dinner was whisked away.

My stomach rumbled hideously in protest. I had been so sure that we would be given a giant meal as a reward for our generosity. We can't possibly do this much exercise without food! We'll end up in hospital at this rate! All the unlucky victors complied with the request and handed over the grub.

Then it was over. I just knew I was going to get some big reward: that fish supper must have been cooked for someone. After a small delay, two very large oil lamps were lit and put on the end of heavy metal poles.

Ekken talked.

I listened carefully. I was sure I heard the Japanese word for 'rice' in there.

'He says it's time for "moving air" trial and that we should walk to edge of mountain in line.'

At this time of night? I was feeling like I was beginning to lose the plot. 'Are we not sleeping here?'

'Yes, we sleep here to protect against bears.'

'But not now?'

I was getting really annoyed – almost delirious with lack of food, sleep and a distinct sense of misery.

'*Okidamo!*'

We dutifully lined up and it was then I discovered what the lamps were for: one was carried at the front of the line, the other at the back. This was supposed to light the way but it merely lit it for the two people at the front and back of the queue. There were twenty of us, which left sixteen unenlightened.

We walked along crumbling rocky paths that endlessly undulated and wove upwards. There was no carved-out route so we were constantly stumbling up or down. If you fell or stumbled, your hands were cut on the stone and I was constantly bumbling into someone. By the time we got to where we were being led, I was cut and bruised.

'Here is meditation peak.' Ekken had spoken in English, which made me jump.

I looked at the peak and, to my horror, it was at the end of a length of rock that was less than the width of my shoulders. It was not very long, perhaps ten big strides to the end, but in the dark it seemed a huge challenge. The wind was getting up and I started to wonder if I would be blown to my death. Everyone sat down and started talking but all I could hear was the wind howling.

Each of us was given the chance to crawl to the end of the peak and sit until the horn blew. I was the first to be chosen.

The moon lit the way perfectly and I could see the stretch of rock silhouetted like a silver road before me; a jagged walkway made of spikes of rock that reflected in the moonlight. I looked back and everyone was watching me attentively. I couldn't help but think, 'They're all just waiting to see if you fall, Martin.'

I crawled along the edge, shards of razor sharp rock scraping through my robe, which was rapidly becoming covered with twigs, slimy moss and even some long-dead thorns – none of which left me feeling confident. The very top of the ridge, though, appeared dry and, though spiky, was easy to grip. As soon as I eased my hands to the side, I discovered that also was wet and coated in slime. As I looked over the edge, I couldn't judge how far the drop was, but whenever I dislodged something, I could hear it bounce off the cliff, each contact of rock on rock reverberating around the mountain. It was definitely a long drop. My shoulder was killing me: each stretch pulling me towards the peak yanked at an already exhausted and inflamed muscle.

As I got closer to the end, the area widened, but fear was rising: would the peak hold me? I knew the fears were illogical and that in truth the Yamabushi had set the situation so there was no real risk, but rather a challenge to the mind, but in that moment a flood of negativity started to overcome me. I reached the precarious outcrop and gingerly sat cross-legged almost at the very edge. It was completely dark beyond, but a canopy of stars and the ever-watchful moon gave me just enough light to see. The height made me feel slightly dizzy; the wind was a pleasant breeze, which was fine at first, but then it began to buffet me. I was terrified. I had to keep my head. If fear overcame me, I might do something stupid and lose my concentration and co-ordination. A gust of wind buffeted me again, this time from a different direction. It was terrifying not knowing in which direction I would be pushed next. I was afraid to over-adjust my position in case I fell. Over the edge there was only darkness, a bottomless pit. Nevertheless, I felt some relief when I could hear others coming behind me and sitting near to me.

I started my earth *kuji*, nerve-racking because it involved moving my hands above my head, but I carried on and began to realise that the wind was nowhere near as strong as I had thought. It would never harm me. I understood that this was a challenge of fear, not of reality. If someone put a plank of the same width on the floor, I would be able to walk along it with ease.

A lovely feeling of calm came over me and seemed far more powerful than any winds or elements buffeting me up there on the cliff. Then, unbidden, my feelings of serenity and confidence swung back to terror. I worried that if I felt too calm, and became too confident, I might fall. This fluctuation between calm and terrified continued for a while. I remained alert but not over-emotional, trying not to over-process my thoughts and, eventually, I settled down.

At last the horn blew. I had defeated the wind element. I stood up and calmly walked back along the route I had crawled. And then I saw what looked like a crumpled robe similar to mine at the bottom of the same deep crevice just to the side. Had someone previously been too hungry, tired or confused to make the walk safely? Why would I put myself at such risk when I had a family to support? I looked again and as my eye adjusted I could see it was only a light-coloured rock reflecting in the moonlight.

Soon the command came for us all to return, this time in a line with a teacher at the front and back.

Okidamo!

People were so tired that they were practically sleep-walking. I couldn't help but mull over my fears. I could understand the concept of facing falls but not while thirsty, tired, and in the dark it was really hard to keep positive. It was almost impossible for me to control my confused emotions. This was just plain madness.

I held my tongue and brooded. Why did they make me give away my dinner? What lesson could it have taught me, other than that it pays not to try? Anger rose inside me. This was *really* stupid and I was going home. There was no wisdom in these mountains. As my negative emotions rose, for a moment I felt like I'd been seduced by the culture and promises of enlightenment.

As we staggered back, I found myself glaring at Yamabushi Ekken and his son.

When we finally got back to the hall, we were each given a mat to put on the floor. I went to sleep in an instant but woke up to the stench of twenty unwashed people who had walked all day. Nausea rose in me and every sound jarred my frazzled nerves. An old man was snoring and I felt like throttling him. I was so hungry that I was permanently angry and wired. How could I not sleep when I was so exhausted?

Eventually I dozed, only to wake again in a state of uncontrollable restlessness. I was at the end of my tether – was I about to go mad on the mountain?

30

Journey into the Underworld

◆

*We all have inner demons to fight. We call these demons 'fear', and
'hatred', and 'anger'. If you don't conquer them, then a life of a hundred
years . . . is a tragedy. If you do, a life of a single day can be a triumph.*

Yip Man

I felt as if I had woken up within minutes of going to sleep. I was
still thinking of sheer drops and *tengu sumo*. Everything seemed
very different in the daylight. Around me, my fellow *yamabushi* were
still slumbering. I was in what I had assumed was the training hall
but it was not just a hall, it was a house. Unlike the *shukubo*, this was
a proper concrete house with a kitchen, stairs and even carpets. Last
night the plain wooden doors were closed; today they were flung open
so I had a view of the other rooms. Light was streaming through
the windows. I decided to get up and explore and went in through the
main doorway. To my surprise, the door didn't have hinges: it slotted
into the doorway. When an opening was required, the door was merely
removed and laid on the floor.

I navigated the house silently and cautiously; the last thing I wanted
to do was wake someone up or walk into a room I was not supposed
to. I had no idea which room the teachers were sleeping in. The
corridor was lined with green *tatami* mats. On one wall there was a
felt picture of two anthropomorphised white rabbits fighting with
hammers. They were using grain mallets, used for powdering rice. I
knew the second mountain – Gassan, or 'Moon Mountain' – was
sacred to the rabbit so perhaps this was a Shinto myth or symbol.

The main living area had the sliding door open and a faint light on, so I walked in. It was large and airy but the roof was very low. The same green *tatami* mats covered the floor, and a couple of tables with cushions were placed at one end, no doubt left over from dinner.

On the far wall a big wooden altar was covered with a cloth. It was positioned under a kind of gate made from sacred rope constructed with twisted straw, known as a *shimenawa*, with the now familiar *shide* or white-paper lightning bolts hanging from it. The rope indicates that the area is a sacred space for the gods. All sorts of items stood on the altar: a classic *kamidana* (house shrine or 'seat of the gods') plus the usual accoutrements, most of which I recognised as they were similar to what I had seen in the shrine at the Quest Center in Dayton. Vases filled with evergreen leaves, pots containing ritually purified *sake*, jars of water and a dish of salt. I recognised a *bonten*, a phallic symbol of creation used in some of the rituals.

In the half-light, I noticed something else: someone appeared to be looking back at me from behind the altar. The face resembled that of Prince Hachiko, the Indian who had opened the mountain, but as I leaned closer it reminded me of a mummified body. I knew the *yamabushi* had evolved by incorporating many different influences, Buddhism, Daoism and other religious forms, until they emerged recognisably in the medieval period as what we now call *shugendō*. However, this figure, of what seemed to me a demonic Indian yogi sitting in a meditation position, seemed out of place in Japan. I continued to stare at it, transfixed.

'Immortal Teacher.'

I swung round. In the doorway stood a young boy dressed all in white. He was carrying huge rucksacks, four or five of them. It was first thing in the morning and the sun was behind him, obscuring my view of his face.

He pointed at himself. 'Teacher Priest's son.'

Following my line of vision, he glanced towards the rucksacks. There was a pause, and then he said, 'England. Thank you.'

I had no idea what he meant, but it seemed nice.

He bowed. So did I, lower than him. He looked confused and bowed again even lower.

'*Watashi wa o namae wa Martin Faulks desu.*' I used what little Japanese I knew.

He looked a bit confused but, after a pause, pointed again at himself. 'Hibiki.'

It was then I finally recognised him. He was Ekken's son. I had seen him after the *tengu sumo* the night before. Now he walked into the room and pointed at all the photos on the wall, high up near the ceiling. They featured generations of *yamabushi* all dressed in perfect white robes standing before a temple. He pointed to a picture of all three mountains. 'You go walk three mountain. Buddha Kannon is Haguro, Buddha Amida is Gassan Mountain, and Buddha is Dainichi yudola san.'

It took me a few moments to understand what he was saying, as he was using Japanese sentence structure yet talking in English. He was telling me that the first mountain was sacred to the many-armed female Buddha of compassion, and that the second mountain was dedicated to Amida, the Buddha of rewards for good actions. The third and final one was sacred to Dainichi Buddha, the cosmic divine golden Buddha of your full potential.

'Autumn Peak.' He gestured at another picture.

It showed a procession of resplendently dressed *yamabushi* carrying a portable altar decorated with flowers up the mountain on the very pathway I had walked a few hours ago. It looked like a funeral, with a man wearing a giant bonnet holding the *bonten* staff I had seen at the front of the altar and with the surrounding *yamabushi* blowing conch shells.

'*Shugenja* is you, person who just start training.'

This was starting to sound useful.

'Can you help me understand the training that's to come?'

He paused for a moment.

I said: 'Just quickly explain what is going to happen and give me some advice.' English speakers were a rare thing so I knew I should take advantage of him being there. I could see he was thinking.

'You come special place.' He walked to the door and put on some white *tabi* to match his white uniform. I put my muddy shoes back on, which now didn't match what I was wearing in any way.

'Very secret.'

He smiled at me in such a way that I couldn't understand if he was playing with me or not. We circled around the *shukubo* and into the woods. We walked for a while through the trees, and all the time he looked a bit irritated. I was finding the emotions of the Japanese hard to gauge and his seemed to change in the blink of an eye. As we came to a very small clearing in the undergrowth he took a mobile phone out of his pocket.

High in the mountains, we seemed closer to the sun and the light was perfect. Before me, there were six beautiful stone statues, which initially looked like women standing in a semi-circle, some with many arms. Or were they metal? In the light, I couldn't tell, but they didn't seem to have any shelter, which made me wonder why they had not rusted. Hibiki had stopped fiddling with his phone and pointed at them. 'The dummy.' He paused and frowned. He knew his English wasn't right. 'The model people.' He looked at me for help.

'Statues?'

I suspected he was using his phone for translation.

He nodded excitedly, 'Yes! Statues. Bodhisattva Kannon, or Avalokitesavara. People pray to Kannon for peace and tranquillity in this life, in each of the six realms. Do English man know six realms?'

I shook my head. 'Like the five elements?'

'Connected to elements, there six realms.'

He paused to fiddle with his phone, which beeped and chirped at him. As it moved, the angle caught the sunlight and blinded me. For a few moments I couldn't see anything.

'This very old statues, old order, old way, little different than in books.' He thought for a while.

I was about to ask him how it differed, when he carried on. 'Listen careful to six realms.'

I made sure he could see I was going to be quiet and pay close attention. It was hard to hear what he was saying over the incessant rhythm of the cicadas.

'Six realms are hell realm, hungry ghost realm, animal realm . . .'

He paused, looking at the statues again. 'Human realm, junior god realm, heaven or god realm.'

So, devils, ghosts, animals, humans, demigods, then gods. Seemed similar to images of the 'other worlds' in Western religions.

'Don't be confused Mar'in.' He smiled, suddenly looking old beyond his years.

'Martin,' I corrected him, and immediately felt pedantic. His English was infinitely better than my Japanese.

'True both ways.'

I had no idea what he meant.

'Think real.'

He'd totally lost me now.

'Real people.'

Blank look. This was getting embarrassing.

Then something happened as he started to explain each realm in detail and I began to realise something. The words were broken and confused but, using a form of philosophical charades, the message unfolded loud and clear. Later when I returned to England, I read more about this fascinating subject.

The realms were not distant spiritual places or, at least, if they were, it was, as he said, 'true both ways'. The categories were tendencies in human nature and each statue was a goddess that helped those in that particular realm.

They consisted of the following:

The Hell Realm is literally a 'hellish' place to live. It is a life of pure battle and everything is hardship; the worst place to be. You may have known a person who lives in the hell realm, full of aggression, confused and angered by everything. They have no effective strategies in life; all they know how to do is attack that which they feel is the cause of their downfall, although others know the cause is actually their ignorance. They blame the world for not giving them a break and feel that it should change, not them. Many people like this are in prison.

People in this realm tend to kill, hurt and maim other beings also caught in the 'hell realm'. They will push away any help and want to be around others like them. If you try to give help to a 'hell-being' or 'devil' he will use it to hurt others and can't escape as he sees everything, including your actions, in terms of battle.

This realm corresponds with the earth element and is protected by the holy one, Shō Kannon, a beautiful goddess, who holds a lotus flower in one hand and smiles beatifically.

The Hungry Ghost Realm is filled with people who always want more. Their ruling tendency is to create lack in their life. Think of someone who is always craving objects, attention or stimulation. They want the newest gadgets or the most attention. Because of this they cannot be still. They are overtaken by addiction, obsession and compulsion. The terrible irony about the 'ghost' is that they consume everything and create lack. They spend every penny they have, tire out friends and cheat on loving partners. They end up with the lack they fear so much. If you try to help a ghost escape, they will seize the opportunity for attention and perhaps for wealth. They think they want to escape the realm but to them escape just means satisfying themselves with further attention or stimulation. Ghosts are experts in creating drama and at drawing you into their realm.

This realm corresponds to water and is protected by Senju Kannon, a beautiful woman with many arms, holding multiple objects.

The Animal Realm consists of people entertained by simple activities and hobbies; they wander from one thing to another, just grazing. They tend to deal with things by distraction or displacement activity. 'Animals' can be recognised by their urge to avoid discomfort at any cost. They don't learn very easily, tend to ignore truth and have little urge for self-improvement. They find change scary and negative, and often show a marked complacency towards others. It is hard to get out of the animal realm, as lack of awareness traps you. Animal people will see any attempt to save them as hassle and they run away.

This realm corresponds to the wind or air element and those stuck in this realm may call on Batō Kannon, a horse-headed woman in a dress.

The Human Realm's inhabitants are moved by purpose. They have goals (good or bad). They move to change the world around them, to build things, and are focused on the effect they have on others and the environment.

This is the only realm in which cause and effect are obvious and viewable. In the other realms, you are either rewarded or punished for your past actions and it seems very hard to change what's happening. Humans try to convert others to their motivations and because of this they are often haunted by a ghost or hell-being they aim to liberate. Therefore, trying to save someone from other realms is dangerous. 'Let's get you out of here,' he says to the hungry ghost. The problem is that the hungry ghost hears, 'I will give you attention,' and never fully engages with the goal of liberation from their prison of lack. They see things in terms of what they can get in the here and now and thus can never escape. As soon as the attention stops, they feel betrayed and try to restart the process. The human soon becomes exhausted by the unsolvable problem. Like a drowning person pulling you down with them, the ghost creates lack in your life too.

A 'devil' is far more dangerous to save. If you try to protect them or stop the fighting, they think you have come to aid them in their battle. They don't understand anything but conflict so whatever you say will be part of that battle. If at any point you stop actively helping them compete with and hurting others directly or indirectly, they will feel you have turned on them. After all, if you are not with them you are against them.

The human realm corresponds to fire, and humans can call on Juntei Kannon, the Pure One, who sits meditating on a lotus flower, for help. This realm is the only one where enlightenment is achievable and where you can work on your spiritual journey.

The Demigod Realm is that of achievers, normally individuals or couples who have risen above the status and wealth of most people. They are more effective than most but fear falling back. Their life is full of paranoia and jealousy. They are focused on status, riches, power, fortune and fame, and are in constant battle with other demigods, competing on all levels. Those in this realm often feel that people trying to help them are trying to get one over on them.

The demigods often feel superior and will usually look down on others but forget that we are all impermanent. This realm is ruled by the void and by Jūichimen Kannon, a woman with eleven heads.

The Heavenly Realm is where the 'gods' live, people with such wealth that they can buy anything they like, fame, fortune, success, sex or anything material. The gods can spend whole years in meditation or trance. They lack awareness due to their state and are in such pleasure that they can't focus completely. They often suffer from boredom and despondency and can be capricious. They are often very wise but have forgotten the awareness that leads to their wisdom and position.

This realm also corresponds with void and is ruled by Nyoirin Kannon, who holds a wish-fulfilling jewel and the Wheel of Power.

Hibiki finished his description of the realms, pointing to each statue in turn with the torch on his mobile phone.

'When you travel through the mountains, you will travel through all these realms. On your trip, you pass through the elements of the realms and the problems you have. Your vices or downfalls transform to good things. Bad things grow as seeds to good things when you learn to live in the different realms proper OK way.'

He glanced at the time on his phone and seemed to wake up as to how long this had all taken. We started to walk back at speed. As we walked, he continued to talk. 'Trials different now. Shinto *yamabushi*, you have good luck English.'

We got to the door. He grabbed the rucksacks and was gone.

I went back to my mat with one thought in mind. 'What realm am I in?'

31

Through the Looking Glass

As above, so below
As within, so without
Hermes Trismegistus,
Hermetica: The Greek Corpus
Hermeticum

Before I knew it, the horn was blowing once again and we all lined up. Worryingly, Jasmine was nowhere to be seen. The masters were at the front, including the twenty or so *yamabushi* who had overseen our *tengu sumo*. They talked among themselves and then we heard the call to move again. Where was my translator? This was going to be pointless if she had decided to do a moonlight flit. I had little idea what was going on at the best of times!

The day continued in the same way as before, sitting on cobbles for two hours followed by a breakfast of rice, miso soup and two red pickles. The meals now tasted divine. I was always so hungry by the time we were presented with any food that I almost entered a state of rapture on placing the first morsel on my tongue. The premise of mindfulness, of living in the moment and savouring every small thing, was now paramount in my mind. Whether this was due to a new sense of enlightenment or merely that I could not function at any other level, I wasn't sure, but it meant that each tiny morsel of food was exquisite and the flavours burst into my mouth, leaving me with a feeling of satiation that I hadn't experienced before.

The pace was often such, though, that there was never any time to reflect on or rejoice in our trials or accomplishments. The pain

I was going through with my shoulder had reached another scale. As I walked, it hurt; if I stopped, it hurt. I kept changing the arm I was using to hold my staff, but that didn't make much difference. My feet were cut to ribbons from walking on uneven and sharp rocky surfaces.

That day and the next few days followed the same routine. During this time, the waterfall training became a welcome pleasure. I found it gave some relief from my shoulder pain and it was as close to washing as we got. I felt sorry for some of the others – if they stumbled out shivering and spluttering a *yamabushi* monk would simply push them back into the flow. Afterwards we would always settle in a room, hall or sometimes even a cave for the smokehouse. After that first time, I had got the hang of the chilli trial, if only from the point of view of dealing with the pain. However, as we continued to practise I found it became more surreal for me. I don't know if this was due to tiredness, or something else in the 'incense', but I was haunted by terrible waking nightmares every time it took place. I became paranoid about the safety of my family back home, and sometimes had hallucinations of their being attacked or hurt by the people who had harassed us. I would see demons or scenes of death and destruction in the smoke before me. At times, my body felt so fragile that it seemed it would fall apart if I moved. I hated that smokehouse but found a way of being OK with hating it. Many of the older members found it increasingly hard and, after a while, were excused from taking part.

Then the meditation on a peak in front of a sheer drop. It never again took place in darkness or twilight but always during the day. In the evening, it was *tengu sumo*. I spent most of my day dreading it. For the next two weeks, that was my life. Uncomfortable meditation, walking miles, standing under a waterfall, walking miles, sitting in a confined space with chilli fumes, meditation on a mountain peak or edge of a cliff, on two meals a day, both rice and miso soup.

My mental state was not normal. As I walked, I would often float into full-scale dreams and wake up, moving like a machine up the steps.

We walked across all three mountains in sequence and sometimes slept in the open, at others in different halls. Even though I was continually exhausted, I still found it hard to sleep; often you could hear bears grumbling in the distance. Whispered conversations among the group continually expressed the hope that the bears had plenty of other readily accessible food: the last thing we wanted to be was bear-chow.

One day when passing a more inhabited area, I saw a sign that had a slightly comical picture of a man punching a wild cat in the face. I took it to mean, 'If attacked by wild animals, fight back!'

The routine was constant. I never had time to think or digest, and it was only after several days that it dawned on me that sitting on cobbles was the earth trial. Soon I stopped using *kuji* and learnt to 'endure'. It's hard to describe but I eventually found somewhere inside that was not hurting, even though everywhere outside was. I harked back to Stephen Hayes's wisdom about having something to ignore while meditating.

As time passed some of us just 'found it' – you could literally see it happen. The nun, Meyoke, seemed already to have learnt that lesson, most likely from the advanced meditation training her sect offered. However, for the rest of us it was waiting in the form of a sudden epiphany or 'eureka' moment, sometimes under a waterfall but equally when just enduring a strenuous mountain walk or while stretching ourselves to the limit of our fears. For me the moment came on our third day on the 'Forbidden Mountain'. I had completed several element trials and now we were involved once again in waterfall practice. I could stand under a waterfall in the freezing cold; I was able to put up with different fumes, including the chilli and some other unknown ingredient that had made me experience those fearful visions; and I had faced my fear of heights. I could now sit for two hours on seriously uncomfortable rocks, in calm meditation. However, although I was focused on what I wished to achieve, I felt I was failing. I was still focusing on the suffering, not the exercise.

This feeling came to a head one afternoon as I sat under the waterfall: all I really wanted to do was escape from the unbearable mountain and the torture it brought me. But in that moment I found a part of me that actually didn't mind. As the freezing torrents of the waterfall beat down, I felt a spark deep inside and my attitude transformed. I could finally see beyond the discomfort we were all putting ourselves through; my mind-set changed in an instant and I began to release the chains of suffering. Others in our group continued to suffer for the remainder of the trip, but I had achieved the great clarity in focus and understanding I had hoped for.

The rest of the journey started to flow and I looked forward to each trial as a real spiritual challenge, not just a physical one. I enjoyed seeing if I could do better than last time. Each trial unlocked another chamber in my being – every mountain scene, every glass of water, every meal was almost literally divine, a feast for my senses and a balm for my soul.

Despite that, my shoulder injury nagged at me. I felt weak and vulnerable and I couldn't do anything about it. I couldn't recover, stop or do anything to improve it. The injury became a symbol of the human condition. I was trapped in a weak, limited body, having to fight forwards with no chance to rest or recover. I couldn't sleep or do anything without pain and I never came to terms with *tengu sumo*. However, similar to my new-found unchaining of the spirit, my physical condition also adopted my almost resigned state of mind and made me more open. With hours and hours of silent walking, I had time to think but also to feel.

I definitely felt freer and, as I walked, I tried to define it. It was something about my relationship with myself, my errors and mistakes. But also in there were my accomplishments and good works. There was no tangible change in my demeanour, nor had I had a massive revelatory epiphany, but I did feel an overwhelming sense of relief. As I walked endlessly up and down the mountains, I felt like a small cog in a big mechanism, and I realised that many of my goals were simply too great for one person to achieve.

It wasn't down to me to secure happiness and fulfilment for the people close to me. It wasn't possible to reach perfection. Nor was it essential that I earn huge sums of money: cash wouldn't change who I was or who I was born as. Money is a temporary accessory. Most importantly, I realized that life is a balancing act; pleasure and pain can – and always will – co-exist. I could not find a place beyond suffering and risk. Many of my limitations were inbuilt, not due to lack of effort or learning: they were just there. The rabbit is reputed to have poor stamina, the mole bad eyesight; we all have our limitations.

This realisation unburdened me. I felt calmer, liberated, and was able to complete the trip in a far happier state. Sure, the rocks still hurt and the flames could still burn me, but I was able to see through the pain with the comforting fact that I was just human. This was a hint of what was to come: something was forming beyond words. Something that one evening, at the end of my time in the mountains, was to change my view of life completely.

We made our way in silence down the mountainside, weaving along narrow steps while the crickets and cicadas chirruped noisily in the bushes. The air was incredibly humid and the waterfall training had left us all soaked. I couldn't help wondering how many other monks in our queue had had a similar experience to mine. I scanned them for any sign but I could see nothing in their faces and our vow of silence prevented me from asking.

Then it started to rain. The steps under my feet rapidly became treacherous and my *tabi* boots, with their polished leather soles, didn't help. I was slipping continually, so I dug in my staff in order to hold on. Suddenly another monk slipped and fell; as she did so, she reached out for me and I, too, toppled.

As we flailed around on the steps, the line stopped. By now, we were both covered with mud. The others, in a bid to see what was happening, also slid around unceremoniously. I tried to regain my demeanour but I became distracted by the scene around me: the ground was teeming with frogs! It was as if they had appeared from nowhere, swept in on the streams of water. They must have been lurking in the undergrowth but were now thoroughly enjoying the rain. I couldn't imagine why we hadn't seen them before: they were so vibrant and positively croaking in delight at the huge splashes of rain beating down on the rocks.

I attempted to struggle to my feet. As I did so, a hand reached out to me and I grabbed it to pull myself up. Then I realised my mistake: it was Sensei Hayasaka, the head of the order from the *shukubo*. Why was he here? I had just covered his immaculate robe with muddy handprints. In panic, I let go and fell back on my rear end. Then something terrible happened: I apologised. So natural for an Englishman, but in the company of a row of monks on the last day of a silent retreat, it was a complete *faux-pas*. Everyone tensed, paused, cringed and ignored it.

Then I discovered what had happened: instead of offering a hand to help me up, the master, holding pieces of paper, had been walking along the line handing one to everyone. He was still standing before me, proffering a soggy sheet. I sheepishly took mine and he moved on to the next person.

I looked at it. Unsurprisingly, it was all in Japanese. I turned it over and was relieved to see that someone had kindly handwritten in English on the other side. I read the title of the text: *The Heart Sutra*. Hatsumi Sensei had mentioned it often, and Stephen Hayes had produced DVDs on the subject. I had always shied away from it, as I had never really been interested in Buddhism. I was aware that many different traditions had contributed to this order but was still surprised to see the text: the monks here were Shinto, not Buddhist.

As we started to walk slowly, I read the first lines: 'Avalokiteshvara, the Bodhisattva of Compassion, meditating deeply on Perfection of Wisdom, saw clearly that the five aspects of human existence did not exist in their own right, and so released himself from suffering.'

I had no idea who the figure was but I suspected it must be a different name for Kannon, the female figure who represents compassion. What struck me was the experience described: it was just like my experience under the waterfall, where I had gone beyond suffering and found a sense of unity. At the time, to me, the five aspects were the five elements or senses. I was transfixed.

The monks started to chant: 'Hanyaaaaaaaaaaaaa sssssssssssssssyyyyyy yyyyyyyyyyngooooooooooooooooooooooooooo.'

I contemplated the heart and the sword symbol that makes up the Japanese word 'ninja'. I saw in my mind's eye the symbols of the ninja and a sudden insight hit me – the heart has four sections, the four elements, but as a whole. I read on:

> Body is no more than nothingness;
> nothingness is nothing more than body.
> The body is exactly empty,
> and emptiness is exactly body.
>
> The other four aspects of human existence,
> feeling, thought, will, and consciousness
> are likewise nothing more than nothingness,
> and nothingness nothing more than they.

I realised that the emphasis here referred not to the idea that there was nothing but to the fact that there was nothing in its own right. Nothing has ultimate substantiality, which in turn means that nothing is permanent and nothing is completely independent of everything else, including human existence. I understood in that moment that I had been trying to do something impossible because I had believed, on some level, that I was a separate entity. I thought I could build up my own permanence; if I gained enough fame, or impressed enough people, I could go beyond death, illness and criticism.

I read further:

> All things are empty:
> Nothing is born, nothing dies,
> nothing is pure, nothing is stained
> nothing increases and nothing decreases.
> So, in emptiness, there is no body,
> no feeling, no thought,
> no will, no consciousness.
> There are no eyes, no ears,
> no nose, no tongue,

no body, no mind.
There is no seeing, no hearing,
no smelling, no tasting,
no touching, no imagining.
There is nothing seen, nor heard,
nor smelt, nor tasted,
nor touched, nor imagined.

After reading this, I felt a sense of relief. All this struggle, to be something or seem something, when I was just a wave in the sea of life. Everything in this world is interconnected and in constant flux. In that moment I realised that it was not building the sense of self that would solve the problem but the exact opposite.

Was this enlightenment? I looked around: everything seemed so clear and bright. I felt oneness and beauty like never before. I was in for a shock as I read on.

There is no ignorance,
and no stopping of ignorance.
There is no old age and death
and stopping of old age and death.
There is no suffering, no cause of suffering,
no stopping suffering, no path to follow.
There is no attainment of wisdom,
and no wisdom to attain.

Well, that hit me like a brick. If wealth and fame and pleasure didn't matter, then surely good works and gaining insight were worthwhile. My mind struggled to find meaning. I read the rest of the text:

The Bodhisattvas rely on the Perfection of Wisdom,
and so with no delusions,
they feel no fear,
and have Nirvana here and now.
All the Buddhas,
past, present, and future,

rely on the Perfection of Wisdom,
and live in full enlightenment.
The Perfection of Wisdom is the greatest mantra.
It is the clearest mantra,
the highest mantra,
the mantra that removes all suffering.
This is truth that cannot be doubted.
Say it so: '*Gaté, gaté, paragaté, parasamgaté. Bodhi Svaha!*'

The last sentence means, 'Gone, gone, gone over, gone fully over. Awakened! So be it!'

Then something started to form, an awareness. I asked myself, could enlightenment be in my grasp? If we dare to imagine that among more than six billion people in this world, there are a few enlightened ones or saints, people who understand the ultimate truth in life? We could refer to each of them as 'Buddhas'. Their understanding of the world is so different from ours, so much better that it is almost as if they live in another world. Let's call the world they live in the 'other shore'. The rest of us have a far less realistic view of existence and are confused by our emotions and misperceptions. Our view of existence is so distorted by illusions that the world is very different from the Buddha's. Let's call this more common perception of the world 'this shore'.

In that moment, I had a sudden insight into the difference between the two perceptions. Those of us who live in 'this shore' are focused on the 'self'. I realised that this focus makes us separate from the flow of the universe, like a stone in a bucket of water, not willing to dissolve into the water of time and space.

Most of us interact with the world with a complete self-centred approach. Do I like this? How can I change it? The mind distinguishes things that are 'my will' and 'not my will'; what I 'want' and what I 'don't want'.

The enlightened ones who live spiritually on the 'other shore' have a completely different mind-set. They are at one with whatever events or surroundings they come into contact with. An enlightened one is mindful and lives in every moment, life in every breath. This attitude towards living in this world is like a grain of salt dissolving into a bucket of water. It is gone but every last drop of the water is salty. If the water and bucket represent space and time, there is no more ego-self to be found. Instead, it has dissolved into one with the entirety of existence.

The enlightened one shines out like an endless light and fills up all of space, an endless life span that lasts throughout all time. Because enlightened ones are beyond ego and because they have seen through the illusion of separateness, there is no barrier between them and the outside world.

A cell in our body could be seen as a separate organism: it has a life of its own.

The enlightened ones know this but on a higher level. Whatever places they happen to live in, they dissolve themselves into that situation or environment without any personal involvement. When they see the blossom on the tree, *they* are the blossom, *they* are the fragrance. When an enlightened one listens to the rain, he thinks, I am the rain. I am the sound of the rain. When an enlightened one is born, grows older, get sick, dies – he cries, I am birth! I am ageing! I am illness! I am death! Because the enlightened one is without ego, he is able to remain selfless and sincerely embraces all changes in the external world.

I looked around as our path continued. By now, it was getting dark and we were walking through heavy woodland, heading back to the temple lodgings. We were all quietly reflective.

So why was all this important to the ninja? The answer was startling. The ninja were not really aiming to blend in: they were aiming to be at one with everything.

I thought I had come to *ninjutsu* to fulfil a goal. In fact, I had come to find my true goal.

By now we were at the *shukubo* again, the one I had stayed in on the very first day I arrived. We looked at it with tired eyes. We had not eaten since morning and were all totally drained.

'We are going to get so drunk!' Akira looked at me with happy, excited eyes. I raised my eyebrows in disbelief. What a bizarre thing to say.

A command was given and I understood the Japanese for the first time during the trip. We were told to wash, get changed: there was going to be a meal.

Wash! We all looked at each other with excitement. The horn blew. 'Okidamo!'

It took me a moment to realise we had started walking in the wrong direction – away from the *shukubo*. I asked Devil Man what was going on. He turned to me with remarkably bloodshot eyes; in fact, he looked in pretty bad shape. 'We have to go jump over fire before we can go back to normal world. Then there is feast and we get drunk.'

His English was so good! I wish I had been able to talk to him before but the *yamabushi* vow of silence prevented it.

We were really going to get drunk? The idea might have appealed to me if I hadn't felt as if I'd gone ten rounds with Mike Tyson and hadn't just discovered the meaning of spiritual enlightenment! Nevertheless, it was all extra calories, which I was seriously in need of, even if it was in liquid form. I still couldn't quite believe that the *yamabushi* would do such a thing, when we were supposed to be purifying ourselves and losing our base nature. I asked Devil Man why we were being allowed to get drunk.

He responded with a seriously cheeky grin. 'We have become too pure for the normal world, so before we return to life we need to eat, drink and become impure.'

Why undo all the work we had done? 'Hang on a minute.' My brain backtracked to something more pressing than getting hammered. 'Did you just say "jump over fire"?' I was having a problem walking, never mind jumping!

As we turned the corner, I saw it, a kind of small coal fire, burning with a blue flame. Beside it, I could see a bottle of fire-lighting fluid that presumably had been used to give it that eerie hue. So, I had to jump those flames, then got to wash and eat . . . and then it was all over. We lined up. I was more nervous before this final trial than any of the others but comforted myself with the fact that I had completed them with no problems. I would be able to do the final little jump – after all, the flames only came up to my hips.

As the queue moved forwards and I came nearer to the fire, I could feel definite warmth. Then, as my turn came, Ekken leapt up and squirted more fuel on it. Everyone laughed as I watched the flames lick each other and grow until they were level with my chest, then climbed further so they were at shoulder height. When they were level with my face, the oppressive heat was like a fiery wall.

I knew I could just jump through it and be OK. I was quite sure it would be like a finger passing through a lighter flame. I moved back as if readying to run for the jump and closed my eyes: the smoke was making them sting but I also wanted to add drama and delay things for a second so that the flames died down. I could hear the whoosh and surge of the fire. I had visions of going up in smoke myself and was grateful the *yamabushi* robe I had on was not made of artificial fibres.

I opened my eyes. The fire had died down to about waist level, so I ran the best I could, which was a high-speed hobble. My tired muscles strained to keep my legs in a straight line. One of my *tabi* boots was so loose that it flopped around clumsily during the last few strides. Then I jumped, lifting my feet high into the air, and a loud cheer rang out.

The moment I hit the ground I was taken aside by a large, elderly man in full *yamabushi* robes. He led me away from the group, then looked at me seriously. I wondered if I had done something wrong.

'You do well at *yamabushi* trials on this course in this sect.' With that, he handed me some photos. I flicked through them. I could tell they had been taken secretly and that he didn't want the others to see he had given me such a gift. I gulped back my thanks. Words didn't seem appropriate at such a solemn moment. He looked straight into my eyes and gave an almost imperceptible nod.

I had been dismissed. The only other words he uttered were to tell me to head back to the temple lodgings.

When I got there, everyone had gone to the washrooms. The men's had one giant bath filled with scalding water. First, though, you had to shower, with soap, shampoo and a medieval-looking scrubbing brush. As I walked in everyone was sitting on stools under the shower just chatting naturally – a far cry from the icy silence under the waterfalls. There was only one free shower, so I grabbed a basket of washing equipment and went to work. It was heaven after so many days without washing –

my whole body had become one stinking itch. When I stumbled out of the shower I caught sight of a man in the mirror – who the hell was he? He wore a full beard and was remarkably gaunt, his skin tanned. I was startled by my own reflection. I looked like a tramp or a madman.

My hand shook as I tried to shave my face. I could see new lines, caused by pain. After the arduous days of climbing, walking and extended periods of meditating on rough, uncomfortable surfaces I seemed to have gained a look of anguish and a hunched body posture that protected the shoulder injury. Once shaved, I stood up to take a bath. No one else had finished washing. I had never washed so much, but the Japanese were just washing over and over again. I sat down in the shower and washed some more.

As the other *yamabushi* arrived, people started getting into the bath. By then I was beyond it. Why would I want to get into a bath with lots of other nude men anyway? I was starving and clean beyond compare, so I got dressed in my normal clothes and exited the room. I went directly into the garden and sat there. I could see a giant feast being laid out in one of the rooms; small, low tables with cushions lined up for us to sit on. It looked like paradise to me – food, drink and the chance to sit on something other than rocks. Don't get me wrong, I had experienced the spiritual trip of a lifetime but sometimes it's nice to feel your feet on the ground again.

Ekken, his mother and sister were laying out plates with some form of breaded fish or chicken and a glutinous brown sauce. I felt very strange to be dressed in jeans and a shirt. I looked at my reflection in the pool and felt confused – it seemed I was no longer comfortable in normal clothes. 'I suppose it'll take time to adjust,' I said aloud.

The young girl laying the table looked at me. She smiled. 'No, I don't speak English.' I took that as a vague invitation to go and sit down. The room was beautiful, light and airy, statues of Buddhist and Shinto figures dotted along the front wall. By now the rest of the group were emerging to sit at the table. Great barrels of beer and crates of *sake* were brought in. We were indeed going to get drunk!

We sat waiting to eat but everyone was drinking freely while the others filed in. Soon everyone was there, including Jasmine, who sat across from me. It was strange seeing her after her unexplained absence. As people milled about in their normal clothes you could work out more about them. Suddenly you could see people's personalities, class status in society. Devil Man was in a T-shirt with a depiction of Fudō-myōō, the guardian deity, on it.

One of the older Japanese men was already so drunk that he was singing; nobody seemed fazed by this and people round him were clapping and cheering. The lack of food and drinking on empty stomachs was not a good combination. Meyoke and Akira sat next to me; we really wanted to talk but the language barrier was in the way. Luckily, Jasmine stepped in; she was not drinking, so had a perfectly clear mind for our conversation.

'Akira has also trained with Mr Hatsumi and takes part in ninja competitions in Tokyo.'

Akira showed me a range of pictures on his phone of people dressed, bizarrely, as ninja throwing stars and climbing crazy-looking obstacles.

With a smile, Meyoke reached over and gave me a little red book with the Heart Sutra written in it. I was about to thank her when my attention was drawn to something moving in the room. A large long-legged insect was scuttling along at the front; as it paused, I recognised it as a praying mantis. The raucous banter in the room fell silent as it stood in front of the statues of the three mountain deities. Its feet kept catching on the material of a prayer mat and it couldn't move properly. It appeared to be dancing or bowing as it tried to free itself to move forwards.

Everyone was talking all of a sudden.

'Martin, it's the mantis they are talking about!'

I looked at it and it seemed so happy, so comical but special.

Wham! All of a sudden, the old drunk Japanese man who had been singing squashed it and laughed. I was appalled. Hungry, tired and sensitive, I just burst into tears. Through a blur, I looked at Meyoke and then at Jasmine, both of whom were crying too. It just seemed so horrible that someone could snuff out the insect's life.

There was a moment of stunned silence, then the horn blew and

Ekken was there, giving us the command to eat and for the final time we responded, '*Okidamo!*'

The meal was delicious. My plate was constantly refuelled and, in the end, I gave in and drank a beer.

Throughout the meal Devil Man was going from person to person, giving them some form of massage, then hovering his hands over various parts of their body. I asked Jasmine what he was doing but it was Meyoke who responded. 'This is my teacher. He is an advanced *ki* master.' She held her hand out to me in a gesture that indicated I should do the same. Her hands hovered over mine. I could feel a tugging, tingling sensation. Devil Man saw the demonstration and came over.

He talked via Jasmine, even though I knew he could speak reasonable English. 'Do you have injury?' I explained my shoulder problem and he started to rub my shoulders and back, then moved his hands over the affected area. Almost immediately, I felt a searing heat, which was almost as painful as the injury. The heat he created penetrated the injured joint and I couldn't tell whether it had helped or not – it actually felt like the bones themselves were heating up inside and made me feel slightly dizzy.

I swallowed heavily, trying to control a rising feeling of sickness. 'Is this *reiki*?'

The *yamabushi* had created the *reiki* system of healing.

'No, this *yamabushi* breathing,' Meyoke corrected me sternly.

Devil Man moved on to the next patient and I continued eating. As etiquette demanded, the mother of the house was brought in for our effusive thanks and then we were allowed to leave the table.

I was deliciously full and so tired. I wandered to the hall and instantly went to sleep.

I woke up first thing in the morning – well, I say first thing but it was the latest I had been up in weeks. My whole body was just a ball of tiredness but most of all I was aware of an exaggerated almost unearthly tiredness in my injured shoulder. It was so weak I could barely move or lift it. It dawned on me that I was feeling pure fatigue: it didn't hurt any more.

The *ki* master had fixed my shoulder. I was so happy – but also disappointed. What a fool I was not to ask to learn from him while I'd had the chance. I had come all the way to Japan to learn and when I met a genuine master of *yamabushi* healing breath, I'd let him go without any questions at all.

I wandered through to the hall to be greeted by the lady of the house and sat down for an amazing Japanese breakfast, complete with rice, raw eggs and lots of fish.

Devil Man, his wife and Meyoke appeared and sat down for breakfast. Thoughtlessly, I jumped up to greet them, but instead blurted out, 'My shoulder is better! I want to learn the healing technique. I want to learn *yamabushi* breathing . . . please.' I felt like an over-enthusiastic schoolkid. They paused for a few seconds to talk to each other.

Devil Man looked at me seriously. 'Yes. The course you just did means yes.'

My tuition started immediately.

'Everything has spirit in it. The food you eat has spirit, so you should always focus on receiving from food when you eat. The air you breathe has air spirit. Herbs, places and trees, places of nature, all these can help you with their spirit.'

He held his hand over his food for a moment in prayer. His wife and student did the same. Then we started to eat.

I wanted to ask his name but we were obviously supposed to be eating in absolute silence, concentrating on our food and absorbing the spiritual force in it. When the last morsel was consumed, he spoke again: 'I will be here with my family for the next few days and, if you like, we can walk in mountain as a manner of teaching.'

I was totally humbled. 'Yes, Master, thank you. But what is your name?'

I could see him thinking for a few moments. He turned to Meyoke, whispered something quickly and she slipped from the room.

'In England I have no name, do you understand? You don't put my name or anything I teach you in your book you promise?'

Jasmine must have told him.

'I promise.'

'Marain.' He struggled with my name. 'Don't teach until you completely understand. The breathing is for healing yourself and others, and makes sure you have a long, happy life. I think you have spent too much of your life searching how to fight and defend. This is from fear.'

I was a bit insulted.

Meyoke re-entered the room with a scroll and handed it to him.

'The fear is making you want to fight and defend. You want to save others but it is really you who is in trouble. Now you want to heal others but it is you who needs to heal first.' He opened the scroll. It was a picture of the mountain but in a strange two-dimensional form with pictures of little people doing things like tilling the fields and leading cattle. A giant river with three waterfalls was depicted down one side of the mountain.

'The mountain has the spirit like we do have.' He pushed his hand down my head, stopping at the back of my neck to press, then continuing to the point between my shoulders, finally pressing my coccyx firmly. He traced the picture, pressing each waterfall in turn. He pointed at the five-storey pagoda, then pressed a point just below my navel.

I could see now that the diagram was not only a depiction of Haguro but also of the human body, with each organ shown as an animal and all the acupuncture points hidden in code.

Meyoke said, 'We will walk the mountain and learn about the places in the body for breathing for three days or two. We practise the circulation breathing at each point in the mountain and focus on point in you too.'

They nodded at me.

His wife, who was still sitting there patiently, suddenly started talking excitedly. He listened carefully, then turned to me. 'Never heal people who misuse health to hurt others. If the illness is self-cause, don't heal twice. Never charge money for heal – always keep them at doctor too.'

He stared at me with eyes that went back to the dark ages. 'You no drink or smoke or any drug from now on. You pray every day for help healing.'

I agreed.

The master started again: 'Now that the mountain has taught you more about who you are, and what is important, I hope you are ready to learn. This is not three-day art but three-year practice. For English, very hard as practice slow and not exciting. You need to come back and show you are master for next exercises.'

They stood up and went to the door; it looked as if we were starting that very minute. They put on their pilgrim's hats and shoes and picked up their *yamabushi* staffs. I was about to rush back to my room to get the same, when he stopped me. 'The teaching is over now, Mar'in, you have some days off.'

As I watched the couple leave I found myself thinking, 'Perhaps there is more to the stories of the ninja's supernatural powers. If *ki* is real and can heal, what else is possible?'

32

The Rainbow Body

_Be careful to perform your allotted task while it is yet day, continue
to listen to the voice of Nature, which bears witness that even in this
perishable frame resides a vital and immortal principle._

Masonic ritual

'Why don't you visit the hot springs?' The elderly woman at Tsuruoka Tourist Information Centre peered at me over her glasses; her steel-grey hair looked almost plastic with its perfectly formed ringlet on either side of her ear.

There were hot springs? Did this mean there was a volcano? I asked.

My question stirred a response from her young assistants; they looked up and gave me their full attention. The boy had a pair of glasses, with lenses so thick you could hardly see his eyes.

She pursed her lips, 'Yes, but it never erupts any more.'

'That was Mount Asama,' the boy interjected.

Not one of the ones near here. I thought back to earlier that morning. I had been sitting in my room at the _shukubo_, reflecting on my _yamabushi_ adventure, and it had seemed clear to me that I had discovered the truth about the ninja. There, the unbroken tradition of challenging yourself against the elements continued. But, unlike their reputation, the ninja were honourable, philosophical men. Because ninja warriors operated independently of the rest of the army, and because they used such dark techniques, their hearts had to be pure, and their intentions absolutely in order.

By testing myself against the elements, I had found an inner sense of enlightenment. But there wasn't anything supernatural about it: it was simply a clearer vision of exactly what was happening.

In truth, I was still in search of the supernatural. I found myself drawn to one last quest. I was going to find one of the most sacred relics in the mountain, this being the body, or rather the preserved remains, of a saint who had achieved the ultimate in *yamabushi* spirituality.

It is said that such a saint, the great master of the arts of *tantra* and, in this case of *shugendō*, doesn't die but, rather, transforms his soul to live for ever. In the Esoteric Buddhist, the *yamabushi* and the Tibetan Buddhist traditions, this is called 'achieving the rainbow body'.

In Tibet, the body shrinking and perhaps even disappearing characterises it. In Japan, it is believed to have been achieved when, upon death, the body does not rot. Yamagata is the only area of Japan where this practice took place.

I jerked out of my reverie as I heard the young boy say something to me: 'We have a protector!' He smiled, nodded eagerly and turned back to his computer. Beside him was a long strip of white candy. He ripped off a piece and put it into his mouth as he continued typing with one hand.

The woman shot him a withering glance, but said, with a tight smile, 'The whole area is protected.'

It had started to rain outside and I was the only person in the centre. With the whole day to spare and nothing planned, I decided to press them further. 'Who protects the area? Is it a spirit, to protect you from volcanoes?'

The woman responded, with an irritated shake of the head, 'It's just a folk tale. Look . . . here.' She jabbed a heavily lacquered red fingernail at a guidebook; luckily for me it was in English. Before I could pick it up, she whipped it from under my fingers and started to flick through the pages. Once she'd found what she was looking for, she spread the book open on her desk.

'Living Buddha . . . a local saint,' I read aloud.

'Mmm, yes, he sacrificed himself to prevent volcanic eruptions.'

'It was to stop the crops failing,' the boy corrected, still chewing and typing.

The woman winced. She had been flicking through some information sheets and showed me a crumpled photograph. It was of a dark, withered figure robed in red, with a hat – the caption read:

'*Sokushinbutsu* – self-created, living Buddhist mummies . . .'

I'd seen mummies in Egypt but I'd had no idea that it was a practice that had been used in Japan. My mind flashed back to the figure I had seen in the painting in the training hall, the one that had looked Indian. Perhaps that had been a rendering of one of these 'living saints'.

'How does someone mummify themselves . . . alive?'

The woman looked at me pointedly. 'You really want to know?' Her eyebrows arched high above the rim of her glasses.

I nodded vigorously.

'My mother told me . . . years ago.' She waved a hand as if to discourage questioning while she spoke. 'These monks looked for spiritual purpose, and trained in ways that most of us wouldn't dream of. They were *kinyoku-tekina* . . . maybe you say "simple living"? They did not eat ordinary food but had special diet of pine needles. They starve themselves. Then become mummies.'

'For years, they slowly starve . . . for years!' The boy's voice was delightfully melodramatic. He was now unwrapping something pink and sticky and rolling it between his fingers.

I looked between the two of them. 'These monks actually starved themselves into a mummified state? How did they die? How long did it take? What else did they do? Was there any magic or meditation?' I faltered as I saw the look on her face.

The woman sighed deeply. 'Why you not use computer to look up?' She was obviously getting fed up with trying to put all this into English.

I scrambled gratefully into the empty chair set before an ancient PC with an English keyboard. It whirred into life and eventually I was online – Google was about to become my new best friend.

I quickly typed in *Sokushinbutsu* and a raft of entries appeared. I clicked on a link to Wikipedia – might as well start with the basics:

Sokushinbutsu refers to a practice of Buddhist monks observing austerity to the point of death and mummification. This process of self-mummification was mainly practised in Yamagata in Northern Japan between the eleventh and nineteenth century, by members of the Japanese Vajrayana school of Buddhism called Shingon ('True Word'). The practitioners of *sokushinbutsu* did not view this practice as an act of suicide, but rather as a form of further enlightenment. Those who succeeded were revered, while those who failed were nevertheless respected for the effort.

It is believed that many hundreds of monks tried, but only twenty-four such mummifications have been discovered to date. There is a common suggestion that Shingon school founder Kukai brought this practice from Tang China as part of secret tantric practices he learnt, and that were later lost in China. Today, the practice is not advocated or practised by any Buddhist sect, and is banned in Japan.

Well that told me something, but what about the actual process? I read further and found a PDF of a book called *Living Buddhas: The Self-mummified Monks of Yamagata, Japan** by Ken Jeremiah, which covered the whole subject.

After a while, I began to get the full picture. If I'd thought the training we had just completed on the mountain was extreme, then the process of *sokushinbutsu* ('becoming a Buddha in this very body') put it into perspective. To attain this state of near divinity would take roughly ten years or, as mentioned in several writings, three thousand days. During this time, the monks would slowly starve themselves on a special diet (known as *mokujikigyo*) that excluded most cereals but included nuts, berries, seeds and, essentially, pine needles. There is no concrete proof but, consistent with other traditions where a similar process is used, pine needles and/or pine resin do seem to be a consistent part of the diet and may have acted as a natural preservative. A first stage lasted a thousand days and would combine this diet with strenuous activity. For the next thousand days, they would don white robes, grow their hair and retire to meditate and pray in an

---

* *Living Buddhas: The Self-mummified Monks of Yamagata, Japan*, Ken Jeremiah, McFarland (2010).

area aptly named 'The Swamp of Wizards'; their diet would be restricted further to bark, roots and finally just pine needles and resin. A drink made from the urashi tree (*Toxicodendron vernicifluum*) was drunk and the sap collected and eaten. This would cause severe vomiting and diarrhoea. Interestingly, the leaves, bark and flowers of this plant are used in Chinese medicine to expel parasites and reduce bleeding. It is also known as the Chinese lacquer tree, its sap being used as a highly durable lacquer and preservative for furniture and decorative items. All these things combined add up to a strong case that the monks were intentionally poisoning themselves while creating a perfect internal environment of bodily self-preservation. The anti-parasitic and poisonous properties of the urashi tree would make sure that no maggots, worms or other parasite would destroy the flesh – and the sap, well, it effectively lacquered them!

The final thousand days would be spent in achieving *nyūjō*, a deep state of meditation or prayer. In their last days the monks would enter a cave or specially dug tomb and be sealed inside. Seated in the classic lotus position of the Buddha, in darkness, awaiting death and purification, their only contact with the world from then on was via a breathing tube made from bamboo and a bell, which they would ring once a day to let the other monks know they were still alive.

'"When the bell stopped ringing the air tube was removed because the monk had died. Then monks would leave him until he became mummy . . . or didn't. Once the monk had been proclaimed dead in his tomb, he would be left until he was unsealed three years later to see if he had achieved self-mummification."' I looked up from the screen and realised I had been reading aloud. The boy was grinning.

The woman resumed the story. 'The monks that dress as rabbits are the ones that eat only leaves.'

I took her to mean the *yamabushi* and I certainly knew them.

'They practise special miracle feats: learn to hold sword blades that are heated to high temperatures, walk on hot coals and climb ladders made of swords. They mark these achievements with stone markers in a sacred place only they visit called Swamp of the Immortals.'

Hmm, did she mean 'The Swamp of Wizards'? Then my mind flashed back to an area of grassland that we had rested in, one that had had stones, which I had assumed were grave markers. I suddenly recalled our earlier conversations. 'So who is the protector, and how is he connected with the mummified monk?'

'Shinnyokai Shonin.'

I repeated the name back to her.

'Yeah.' She nodded. '*Shonin* is a title that means "holy man" or "saint". Shinnyokai is his Buddhist name.'

Had I been mishearing what was said about Ekken, the priest on our retreat? I'd thought they were using the ninja term '*jonin*', meaning 'top man', not '*shonin*' meaning . . . Had I been in the presence of a living saint?

'His story is a great one,' she continued. 'He was a farmer from here, born in this very town, a very strong man who worked the land. Born here, this time.' She wrote '1700' on a bit of paper, his year of birth. 'It all here . . . in book.' She pushed the guidebook I'd seen earlier towards me with her fearsome nails.

Now I got it. Shinnyokai Shonin was the self-mummified monk and protector saint of Tsuruoka and the surrounding area. I settled back to read more about him. He had been a well-known, very pious farmer who one day, while walking home carrying a bag of manure from his livestock, knocked into a samurai in the street and possibly tainted the warrior with the waste. In those days, samurai were judge, jury and executioner, and could kill a peasant for any perceived insult.

The warrior was offended and drew a sword to kill Shinnyokai. Worried as to who would look after his family, he thought of his responsibilities and evaded the blow, fighting back with his walking staff. According to the book, he killed the samurai with repeated blows to his head. Realising the severity of his crime – to kill a samurai meant certain death – he fled to Dainichibō Temple, where he was sheltered by the priests and became a *yamabushi*.

I noticed movement beside me: the boy had got up from his computer and was chewing noisily next to me. He jabbed his sticky finger at the photo.

'After he became monk no one would get him. He became powerful wizard and he learnt about the secrets of becoming a living Buddha after his teacher became one. He was good man and wanted to look after people. When the volcano killed people, he decided to become living saint and protect us. He still does now.'

The woman interjected, 'No, was not here. It was miles away at Mount Asama and it was Shinnyokai's teacher,' she poked her finger at him triumphantly, 'who became an ever-living immortal after that.'

The boy shrugged. 'Well, our protector became mummy after the crop failed but now we have Western monk here, he can protect us!' He burst into peals of laughter and with that left the room.

It was then that I realised they had known all along who I was and why I was interested in these subjects. I guess news travels quickly in a small town. I peered at the caption under the photo of the figure. It was Shinnyokai Shonin. His preserved body now resided in Dainichibō Temple in Yamagata, where he'd gone all those years ago to hide. 'Where is the temple?' I pointed at the picture in the guidebook.

'What temple?'

'Dainichibō Temple! Where the monk is?'

'Oh, it's a couple of miles from here.' She said it so nonchalantly, as if I had just asked where the station was.

'Can you show me on a map where the mummy is?'

She paused for a few minutes but looked at the *yamabushi* staff I still carried, with stamps showing I had visited all three sacred mountains, and relented. She marked the position on a map for me. It was time to rent a bike and get going – this was far more important than hot springs.

I thanked the woman in the tourist office and she directed me to where I could get a bike; the only one they had left was a women's model. I felt a little strange, riding a bike with a big basket on the front and a brake that only operated by pedalling backwards. Realising I had no idea where I was going, and how hungry I was, I decided I needed some supplies. I wobbled to a stop at one of the local shops and stocked up on some sandwiches with an unidentifiable filling and a couple of bottles of drink.

Now to find the mummy. I looked at the map and it was clearly in an area of woodland. Of course it would be, hidden in the mountains away from the profane. I looked at the roads, lined them up and took in the Japanese phrasing. I thought I knew pretty much where to go, but it was a long way.

However, my confidence in my navigational skills soon began to wane and I was at the point of giving up and decided to ride back. As I passed an industrial area, I couldn't believe my eyes: in front of me were two men who had been on the *yamabushi* trip – Akira and a bald chap whose name I couldn't recall. They also had bikes and were aimlessly riding around the place; we greeted each other like long-lost brothers. Though they knew hardly any English and my Japanese was terrible, it became apparent that we were looking for the same thing. Their map had a slightly different marking, which made it obvious that my expectations had confused me. It wasn't in the mountains. It was right in the centre of what appeared to be an industrial area.

The man with the shaven head was obviously interested in Buddhism. I found myself looking at him from behind and wondering if I had mixed him up at certain points with Meyoke during the mountain trip.

We cycled around, Akira balancing the map on his handlebars. More than a few times, we mistook a building for the one we were searching for – the area was a perplexing mix of industrial units and residential houses. Then we saw it. Right next to an area where they made gravestones, we saw a house with two levels, normal in every way but for the markings of a temple, the red gate showing it was a holy place and sacred gravestones, called stupa.

We walked up a flight of steps and tentatively rang the bell. Without waiting for a response, the two men walked straight into the room, taking their shoes off and shouting what I assumed were their names – I recognised 'Akira'.

An elderly woman with no teeth appeared, her face eerily whitened with what looked like chalk dust. I decided she must be a *miko* (a 'shrine maiden' or 'female shaman') due to her attire, which was traditional red *hakama* trousers and white kimono jacket. Akira, I presumed, was enquiring whether we could see the mummy but she seemed very reluctant, shaking her head so vigorously that specks of white dust danced like moths in the stream of sunlight that filtered through the rice-paper wall. Akira rummaged in his rucksack for his tablet computer. He typed quickly and pointed to some pictograms on the screen. Ah. She nodded solemnly this time and glided over to some sliding doors. We started to follow, Akira a bit too eagerly. He found himself up against a firmly raised hand and the sliding doors slid firmly shut in his face. 'I think we wait.' He chuckled, looking back at us both with an embarrassed grin.

After some delay, she reappeared and led us back down the steps out to the front garden. A short walk around the house took us to another entrance; once again we removed our shoes and bowed.

I wasn't too sure what I was bowing to as it took a few moments for my eyes to adjust to the hazy gloom in the room. Then I made out the outline of a seated figure and the hairs on the back of my neck stood up. There he was, a wizened yet obviously human-featured skull appeared in my line of vision, enveloped in an over-large red cloak and hat, skeletal hands clutching a set of prayer beads. We stood motionless, a sense of fear, of being in the wrong place. The old woman came to us, walking in front of each of us in turn with what looked like three bits of flat wood about the length of a school ruler, which had a red stamp on them. I didn't know what these were for and turned one over and over in my hands.

Akira whispered, 'You write on. Um, they burn and it come true.' He motioned to get his tablet computer out to help further using his translation program, but the *miko* wasn't having any of it. She swatted angrily at him, 'You not film here!' and said something in Japanese. The computer was put away very quickly.

The two men knelt on the floor and started writing. I followed suit and wrote that I wished the spirits would make sure that my wife and daughter were safe in my absence. Worry had started to overcome me during the last few days of my stay, and I found myself scared for their safety. I felt so distant, as if I'd been taken permanently away from them. The *miko* had silently observed us; she motioned for us to approach the figure – a few metres away – and put the wood in some form of offering box. We approached, bowed, prostrated ourselves almost flat, and finally put the pieces of wood in the box. As we did so, something happened that I'll remember for the rest of my life. All three of us found ourselves stepping back as if dazed, confused or pushed by an outside force – I may even have swayed. My eyes felt wide, yet heavy, the same kind of feeling I would get if I drank too much caffeine or smoked a strong cigar.

I heard Akira swallow hard. Without *any* prior communication or indication, all three of us involuntarily started performing some form of ritual or supplication. It involved the clicking of fingers two or three times to one side, then a bow on the other, putting our hands together, kneeling down, and raising the palms of our hands above our heads. All this happened in perfect unison without any prompting, understanding or control. I didn't feel any sense of resistance. I was barely aware of what was happening; it was like watching a film. The atmosphere felt sinister and confusing.

I believe the woman had only let us see the mummy because we had explained we were *yamabushi*. At the time, I had no idea what I was doing and wondered if our connection with the tradition had made it feel like some strange possession. I later read that the spirit of the shrine possesses the *miko*. I had a feeling that she had been guardian of that particular shrine for a long time and still controlled the magical powers of the old tradition.

We almost simultaneously shook our heads groggily and stepped back out into the hall and the light, blinking in surprise. The elderly *miko* didn't seem surprised but responded as if we had been good boys. She smiled, nodded, and the door gently closed behind us.

'Wow! That was crazy!'

I just looked at Akira. He grinned, tried to get onto his bike and caught his feet in the pedals. All of us were faintly confused, as if we had been given a very subtle sleeping draught and had just awoken, emerging back into the brightness of the world from somewhere beyond time and space.

'That has to be the understatement of the century.' I shook my head in disbelief. What had just happened back there? More importantly, had our written prayers been answered?

I tried to ascertain if they knew the ritual? Was there some way I already subconsciously knew it? Without any success. My shaven-headed friend started to cry. He seemed extremely scared and shaky. Akira offered some words of comfort, which seemed to have the desired effect as he pulled himself together. Unable to think of anything else to say, considering the language barrier and what had just occurred, we gestured that we were heading back to our respective lodgings.

'Ah,' Akira said, 'Facebook!' and wrote his name on a piece of paper for me. The other man did the same, in Japanese script and in attempted English. I tried looking them up when I got back to the 'real' world but never found them.

It was only as I rode my bike back that the full impact of what had happened sank in. All three of us had performed the same ritual at the same time, through some form of possession, so a non-physical force must have made it happen.

As it had taken place in the presence of the venerable mummy, it's logical to believe that it was somehow connected. If that was true then, at least for the mummy, it appears there actually *is* some form of life or power after death.

As I approached the rental company to hand over my bike, a feeling overwhelmed me. I realised that, in a sense I'd been lying to myself, and that all this time I hadn't just been looking for *ninjutsu*. I hadn't only been wanting to train in those arts: it had been a means by which I could allow myself to search for the spiritual, the supernatural. The ninja, like my childhood focus on superheroes, was the closest I could find to the inner calling I felt. On this trip I had found both genuine enlightenment and also, inexplicably and undeniably, supernatural events.

I had found what I was looking for and could finally be honest with myself. As I got on the bus back to my lodgings, I was full of awe and inspiration. Actually, I didn't know if I was scared or inspired. I realised that maybe we all find ways that we can allow ourselves to do things that we haven't quite admitted to ourselves. Perhaps, in truth, Stephen Hayes and Michael Pearce, in their own way, had known me better than I knew myself.

As I arrived at the *shukubo*, I walked past a statue, one of the earliest representations of Kannon, the goddess of compassion and enlightenment. In that moment, I had another realisation. Ninja were warriors, men of warrior castes who fought and used psychology, deception and studies to achieve their goals, but now I could not deny that Stephen Hayes was completely correct: enlightenment was part of their training. I could no longer dismiss the idea that they had supernatural abilities. Neither could I say that, for me, this was the end of a quest. Rather, it was the beginning of a new journey, which was to find the truth about enlightenment and these supernatural abilities.

Was it possible to see the world truly as it is, beyond the limitations of being human? Was there a state of higher consciousness that could be reached to travel outside the body, to achieve some form of immortality? If that was possible then what was the true limit of human potential with these arts? In that moment I realised I had finally found my calling, what I truly wanted to do with my life. And now that I had had this experience nothing would stop me achieving my goal.